This book shows how England's conquest of Mediterranean trade proved to be the first step in building its future economic and commercial hegemony, and how Italy lay at the heart of that process.

In the seventeenth century the Mediterranean was the largest market for the wool, spices and colonial products which were exported by English merchants, as well as being a source of raw materials (Spanish wool, Puglian oil, oriental silk) which were indispensable for the growing and increasingly aggressive domestic textile industry. Italy lay at the centre of this trade network: Venice, Genoa and Florence had been major centres of trade for centuries, and remained rich and powerful. In addition the new free port of Livorno became the linchpin of English trade with the Mediterranean as a whole and, together with ports in southern Italy, formed part of a system which gradually enabled the English merchant fleet to take over control of the region's trade from the Italians.

In her extensive use of English and Italian archival sources, the author looks well beyond Braudel's influential picture of a Spanish-dominated Mediterranean world. In doing so she demonstrates some of the causes of Italy's decline and its subsequent relegation as a dominant force in world trade.

CAMBRIDGE STUDIES IN ITALIAN HISTORY AND CULTURE

ENGLISH MERCHANTS IN
SEVENTEENTH-CENTURY ITALY

CAMBRIDGE STUDIES IN ITALIAN HISTORY AND CULTURE

Edited by GIGLIOLA FRAGNITO, Università degli Studi, Parma
CESARE MOZZARELLI, Università Cattolica del Sacro Cuore, Milan
ROBERT ORESKO, Institute of Historical Research, University of
London
and GEOFFREY SYMCOX, University of California, Los Angeles

This series comprises monographs and a variety of collaborative volumes, including translated works, which will concentrate on the period of Italian history from late medieval times up to the Risorgimento. The editors aim to stimulate scholarly debate over a range of issues which have not hitherto received, in English, the attention they deserve. As it develops, the series will emphasize the interest and vigour of current international debates on this central period of Italian history and the persistent influence of Italian culture on the rest of Europe.

For a list of titles in the series, see end of book

ENGLISH MERCHANTS IN SEVENTEENTH-CENTURY ITALY

GIGLIOLA PAGANO DE DIVITIIS

University of Calabria

TRANSLATED BY STEPHEN PARKIN

CAMBRIDGE
UNIVERSITY PRESS

CAMBRIDGE UNIVERSITY PRESS
Cambridge, New York, Melbourne, Madrid, Cape Town, Singapore,
São Paulo, Delhi, Dubai, Tokyo, Mexico City

Cambridge University Press
The Edinburgh Building, Cambridge CB2 8RU, UK

Published in the United States of America by Cambridge University Press, New York

www.cambridge.org
Information on this title: www.cambridge.org/9780521580311

Originally published in Italian as *Mercanti inglesi nell'Italia del Seicento: navi, traffici, egemonie*

by Marsilio Editori 1990

and © Marsilio Editori, Venice 1990

First published in English by Cambridge University Press 1997 as *English merchants in seventeenth-century Italy*

English translation © Gigliola Pagano de Divitiis

A catalogue record for this publication is available from the British Library

Library of Congress Cataloguing in Publication data
Pagano De Divitiis, Gigliola.
[Mercanti inglesi nell'Italia del Seicento. English]
English merchants in seventeenth-century Italy/Gigliola Pagano de Divitiis:
translated by Stephen Parkin.
p.   cm. – (Cambridge studies in Italian history and culture)
Includes bibliographical references and index.
ISBN 0 521 58031 5
1. Italy – Commerce – England – History – 17th century.
2. England – Commerce – Italy – History – 17th century.
3. Merchants, Foreign – Italy – History – 17th century.
I. Title.   II. Series.
HF3588.G6P3413   1997
382'.0942045 – dc21   97–1846   CIP

ISBN 978-0-521-58031-1 Hardback

For Marcella Pagano

CONTENTS

LIST OF TABLES

PREFACE

The seventeenth century is normally regarded as a time of crisis for the Mediterranean world, in which the centuries-old commercial domination of the maritime and industrial cities of northern Italy was in retreat before the ascendancy of England and Holland, whose global economic strategy first began to be built in the Mediterranean.

Generalisations have often sufficed to describe the period and despite the recent appearance of studies devoted to the decline of Venice and Spain (Rapp, Kamen) as well as to the activity of the Dutch in Mediterranean trade (Israel), the inter-relations of Italy and England, the two countries most closely involved in the century's developments, have not been explored in detail. The expansion of English trade in the Levant has been studied by Wood and by Davis, but there is no extended examination of English commercial activity in the central and western Mediterranean. The present work seeks to clarify the ways in which England came to replace the cities of northern Italy as the guiding force in the organisation of Mediterranean trade over the course of the seventeenth century, and the reasons why it was able to take on this role.

While the study takes account of wider contexts, its analysis of the English conquest of Mediterranean trade concentrates largely on the triangle formed by London, Livorno, and the 'Mezzogiorno' or southern Italy, a pattern underlying the organisation of the entire English system of trade in the Mediterranean region. The discussion is organised by topic, as befits the nature of the inquiry and the sources which have been used, but at the unavoidable risk of some repetition. The discussion of each topic is set within a chronological framework which reflects the development over time both of English commercial expansion and of the closely related Italian situation. Three phases can be identified: the return of northern European ships to Mediterranean waters at the end of the sixteenth century, the choice of Livorno at the beginning of the 1630s as the organisational hub of English trade in the region, and the full establishment of the system together with its absorption into a global network of trade after the Stuart restoration in 1660.

The book is based on many years' research, in the course of which I have accumulated many debts of gratitude for the help I received. The research I carried out in British archives and libraries was made possible by grants from the British Academy and the Consiglio Nazionale delle Ricerche. The attentive help of the staff in the following institutions has been invaluable: the Public Record Office in London and Kew, the British Library, the Kent County Council Record Office, the library of the London School of Economics and Political Science, the Archivio Storico del Banco di Napoli, and the State Archives in Livorno, Pisa, Florence and Naples.

Individual thanks must go to Giuseppe Galasso, for first encouraging me to undertake this research; Luigi De Rosa, for his support in the early stages of the work; Peter Earle, for his unfailing and generous help while I was researching in London; Vincenzo Giura, for following the project with interest and encouragement, and for reading the final manuscript. My work has been greatly helped by individual discussions with Basil Yamey, Sari Hornstein and David Hebb, and by the seminars organised at the Institute of Historical Research of the University of London by the late Professor F. J. Fisher. I should also like to thank Piero Bevilacqua for his valuable advice and Robert Oresko for his precious support. I owe much more than might appear from the book itself to Fernand Braudel, Ruggiero Romano and Maurice Aymard.

Finally, I should like to thank Oreste, Paolo, Marcello and Bianca for their unwavering support and reassurance at moments of doubt and fatigue.

ABBREVIATIONS

Add. MSS	Additional Manuscripts
ANF, AE	Archives Nationales de France – Affaires Etrangères
ASBN	Archivio Storico del Banco di Napoli
ASF	Archivio di Stato di Firenze
ASG	Archivio di Stato di Genova
ASL	Archivio di Stato di Livorno
ASN	Archivio di Stato di Napoli
ASP	Archivio di Stato di Pisa
ASV	Archivio di Stato di Venezia
Banco AGP	Banco Ave Gratia Plena (Annunziata)
BL	British Library – Department of Manuscripts
BNN	Biblioteca Nazionale di Napoli
CO	Colonial Office
CSP	Calendar of State Papers
Eg.	Egerton
HCA	High Court of Admiralty
KCCRO	Kent County Council Record Office, Maidstone
PRO	Public Record Office, London
SP	State Papers
SP46	State Papers Supplementary
SP78	State Papers Foreign – France
SP84	State Papers Foreign – Holland
SP93	State Papers Foreign – Sicily and Naples
SP98	State Papers Foreign – Tuscany
SP101	State Papers Foreign – News Letters
SP103	State Papers Foreign – Treaty Papers
SP104	State Papers Foreign – Entry Books
SP105	State Papers Foreign – Levant Company

CHAPTER I

TIMES AND PLACES

THE ENTRY OF THE ENGLISH INTO THE MEDITERRANEAN

In a dispatch written to the Doge and Senate in Venice on 28 September 1605, Nicolò Molin regretted the passing of the time when foreign merchants had been welcomed into England while those native merchants who traded abroad were few and far between; now it was almost exclusively the English who dedicated themselves to foreign trade, gradually extending their control over the entire commercial network and all its opportunities for profit. Molin added that the Levant Company had drawn up an agreement with the Crown which defined the extent of its monopoly; the Company itself continued to thrive, maintaining its own consul in Constantinople, growing in membership and widening the area of its operations, which now, the ambassador ended, included Italy.[1]

Molin's remarks testify to the shift in the pattern of trade between northern Europe and the Mediterranean. The essential upshot of this change was the exclusion of Italian merchants from English trade, in both the English and the Mediterranean markets, to the point where part of Italy itself, as a trading area, fell under the control of the English company. In 1581 the Company had received its charter from Elizabeth, together with the granting of the monopoly of the nation's trade with the Levant.[2]

From the thirteenth to the sixteenth centuries, trade between

---

[1] CSP, Venetian, 1603–1607, 28 Sept. 1605, p. 276.
[2] All that Nicolò Molin meant by the expression 'Italy' was the Adriatic coast and the so-called 'currant islands', Zante and Cephalonia. After a protracted argument with the Crown, the Levant Company finally succeeded in incorporating the Venice Company, which held the monopoly in the trade of currants, wine and oil ('sweet oil') with Venice and its islands. See A. C. Wood, *A history of the Levant Company* (London: 1935; 1964). 'Charters' were issued by the sovereign to ratify the concession of privileges and exemptions.

I

northern and southern Europe had been controlled by the merchants of
Florence, Genoa and Venice, who had successfully introduced their
manufactured goods into the markets of northern Europe. Venice,
moreover, held the monopoly of trade with the east, from where goods
arrived, along the caravan routes, at the Mediterranean shores of Asia
Minor; whereas Genoa dominated the market for alum, used as a
mordant in the manufacture of woollen cloth (first extracted at Phocaea
in Asia Minor but later principally at Tolfa in the Papal State). It was
Venetian and Genoese galleys and carracks which transported the goods
from the Mediterranean to the north, and returned laden with wool,
essential for the Italian textile industry, and metals such as lead and tin.[3]

A sophisticated financial system lay behind the activities of the Italian
merchants, which enabled them by means of bills of exchange and the
use of a dense network of agents in all the principal trading cities to shift
capital at short notice to where it was needed and to obtain short-term
credit; thus, they were able to subsidise not only their own commercial
operations but also the wars between European monarchs, exploiting
the support they gave them to extract special privileges and commercial
advantages.[4]

The trading relations between northern and southern Europe underwent their first significant change at the end of the fifteenth century and
onwards, with the emergence of Antwerp as a key commercial link
between the two. Various factors favoured the rise of Antwerp as a
centre for merchants and their goods: among them, the choice of the
city as an operational base both for the commercial agents of the Portuguese monarchy, offering the spices and sugars which Lisbon received
from the east and from Brazil in exchange for metals, as well as for the
Papal agents selling alum in northern Europe.[5]

The leading Italian firms also set up branches in Antwerp, from
where they continued to oversee their European commercial and financial strategy:[6] the city was well situated at the point where the roads

---

[3] On the alum from Tolfa, see J. Delumeau, *L'alun de Rome (XVème–XVIème siècle)*
(Paris: 1962). The period from 1420 to 1470 saw the failure of Tuscany's attempt to
rival Venice and Genoa as a maritime power. See M. E. Mallett, *The Florentine galleys
in the fifteenth century* (Oxford: 1967); C. Vivanti, 'La storia politica e sociale, dall'avvento delle Signorie all'Italia spagnola' in R. Romano (ed.), *Storia d'Italia* (Turin:
1974), vol. II, part I, pp. 312–13. The purchase of Livorno from the Genoese in 1421
probably formed part of the Tuscan strategy.

[4] See T. H. Lloyd, *Alien merchants in England in the High Middle Ages* (Brighton: 1982).

[5] C. G. A. Clay, *Economic expansion and social change: England 1500–1700* (Cambridge:
1984), vol. II, pp. 110–11.

[6] On the Genoese merchants in Antwerp, see C. Beck, 'Eléments sociaux et économiques de la vie des marchands génois à Anvers entre 1528 et 1555', *Revue du Nord*

which led through Germany from Venice and Milan reached the North Sea. It was on these roads that the less space-consuming and more valuable Mediterranean commodities were usually entrusted on the journey northwards, while, in the opposite direction, English woollens were sent south to the Italian cities and to the principal ports of the Levant.[7] Bulky goods of comparatively low value, on the other hand, were sent by sea: oil, alum and wine to the north, raw wool, lead and tin to the south.[8]

Antwerp was particularly well placed in relation to England, a mere two days' journey away: English merchants could thus gain easy access to the eastern spices and Italian silks on offer in the city and also find a market for their own kerseys and heavy woollens.[9] On the English side, the Flemish entrepôt gave rise to a concentration of commercial traffic and foreign merchants in London, which helped to promote the capital city over other English ports.[10]

The first English attempt to dispense with Italian middlemen can be dated as far back as 1446, when Robert Sturmy of Bristol sent the *Cog Anne* with a cargo of wool, tin and other goods to the Mediterranean. This voyage, like that of the *Katherine Sturmy*, its successor, chartered by the same merchant, ended in ignominious failure: one ship was wrecked in bad weather off the Greek coast, while the other was sunk near Malta by the Genoese, angry at this invasion of their commercial territory.[11] From this time onwards, English ships continued to venture beyond the Straits of Gibraltar, albeit only occasionally.

(1982), 759–84; and the classic study by J. A. Goris, *Etude sur les colonies marchandes méridionales à Anvers du 1488 à 1567* (Louvain: 1925).

[7] On the role of Ancona in this system, see P. Earle, 'The commercial development of Ancona, 1470–1551', *The Economic History Review*, ser. 2, 22/22 (1969), 28–44.

[8] The export of raw wool from England was made illegal in 1614 (see Clay, *Economic expansion and social change*, vol. II, p. 14).

[9] Kerseys were a cloth of average quality and thickness. The textiles of the 'old draperies' were thick and costly, and generally intended for the markets of northern Europe. The usual procedure was to export them semi-finished to Flanders, where they were dyed. See A. Friis, *Alderman Cockayne's project and the cloth trade* (Copenhagen: 1927); P. J. Bowden, *The wool trade in Tudor and Stuart England* (London: 1971); G. D. Ramsay, *The English woollen industry, 1500–1750* (London: 1982).

[10] Clay, *Economic expansion and social change*, vol. II, p. 112; G. D. Ramsay, 'The undoing of the Italian mercantile colony in sixteenth-century London' in N. B. Harte and K. G. Ponting (eds.), *Textile history and economic history: essays in honour of Miss Julia de Lacey Mann* (Manchester: 1973), p. 23; A. A. Ruddock, *Italian merchants and shipping in Southampton, 1270–1600* (Southampton: 1951).

[11] Wood, *A history of the Levant Company*, pp. 1–2; J. Heers, 'Les Génois en Angleterre: la crise de 1458–1466' in *Studi in onore di Armando Sapori* (Milan: 1957), vol. I, pp. 809–32; F. Braudel, *La Méditerranée et le monde méditerranéen à l'époque de Philippe II* (Paris: 1949; 1979), vol. I, p. 554.

However, in the twenty years from 1550 to 1570, such contacts
appeared to cease altogether. English historians have usually ascribed
this interruption to two causes: the deteriorating situation in the Mediterranean, plagued by piracy and the warfare between Christians and
Muslims, and the proximity of Antwerp which made it a convenient
source for spices and other goods of Mediterranean provenance as well
as a useful outlet for English woollens.[12] Braudel, on the other hand,
argues that the worsening situation in the Mediterranean, if true, would
have affected all shipping in the area. There is, however, a considerable
body of evidence to show that Venetian and Ragusan ships continued
to sail their usual routes in this period. Braudel argues that the reasons
for the interruption in English voyages are to be sought elsewhere: in
the economic crises, for example, which struck continental Europe
during 1540–5 and England a few years later (it was this mid-century
crisis in England which led to the establishment of the Merchant
Adventurers in 1552). A decline in foreign demand for English goods
had come about as a consequence both of the slowing down of trade
and the reduction in colonial imports. The break in trading relations
was therefore due to the fact that Mediterranean contacts were no
longer profitable for English merchants, faced with competition from
the Mediterranean mercantile fleets and the traffic on the overland
routes.[13]

Subsequently, it was the desire for greater profits, stemming from the
growing domestic demand for luxury goods, which induced the English
merchants to reopen links with the Mediterranean world, with Italy and
the Iberian peninsula – although here the process was hindered by the
worsening relations with Spain – and to seek to broaden their trading
contacts to include Russia and the Baltic, North Africa, the Gulf of
Guinea and the Indian Ocean.[14]

The return of the English merchants to the Mediterranean can be

[12] See Wood, *A history of the Levant Company*; Ramsay, 'The undoing of the Italian
mercantile colony'; Clay, *Economic expansion and social change*.
[13] Braudel, *La Méditerranée*, vol. I, p. 556. On the subject of the 'Merchant Adventurers', see E. M. Carus-Wilson, 'The origin and early development of the Merchant
Adventurers' organisation in London as shown in their own medieval records', *The
Economic History Review* 4 (1932–4), 147–76; G. D. Ramsay, *The City of London in international politics at the accession of Elizabeth Tudor* (Manchester: 1975); W. R.
Baumann, *The Merchant Adventurers and the continental cloth-trade, 1560s–1620s* (Berlin:
1990). A similar theory that there was no suitable profit margin in Mediterranean
trade is advanced by Clay to support his argument that the crisis in the Antwerp
market developed before the collapse of the northern entrepôt as a result of competition from other merchants, the Italians in particular, who exploited the advantage of
their direct trading contacts with the sources of supply.
[14] Clay, *Economic expansion and social change*, vol. II, pp. 126–7.

dated precisely: 23 June 1573, when the *Swallow*, commanded by John Scott and sailing from London and Southampton, docked in the port of Livorno. It was carrying a cargo of bells, tin, wool, kerseys and other textiles, although some of the goods which were later to make up the typical cargo of English ships were absent: leather, herrings, salmon and other preserved fish, as well as those which were taken aboard at Lisbon or Cadiz, during the voyage out, such as cochineal, flax, sugar and sapan wood.[15]

Various factors worked together to favour the return of the English ships. In terms of foreign relations, the two interruptions in trade with Antwerp, the first in 1563–4, and the second, of irremediable consequences, in 1569–73, both due to the crisis in Anglo-Spanish relations, led to an increase in the cost of spices; the supply of spices was, in any case, increasingly insecure after Portugal came under Spanish rule, and following the outbreak of hostilities with Spain. In the same period the sack of Antwerp in 1576 marked the end of its prosperity as an entrepôt, while Hamburg, where trade was diverted from the 1570s onwards, was suitably located for northern European trade but not for the Mediterranean area. The Mediterranean itself saw a revival of navigation after the battle of Lepanto and the end of the Venetian war against the Turks.

On the domestic front, foreign merchants resident in London, who had enjoyed a period, from 1539 to 1546, of profitable trade, caused by the level pegging of customs duties in England and abroad, now found themselves subject to a series of restrictions. These new restrictions led to the expulsion of the Hanseatic merchants in 1598 and, among the Italian traders, either voluntary departure or, for the few who remained, assimilation within the English mercantile community.

It was, in Ramsay's opinion, the Italians themselves who were responsible for the return of the English to the Mediterranean: they had taught the English their financial skills, imparted their ability to organise trading links over a wide area, and instructed them in the use of bills of exchange instead of currency; while the Cabots had opened up the route across the Atlantic for English seamen.[16] Among those Italians who most actively encouraged the English was the Pallavicino family from Genoa, who were farmers of alum from Tolfa in north-western Europe and who kept correspondents both in Antwerp and in London. In 1568 they started up a direct connection by sea from Civitavecchia to London, using Venetian and Ragusan ships, and excluding Antwerp. This arrangement lasted for almost a decade, until 1577, when Orazio

---

[15] F. Braudel and R. Romano, *Navires et marchandises à l'entrée du Port de Livourne (1547–1611)* (Paris: 1951), p. 49.

[16] Ramsay, 'The undoing of the Italian mercantile colony'.

Pallavicino, a businessman and courtier, a close friend of the Cecil family and an ambassador for Elizabeth I, commissioned Hawkins to sail from England to Genoa to transport vast quantities of alum.[17] This established a trend: in 1585, we find the Grand Duke of Tuscany recommending the *Appaltatori degli Allumi d'Italia* or 'alum farmers of Italy', his subjects, to the Queen's protection; they wished to use the English ships which reached Livorno and other Italian ports to 'transport their merchandise into Your Majesty's Kingdom, and to other parts of France and Flanders'.[18] The initiative to export herrings from England to Italy also came from an Italian merchant resident in London, Vincenzo Guicciardini, who displayed a very shrewd grasp of the English and Italian markets.[19]

Before travelling on to the Mediterranean ports which were centres for the spice trade, the English ships first navigated the Adriatic as far as Venice, where they stocked up with currants, wine and oil. The man responsible for this inversion of the usual European trade route, a development encouraged by the Venetian postwar crisis, was the Lucca merchant and financier, Acerbo Vellutelli, known as 'Mr Asharbo', who was regarded as the leading Italian importer in the City. In 1575, Elizabeth granted him the monopoly for Venetian imports into England. Venice countered by raising its import duties on English goods, as well as on currants, wine, and oil, which could henceforth only be exported from Venice. In 1582, in response to pressure from the English merchants operating in the Mediterranean, whose business had been damaged both by the monopoly granted to Vellutelli and by the Venetian countermeasures, Vellutelli's patent was revoked. The following year saw the establishment of the Venice Company, initially for a period of six years, which enjoyed the same monopoly privileges which had been granted to 'Mr Asharbo'.

The new company, however, trespassed on the activities of the Levant Company, which had only recently received its own charter in

---

[17] L. Stone, *An Elizabethan: Sir Horatio Palavicino* (Oxford: 1956); Delumeau, *L'alun de Rome*; G. Pagano de Divitiis, 'L'arrivo dei nordici in Mediterraneo' in R. Romano (ed.), *Storia d'Italia* (Milan, 1989), vol. V, pp. 49–72. Orazio Pallavicino, known to the English as Sir Horatio Palavicino, was born in Genoa in 1540. He died in 1600 at his country house in Babraham near Cambridge, after he had amassed immense wealth and extensive estates. He was a friend of Sir Willam Cecil, Lord Burghley (1520–1598), secretary, Lord Treasurer, and minister under Elizabeth I, and of his son, Robert Cecil, Earl of Salisbury (1563–1612), who held the same positions.

[18] PRO, SP98/1, 14, Grand Duke to Elizabeth, Florence 9 Aug. 1585: 'per condurre la lor Mercantia ne i Regni di Vostra Maestà et in altre parti della Francia, et Fiandra'. The Grand Duke of Tuscany at this time was Francesco de' Medici (1574–87), the son of Cosimo I.

[19] Ramsay, 'The undoing of the Italian mercantile colony', 66.

1581: relations between the two were intensely competitive and strained. Until they were formally merged in 1592, there was a series of arguments with the Crown and with other merchants on account of the high import duties which non-members of the Company in England had to pay. The issue was resolved only in 1605, with the granting of a new charter to the Levant Company, under the terms of which, as Nicolò Molin pointed out, Venice and its territories formed part of the protected commercial area which was allotted to it.[20]

The exclusion of Vellutelli from the monopoly on Venetian imports, and the establishment of the Levant or Turkey Company on the part of two English merchants, Edward Osborne and Richard Staper, are indications of the extent of England's readiness to take control of its trade with the Mediterranean. At this point our focus must shift from the Italian presence in England to examine the activities of the English in the Mediterranean.

THE ITALIAN CRISIS

Vellutelli's initiative took advantage of the Venetian crisis in the years following the war with Turkey and the loss of Cyprus. In the same way the new commercial skills of the English needed a favourable opportunity if they were to be put into practice, the kind of opportunity which presented itself in the Mediterranean world in the last quarter of the sixteenth century. It was not only the increase in England's economic strength, but also the decline in Italian power which favoured the expansion of English trade in the Mediterranean. The merchants whose interests in the Levant were harmed by the arrival of the English were Italian, as were the ships which remained in harbour while English vessels for the Mediterranean voyages found themselves in increasing demand.[21]

An analysis of England's commercial conquest of the Mediterranean, therefore, does not simply entail an examination of the changing relations between England and Italy; the flaws which were beginning to appear in the Italian system must also be studied, since it was these which allowed the growing commercial power of England first to infiltrate Mediterranean trade and then to seize control of its key centres, in the process ousting Italy from its leading role.

Historians have long viewed the seventeenth-century Italian crisis as

[20] Ibid., 47; Wood, *A history of the Levant Company*, pp. 18, 35–41.
[21] R. Davis, 'England and the Mediterranean' in F. J. Fisher (ed.), *Essays in the economic and social history of Tudor and Stuart England – in honour of R. H. Tawney* (Cambridge: 1961), pp. 132–3.

one element within a wider European crisis, of which the economic dimension was of fundamental importance.[22] The argument that the sixteenth century, *el siglo de oro*, was followed by one of decline was based on two observations: the continuing reduction in the supplies of precious metals from the New World and the fall in prices, which was held to be directly dependent on the import of the metals into Europe.[23] Both these presuppositions have been challenged by recent historians, who have sought to show, in particular, that imports of American silver continued to reach the Mediterranean throughout the seventeenth century and later.[24] As Morineau points out, while such recent research does not transform our overall picture of the seventeenth century as one of decline, it does alert us to the need for a less generalized and more detailed examination of the 'multiple and variously localized developments taking place within the same limited time span' which are characteristic of the period. If we wish to analyse the European crisis of the seventeenth century – always granting that there was such a crisis – we need to lay aside the construction of systematic chains of cause and effect and concentrate on the train of events as these develop from moment to moment.[25] Morineau also argues that the development or decline, in terms of growth, of a country should be based on per capita estimates of its gross national product, a figure which it is difficult to calculate for the pre-industrial period.[26]

The situation in Italy was directly related to the century's wider economic crisis. Moreover, as Romano has written, 'the seriousness of the Italian crisis was exacerbated by the economic difficulties affecting other European countries at the same time'.[27] In the opinion of some historians, Italy was transformed in the course of the seventeenth century from an urban and industrialised country into a typically backward one, characterised by a total collapse of the manufacturing sector. External trade did not disappear overnight, but its nature changed: by the end of the century, Italy was primarily exporting raw materials and agricultural products to the countries of northern Europe.[28]

---

[22] See T. Aston (ed.), *Crisis in Europe, 1560–1660* (London: 1965).

[23] E. J. Hamilton, *American treasure and the price revolution in Spain (1501–1650)* (Cambridge, Mass.: 1934); H. Chaunu, *Séville et l'Atlantique* (Paris: 1955–9).

[24] See H. Kamen, *Spain in the later seventeenth century, 1665–1700* (London: 1980); M. Morineau, 'Il secolo' in P. Leon (ed.), *Storia economica e sociale del mondo. Difficoltà di sviluppo, 1580–1730*, vol. II (Bari: 1980); H. Roserveare (ed.), *Markets and merchants of the late seventeenth century: the Marescoe-David letters, 1668–1680* (Oxford: 1987).

[25] Morineau, 'Il secolo', pp. 66, 87, 98.   [26] Ibid., p. 101.

[27] 'L'Italia nella crisi del secolo XVII' in R. Romano, *Tra due crisi: l'Italia del Rinascimento* (Turin: 1971), p. 191.

[28] See E. J. Hobsbawm, 'General crisis of the European economy in the 17th century',

Reservations about such a theory have been expressed by Charles Wilson. Wilson takes account of the arguments advanced by Cipolla and supported by Romano; he himself believes that the principal manifestation of the Italian crisis was a decline in the commercial and industrial activity of the country's heartland, the quadrilateral lying between Genoa and Venice to the west and east, and Milan and Florence to the north and south, yet he goes on to ask if industrial decline was not compensated for by greater investment and higher productivity in the agricultural sector, as De Maddalena has shown to be the case in northern Italy. Wilson is of the opinion that no conclusion can be reached until new evidence is available; what can be convincingly argued at present is that, while the economic structure of seventeenth-century England was both more advanced and better balanced than that of Italy, Italy nevertheless remained more economically advanced than Spain.[29]

The seventeenth-century Italian crisis has similarly been re-examined by recent historians; in this context too, as with the more general view of Europe, although the verdict that there was a decline has not been reversed, a more diversified picture of periods and places has begun to emerge.

A distinction of primary importance has been drawn between 'relative decline' and 'absolute decline', where the first can be defined as the loss of one country's economic superiority over other countries within the same economic community. Distinguishing features of this decline might be the disappearance of freight traffic and port industries, a falling behind in industrial competitiveness, and diminishing influence. Absolute decline, on the other hand, may be defined as the growing inability of a country to maintain the standard of living of its population. The difference between absolute and relative decline is that the first involves a comparison of a country's present economic conditions with its past performance, whereas the second

Past and present, 5 (1954); C. M. Cipolla, 'The decline of Italy: the case of a fully matured economy', The Economic History Review, ser.2, 5/2 (1952), 178–87.

[29] C. H. Wilson, 'The historical study of economic growth and decline in early modern history' in E. E. Rich and C. H. Wilson (eds.), The Cambridge economic history of Europe (Cambridge: 1967), vol. v, pp. 33–4; Romano, 'L'Italia nella crisi del secolo XVII'; R. Romano, 'Tra XVI e XVII secolo una crisi economica: 1619–1622', Rivista storica italiana 74 (1962), 480–531; R. Romano, 'Encore la crise de 1619–1622', Annales ESC 19 (1964), 31–7; A. De Maddalena, 'Il mondo rurale italiano nel Cinque e nel Seicento', Rivista storica italiana 76 (1964), 349–426; A. De Maddalena, 'Rural Europe 1500–1750' in C. M. Cipolla (ed.), The Fontana economic history of Europe (London: 1974), vol. II, pp. 273–354.

implies a comparison with other countries over the same period of time.[30]

This distinction has been made by the American historian R. T. Rapp in relation to seventeenth-century Venice, a typical example of relative decline. He maintains that, although this period saw a collapse of the Venetian role in international trade, there was, in compensation, a transformation of the leading industries from export-led production to internal market activities, without any appreciable decrease in the population or in the standard of living. It has likewise been shown that, in the case of Florence, as in the rest of northern Italy, the verdict of decline has been largely based on figures for the production of woollen cloth, an industry which was undoubtedly in crisis at the turn of the sixteenth century, ignoring the fact that for a pre-industrial society there is no such thing as a key industry, as modern analysis would understand the term. It is moreover impossible in this period to apply the modern parallel concepts of developed/industrial societies and underdeveloped/agrarian ones.[31]

In the particular case of Florence, where population, prices and wages were comparatively stable throughout the seventeenth century, the wool industry's leading role in the city's economy was taken over by the largely export-driven production of silk. This transformation was accompanied by the region's almost complete abandonment of the traditional sources of raw material in southern Italy, and a thoroughgoing reorganisation of the financial and managerial activities of the silk industry.[32]

While Florence and Venice in the sixteenth century were the acknowledged leaders in manufacturing industry and commerce respectively, the Genoese had, from the middle of the century onwards, ceased to play a significant role in either. Contemporary observers all agree on the change of direction in the city's financial activities. Giovan Francesco Buonamici, in his *Scrittura in materia di nautica* of 1629, addressed to Galileo, remarked that 'Genoa is preoccupied with other concerns, and prefers to entrust its wealth to the guidance of Spanish decrees rather than expose its ships to the storm-tossed waves of the

---

[30] R. T. Rapp, *Industry and economic decline in seventeenth-century Venice* (Cambridge, Mass.: 1976), pp. 1–13.

[31] D. Abulafia, 'Southern Italy and the Florentine economy, 1265–1370', *The Economic History Review*, ser. 2, 34/3 (1981), 377–88.

[32] J. Goodman, 'The Florentine silk industry in the seventeenth century', Ph.D. thesis, London School of Economics (1976). See also J. Goodman, 'Financing pre-modern European industry, 1580–1660', *Journal of European Economic History* 10/2 (1981).

ocean. The Spanish galleys at anchor in the harbour there are used mainly for the transport of money, and little else.'[33]

Writing in the same period, Lewes Roberts, an English merchant who had lived in Italy for a long time, declared, in his *The merchants map of commerce*, that, in the first decades of the seventeenth century, Genoa was the home of 'the greatest Money-changers and Usurers in the world, who if they would not distrust God with their wealth by Sea, would easily become famous Merchants'.[34]

The 'Genoese century', following the great age of the Fugger family, celebrated in the writings of Braudel, is usually described as ending in 1627, when Olivares began to replace Genoese bankers with the Portuguese Marranos from Amsterdam.[35] However, the withdrawal of the Genoese from Spanish finance signified neither a defeat nor the onset of a crisis for the city; from 1617 onwards, Genoese capital was subject to a 'vast and radical redistribution of financial investment': towards Venice and Rome, where Genoese bankers had replaced the Florentines, towards Naples and Sicily, and indeed throughout Europe, including England – in short, wherever handsome profits could be made.[36] Numerous Italian, principally Genoese, communities were still to be found in eighteenth-century Cadiz: in the words of Braudel, 'Genoa kept hold of its prey.'[37]

In Lewes Roberts's opinion, Genoa reflected the changes taking place elsewhere in the country's commercial activities in the early seventeenth century. Some of the greatest and most enterprising merchants were to be found in Italy, although they hardly merited this title, since their skills were largely absorbed by the financial markets rather than commercial initiatives. It was moreover a widespread view that the Italians preferred to keep their wealth safe at home rather than risk it on maritime trade.[38] Romano remarks that 'there was no lack of money: once again, this is not the real problem. It is rather that the money was

[33] C. Guasti (ed.), 'Scrittura in materia di Nautica del Cavaliere Giovan Francesco Buonamici di Prato', *Archivio storico italiano*, ser. 4, 16 (1885), 14: '[Genova] impiegata in altro, ha più tosto voluto fidare le sue ricchezze all'aurea de' decreti di Spagna, che le vele alle procelle e all'onde del mare. Le galere di Spagna che stanno a Genova, fuore che in trasportare denari contanti, s'impiegano in pochi altri noliti.'

[34] L. Roberts, *The merchants map of commerce*, 3rd edn (London: 1677), p. 214. The work was probably written some time in the 1630s.

[35] A. Castillo, 'Les banquiers portugais et le circuit d'Amsterdam', *Annales ESC* 19 (1964), 311–16.

[36] G. Felloni, *Gli investimenti finanzieri genovesi in Europa tra il Seicento e la Restaurazione* (Milan: 1971), p. 472.

[37] F. Braudel, 'L'Italia fuori d'Italia', in R. Romano (ed.), *Storia d'Italia* (Turin: 1974), vol. II, part 2, p. 2167.

[38] Roberts, *Merchants' map*, p. 189.

invested to increase revenue from property rather than generate profits from trade.'[39] Thus the Italian crisis was less a real economic crisis than a progressive withdrawal, at least in northern Italy, from commercial enterprise accompanied by an increasing involvement, partly due to the very prosperity of the country, in property investment and financial speculation, the profits from which were equal to if not greater than those to be obtained from trading, and were, moreover, without the concomitant risks.

In Venice, as early as the sixteenth century, the nobility had begun to withdraw their capital from commercial activity, showing an increasing preference to invest it instead in property on the mainland.[40] The decreasing importance of commerce in the economic life of the city must already have been apparent in the first decade of the new century; we find Leonardo Donà in 1612 writing: 'It is not that we lack capital; our nobility wants no part in trade. Nowadays things are different . . . wealth is tied up in property and estates, in possessions and private amenities in the city, and the prosperous prefer to invest their money in the financial markets rather than employ it in voyages to the Levant.'[41]

Italy was therefore a wealthy country, and remained prosperous, certainly until the mid seventeenth century; its merchants were, however, no longer inclined to risk their capital, preferring to defend what they had. What caused this gradual financial sterility and the change of attitude which lay behind it? A partial explanation may be found in the ease and comparative security of gain in financial speculation, as well as in the lack of correspondingly attractive investments in other sectors. Moreover, the Italians began to spend enormous sums of money in unproductive ways, since the country's economy, as Hobsbawm points out, no longer offered the opportunities for profitable investment.[42]

The sheer wealth of Italy in this period is indicated by the country's high consumption of caviar, said to account for 97.5 per cent of Russia's total exported production.[43] Until 1658, caviar, together with hides and

---

[39] R. Romano, 'La storia economica: dal secolo XIV al Settecento', in *Storia d'Italia*, vol. II, part 2, p. 1915.

[40] U. Tucci, *Mercanti, navi, monete nel Cinquecento veneziano* (Bologna: 1981).

[41] S. Romanin, *Storia documentata di Venezia* (Venice: 1858), vol. VII, pp. 532–3: 'A noi non mancano i capitali, la nobiltà non vuole aver parte nella mercantia. Hora le cose sono mudade . . . tutto è impiegato in beni e stabili, in possession e delitie della città, e a chi soprabbonda il denaro tutto sta sui cambi, che è quello che potria essere impiegato nelli viazi del Levante.'

[42] Hobsbawm, 'General crisis'.

[43] PRO, SP98/8, Finch to Arlington, 7 Mar. 1667. See G. Pagano de Divitiis, 'Il Mediterraneo nel XVII secolo: l'espansione commerciale inglese e l'Italia', *Studi storici* 1 (1986), 109–48; J. I. Israel, 'The phases of the Dutch *staatvaart*, 1590–1713', *Tijschrift*

other Russian exports, was transported and distributed via the port of Livorno by ships belonging to the Muscovy Company. Commercial relations between Tuscany and Russia, with the English acting as the middlemen, began in 1634; it appears that Tsar Michael I entrusted the English consul in Livorno, Morgan Read, with temporary responsibility for the Russian consulate in the city.[44]

In 1658, when the contract with the Muscovy Company expired, the Tsar, conscious of the importance of the Italian market, sent a special envoy to the Tuscan Grand Duke to negotiate an agreement whereby Tuscany was granted the monopoly on caviar imports in exchange for the payment of an annual sum of money. The Grand Duke, however, offered to pay only half the sum requested in money, with the rest in silk. In response, the Tsar's emissary contacted Charles Longland, the English consul in Livorno under the Protectorate, who set up a joint-stock company, with the participation of Dutch and Italian merchants, which held the contract until 1667.[45] We find what is probably a Dutch ship, the *Sol dorato*, named in the records of a law-suit for the compensation of damage costs brought before the Pisan maritime tribunal by Giovanni Zeffi & Company against Thomas Dethick and other insurers; this ship was under the command of the Fleming, Giovanni Cornelissen, and had been hired by Zeffi and his partners to bring caviar and other goods from the port of Archangel to Livorno.[46]

Given the importance of the business, which brought in profits of the order of 60 per cent, the English resident in Tuscany, Sir John Finch, sought to keep the import of caviar in the same hands when the contract which had been agreed with Longland's company expired; he appealed to Arlington, the Secretary of State, and warned him of the fierce com-

---

voor Geschiedenis 99 (1986), 1–30; J. I. Israel, *Dutch primacy in world trade, 1585–1740* (Oxford: 1989), p. 47.

[44] G. Guarnieri, *Livorno medicea* (Livorno: 1970), p. 183. The Muscovy Company was established in 1555, following Chancellor and Willoughby's expedition in search of a north-east passage to the Far East. Sebastian Cabot was the first governor of the company. See T. S. Willan, *The Muscovy merchants of 1555* (Manchester: 1953).

[45] PRO, SP98/8, Finch to Arlington, 7 Mar. 1667. Sir John Finch (1626–82) was educated at Cambridge and Oxford, and took a degree in medicine at Padua. From 1665 to 1672 he held the appointment of English resident in Tuscany; from 1672 to 1682 he was ambassador in Constantinople. See A. Malloch, *Finch and Baines: a seventeenth-century friendship* (Cambridge: 1917). Sir Henry Bennet (1618–85; he was made Lord Arlington in 1665, and the first Earl of Arlington in 1672), an experienced diplomat and Member of Parliament, held the post of Secretary of State for the Southern Department from 1662 to 1674, when he was appointed Lord Chamberlain. See G. Pagano de Divitiis (ed.), *Il commercio inglese nel Mediterraneo dal '500 al '700* (Naples: 1984), pp. 34–6, 333 ff.

[46] ASP, Consoli del mare, 271/10, judgement dated 26 May 1660.

petition to seize control of the trade which they would face from the Dutch and the Italians. Moreover, the Grand Duke had already written personally to the Tsar on behalf of his own subjects.[47] No further reference to the 'caviar business' can be found in the English State Papers;[48] most probably Ferdinand II's letter to the Tsar had the desired effect, and the monopoly remained, at least for a while, with Longland, Zeffi and their Dutch partners. In 1668 caviar was still arriving in Livorno on Dutch ships sailing via Holland and Spain and on French ships via Smyrna.[49]

There was, therefore, no lack of capital or indeed entrepreneurial initiative among the Italians, when the business in hand held out the prospect of large profits; the objection may still be raised, however, that the Florentine merchants involved in the caviar trade were primarily concerned with revenue, were careful to share the risks with northern European partners, and used Dutch ships. The Tuscan merchants' reluctance to commit themselves to excessive risks and to organise their own transport stems, as we have seen, from defeats sustained more than two centuries earlier;[50] Finch emphasises this reluctance in a dispatch to Arlington written in January 1667:

> The Florentines are so unwilling to trust any thing with their Estates that they will not sell their fabricks of silk without ready money; nor adventure any thing at Sea So that by reason of the Warrs few ships presenting in these Parts to take of their Commoditys and they not daring to adventure them in bottoms of their own, The Florentine Trade is so wholly lost, that they can Scarce keep the poor Artificers amongst them.[51]

Finch acknowledged that the case of Genoa was different: geographical factors meant that the Ligurian republic needed to import food from outside its territory; the Genoese were thus obliged to maintain trade in order to balance the costs of this imported supply.[52] Unlike the Tuscans, 'those damned Genoese', as the brother of the Grand Duke, Leopold, referred to them, were keen to fill the vacuum left in the

---

[47] PRO, SP98/8, Finch to Arlington, 7 Mar. 1667.
[48] Ibid.
[49] PRO, SP98/8, Thomas Dethick to Joseph Williamson, Livorno, 30 Jan. 1668; SP98/9, lists of arrivals in the port of Livorno on 4 Apr. 1668 and 6 Apr. 1668, included with Dethick's letter to Willamson, Livorno, 9 Apr. 1668. Thomas Dethick was an English merchant resident in Livorno. Sir Joseph Williamson (1633–1701), statesman, diplomat, Member of Parliament and member of the Royal Society, was appointed secretary to Sir Henry Bennet in 1662 and knighted in 1672. He himself held the post of Secretary of State from 1674 to 1678. See *Il commercio inglese nel Mediterraneo*, pp. 34–36, 333.
[50] See note 3 above.
[51] PRO, SP98/8, Finch to Arlington, Livorno, 24 Jan. 1667.   [52] Ibid.

Mediterranean when the outbreak of the Second Dutch War caused a temporary hiatus in Dutch and English trading. They put together a merchant fleet of 112 ships, together with 15 warships, and took control of the trade with Spain, which consisted above all in the shipment of Sicilian corn to the Spanish ports.[53] This trade enabled the Genoese both to acquire Spanish pieces of eight reals legally and to make outstanding profits; according to Finch, in 1666, the Genoese made a 100 per cent profit on the consignments of 57 ships.[54]

Trade in exports from Spain was equally profitable: the Genoese managed at the same time to monopolize the import of Spanish silver into Italy, which had until then been controlled by the Dutch. The Genoese organised a convoy for the purpose, in order to protect the valuable cargo, and they made sure they received an extra percentage to cover the costs of protection in addition to those for transportation; a supplementary cost which proved a source of huge income given the value of the cargo the ships were carrying. They even went so far as to claim payment from other vessels which joined their convoys, on the grounds that, although such ships were guaranteed no protection, they nevertheless enjoyed the benefits of greater security, for which, in the Genoese view, payment should be forthcoming. Finch reports in scandalised tones that they had even extorted such a contribution from an English ship.[55]

The strategy of the Genoese was, however, more complex and far-reaching. Their intention was not merely to monopolise the trade between Italy and Spain, but to control the whole network of trade in the Mediterranean, stretching from the Iberian peninsula, a source of valuable currency, on the one hand, to the Levant on the other, using the money acquired from Spain to purchase Armenian silk in Smyrna. At the beginning of 1666, while their ships were sailing, laden with Sicilian corn, for the ports of Spain, the Genoese were planning to revive direct trading links with Turkey, with the establishment of a consulate in Constantinople, and the enjoyment of the same privileges which the Ottomans had already granted to the English. The agreement was drawn up by the Marquis of Durazzo, the brother of the Genoese

---

[53] Ibid. In a document of February 1666, 120 merchant ships and 4 warships are mentioned (PRO, SP98/6, Finch to Arlington, Livorno, 1 Feb. 1660). The Grand Duke at the time was Ferdinand II de' Medici (1620–70).

[54] PRO, SP98/8, Finch to Arlington, Livorno, 24 Jan. 1667. On the export of pieces of eight reals from Spain, Roberts writes: 'It is ever lawful to him that brings Corn to carry out Rials of Plale [plate] in return thereof' (Merchants map, p. 173).

[55] PRO, SP98/8, Finch to Arlington, Florence, 13 June 1667.

ambassador to the English court.[56] The Genoese convoy of three ships sailing for Constantinople and Smyrna, under the command of Durazzo himself, arrived in Turkey in October 1666; Finch estimated its value at 3 million pieces of eight, probably an exaggeration; it was carrying precious gifts and a large amount of money.[57] Their arrival was warmly welcomed by the Dutch and by the English, according to Finch's account at least; much less so by the French. The French wielded great power with their currency, which had given them considerable advantages over the merchants of other countries and enabled them to earn notable profits, even to the extent of being able to sell Levantine silks in France at a rate lower than the purchase price.[58] The Genoese now chose to use the same strategical weapon in order to compete directly with the French. They began to disparage the French 5 sol coin, which they claimed contained 16 per cent less silver than the Spanish real of eight. The Grand Vizir immediately excluded the French coin from circulation in the market at Smyrna, and even refused to postpone the ban for six months and thus allow the French traders to exhaust the supplies of the coinage which were due to arrive from France. The Genoese attack on the French coin was probably motivated by the desire to replace it with one of their own, minted especially for this market, and probably carrying the same value as the real of eight.[59]

The Genoese could easily win control of the export of silk from Smyrna, since the Republic was wealthy enough – according to Finch, it was 'the only city of Europe furnished with vast summs in ready mony' – to be able to buy it all in cash, thus provoking a rise in prices and the automatic exclusion of other traders.[60] The Genoese plan was, even so, considerably more ambitious: to crown the Republic's success

[56] PRO, SP98/6, Bernard Gascoigne to [Williamson], Florence, 2 Feb. 1666. Sir Bernard Gascoigne (1614–87) belonged to an old Florentine family and was a soldier, adventurer and diplomat in the service of the Grand Duke of Tuscany; his real name was Bernardo or Bernardino Guasconi. He moved to England and fought in the Civil War on the Royalist side; in recognition of his services, Charles I awarded him a pension, which was subsequently renewed by Charles II. He became an English citizen in 1661, returned to Italy in 1663, and finally retired in England in 1667.

[57] PRO, SP98/7, Finch to Arlington, Florence, 28 Sept. 1666; Chellingworth to Arlington, Livorno, 27 Sept. 1666. Charles Chellingworth (or Chillingworth) held the post of consul in Gallipoli, but was acting consul in Livorno, where he replaced Joseph Kent who was touring Italy. He moved to take up his post in the Puglian port in the 1670s.

[58] Wood, A history of the Levant Company, p. 100.

[59] PRO, SP98/7, Finch to Arlington, 26 Oct. 1666.

[60] PRO, SP98/7, Finch to Arlington, 9 Aug. 1667; SP98/6, Gascoigne to Williamson, Florence, 2 Feb. 1666.

in the western and eastern Mediterranean, their strategy envisaged the transfer of the Levantine trade in silk from Livorno, where until then English and Dutch ships had carried it, to Genoa. Finch maintained that the Genoese, in sending Durazzo as an ambassador to the Sultan's court, threatened to monopolize Levantine trade or at the very least divert the trade in Armenian silk away from Livorno, which would result in the inevitable decline of the Tuscan port.[61]

The Genoese initiative in the Levant went according to plan, despite the difficulties Durazzo encountered in his official dealings with the Ottoman court, which were in part caused by the French.[62] The three ships returned fully laden with valuable merchandise, accompanied by a fourth ship, which had been chartered from the Dutch.[63] Although it was for the most part destined for Livorno, the cargo of Armenian silk and other goods was unloaded in Genoa. According to some, this was caused by an outbreak of the plague at Smyrna, the port of embarkation, which meant that the ships would not have been allowed to enter Livorno, where the sanitary laws were strictly observed; a much more plausible explanation is that the Genoese wished to show their rival that their city was 'as good a scale for the Levant trade as Livorno'.[64]

Despite the gradual decline in the economic organisation and coordination of the principal Italian cities throughout the seventeenth century, the centres of Venice, Genoa and Florence suffered no shortage of capital or entrepreneurial initiative, and continued to show commercial flair and acumen; with these advantages and qualities, Italy managed to keep a relative superiority, at least until the middle of the century, while ceding its absolute superiority to the trading nations of the north, and in particular to England.

THE TWO ITALYS: THE SOUTH

Braudel observed that 'it is hazardous to use the singular when speaking of Italy'.[65] So far in this discussion on the absolute or relative crisis in Italy's economic status, and on the reversal of direction in the flow of trade between the Mediterranean and northern Europe, leading to the loss of Italian commercial hegemony in Europe, we have concentrated

---

[61] PRO, SP98/8, Finch to Arlington, 24 Jan. 1667. The sum given by the Genoese in exchange to the Armenians amounted to 100,000 'reals of eight' or dollars (PRO, SP98/8, Dethick to Williamson, Livorno, 11 Apr. 1667).
[62] PRO, SP98/9, Finch to Arlington, Livorno, 31 Jan. 1667.
[63] PRO, SP98/8, Dethick to Williamson, Livorno, 11 Apr. 1667.
[64] PRO, SP98/8, Finch to Arlington, Florence, 5 July 1667.
[65] Braudel, 'L'Italia fuori d'Italia', p. 2101.

only on the north of the country, and on Venice, Genoa and Florence in particular. It is almost superfluous to point out that the political and economic reality of the country as a whole was far more complex and varied.

The true contrast between northern and southern Italy lay in their distinct yet complementary roles: the industrialised north, on the one hand, and the agricultural south on the other. Gino Luzzato has averred that Italy 'was in the past, as it is today, predominantly an agricultural country, in the midst of which limited areas of industrialization, varying in intensity from region to region, flourished'; yet he also acknowledges that a distinction between northern and southern Italy existed which was apparent even to contemporaries:

> On the one hand, there are regions where agricultural production is generally inadequate for the needs of the urban population, which have therefore to be supplied partly with imported produce, paid for out of the surplus export of manufactured goods or from the profits derived from commerce or the carrying trade. On the other hand, there are those regions which can afford to export part of their agricultural production but are obliged to turn elsewhere for the provision of manufactured goods which they themselves do not produce.[66]

So, to return to the three great urban centres examined above, in all three, Genoa, Florence and Venice, there was a high demand for food provision, while the south was in the position of being able to export grain and other agricultural produce, above all from Sicily and Puglia. Genoa's geographical position meant that the city's needs could never be supplied from the territory's own resources, a point which the English resident in Tuscany, writing in January 1667, remarked upon and identified as the principal reason for the development of Genoese commerce: 'the Genovese . . . having so barren a territory that they are forced to provide themselves bread from abroad, are necessitated too to drive a Trade that the gain they make of that, may repayr the constant expense of their wealth in necessary Provisions'.[67]

Genoa had imported corn from Sicily since the Norman period and had held the monopoly for its transportation in the Mediterranean until the arrival of the Dutch and English ships.[68] The geographical limitations of Venice resembled those of Genoa; after a period during which it vacil-

---

[66] G. Luzzato, *Storia economica dell'età moderna e contemporanea* (Padua: 1955), vol. I, p. 106.

[67] PRO, SP98/8, Finch to Arlington, Livorno, 24 Jan. 1667.

[68] See D. Abulafia, *The two Italies: economic relations between the Norman kingdom of Sicily and the northern communes* (Oxford: 1977); E. Grendi, 'Traffico portuale, naviglio mercantile e consolati genovesi nel Cinquecento', *Rivista storica italiana* 80 (1968),

lated between Sicily and Puglia as sources of supply, the Republic finally concentrated its interests within its own Gulf on Puglian corn and oil.[69]

Florence too faced continuing problems of provision, despite the extensive and fertile countryside which surrounded the city. It has been calculated that even under normal circumstances the city could only survive on the produce of its own 'contado' or territory for five months in the year; indeed, during the first half of the fourteenth century, the city suffered a long series of famines. Like Venice, Florence imported its provisions in large part from the southern mainland, from where it purchased meat as well as corn.[70]

Aymard's remark on the ending of trading relations between Venice and Sicily: 'those who do not buy, do not sell' can be read in reverse, 'those who do not sell, do not buy', or, if they do, buy only at a high price, with abundant amounts of money. This pattern recurs continually: the country which imports agricultural products and raw materials pays for them in part with its own manufactured commodities but is also obliged, at least at the outset, to make up the total from its currency reserves. This was the problem which confronted the Venetians, and, after them, the newly arrived merchants from northern Europe, in the Levant; it was also the principal obstacle encountered by the developing English and Dutch East India Companies in the Far East.[71]

In the sixteenth century the galleys carried Spanish pieces of eight reals as well as cloth to Messina, and not all the money which came in was transferred to the Levant.[72] At the beginning of the seventeenth century merchants in Florence, Genoa and Lucca were paying 70 per cent of the cost of their imports of raw silk from Sicily in silver, obtained by means of a complex system of multi-lateral trading which extended outwards from northern and southern Italy to include Spain and northern Europe.[73]

As well as exporting its agricultural produce, southern Italy served the industries in the north of the country as a supplier of raw materials; the north then re-exported them as manufactured products to the south.

593–638; E. Grendi, 'I nordici e il traffico del porto di Genova, 1590–1666', *Rivista storica italiana* 83 (1971), 23–73.

[69] M. Aymard, 'Commerce et consommation des draps en Sicile et en Italie méridionale, XVe–XVIIe siècles' in M. Spallanzani (ed.), *Produzione, commercio e consumo dei panni di lana (nei secoli XII–XVII)* (Florence: 1976).

[70] Abulafia, 'Southern Italy'.

[71] K. N. Chaudhuri, *The English East India Company: the study of an early joint stock company, 1600–1640* (London: 1965).

[72] Aymard, 'Commerce et consommation des draps', p. 134.

[73] T. Mun, *A discourse of trade, from England unto the East-Indies* (1621) in J. R. McCulloch (ed.), *Early tracts on commerce* (1856) (Cambridge: 1970), pp. 15–16.

Thomas Mun remarks that 30 per cent of the raw silk imported from Sicily was subsequently sold as 'Florence rashes' – light silks and satins – in Naples, Palermo and Messina.[74] Centuries earlier the same pattern can be found, this time with the raw cotton which Genoa imported from Sicily: the product was different, but the structure of trade is identical.[75]

Naples was the largest centre of wool production in the country, yet continued to import all its cloth, not only to supply the needs of its nobility, merchants and wealthy citizens, but also to dress its clergy and artisans, despite the efforts which had been made by the city's Aragonese rulers in the fifteenth century to develop a local industry, as the Neapolitan economist Antonio Serra noted at the beginning of the seventeenth century.[76] These efforts were renewed in the second half of the seventeenth century, by which time English merchants had taken the place of Italians from northern Italy. At the prospect of an imminent ban on the imports of English cloth into Naples, Francis Brown, the English consul in the city, warned the Neapolitans that, since southern Italy was the largest overseas market for English woollens, if the ban were enacted, 'the Kingdome will loose a great part of the Extraction of silke and oyles, which are returned for the woollen goods'.[77]

Some years later, George Davies, Brown's successor as consul, was much more outspoken in a report written in reponse to a similar proposal: 'if it is thought that England needs oil and will therefore be forced to resort to payment in cash to obtain it, then they are mistaken, for England has no need of oil except in exchange for its woollens, which are only manufactured in order to be sold in the kingdom'.[78]

---

[74] Ibid. Thomas Mun (1571–1641) was a merchant and an economist. On the death of his father in 1573, his mother married the merchant Thomas Cordell, later to become director of the East India Company, who took on the responsibility of bringing up Mun and his brothers. As a merchant, his trading interests lay in the Mediterranean and in Italy. Thanks to his work entitled *England's treasure by foraigne trade*, Ferdinand I, Grand Duke of Tuscany, granted him an interest-free loan of 40,000 crowns to purchase goods for Italy in Turkey.

[75] Abulafia, *The two Italies*, p. 48.

[76] A. Serra, *Breve trattato delle cause che possono fare abbondare li Regni d'oro e d'argento dove non sono miniere con applicazione al regno di Napoli* (Naples: 1613); see G. Pagano de Divitiis, 'Il Mezzogiorno e l'espansione commerciale inglese', *Archivio storico per le province napoletane* III, 21 (1982), 125–51.

[77] PRO, SP93/1, 206, dispatch sent by Francis Brown, English consul in Naples, Naples, 21 Jan. 1668. Brown was consul from the 1640s until 1671. See below, p. 71.

[78] PRO, SP93/3, 6, *Raggioni – per le mercanzie che s'immettono dall'Inghilterra in questo Regno di Napoli*, printed document, in Italian, undated, probably enclosed with the letter from the English consul in Naples, George Davies, to the Secretary of State, sent from Naples on 20 Dec. 1689 (PRO, SP93/3, 21). Davies held the post of

The foreign merchants working in southern Italy were obliged to widen the market for their manufactured products in general and for their textiles in particular in order to reduce to a minimum the proportion of their payments in cash. They faced both local and foreign competition, and for both the support of the governing classes in the south was necessary. From the very first appearance in southern Italy of merchants from the north of the country, there is evidence of close contacts between them and the local ruling classes in a relationship based essentially on an exchange of favours.

Under the Normans, the Crown had already exploited Sicily as a vast reservoir of supply and wealth in alliance with the buyers from northern Italy, who were able in exchange to provide support, in the form of ships and money, for the rulers' military adventures.[79] Over time the system remained intact, and the alliance between local barons and foreign merchants – of whatever nationality, Catalan and Genoese under the Spanish, French under the Bourbons – was an unchanging factor in the economy of southern Italy.[80]

It is this structure, already in place under the Normans, which is held to be the principal reason for the inertia of the south. Aymard maintains that the entire sphere of industrial production and commerce was enclosed in this economic straitjacket; modern Sicily comes to stand for agricultural Italy as opposed to the industrial north.[81] In addition to its immobility, the south was excluded from the international circuits of trade, coming into contact with them only through the mediation of foreign merchants. Finally, the constant presence of this alliance was a formidable obstacle to the development of a local mercantile community and thus to the rise of an effective bourgeoisie within the structure of southern Italian society.[82]

A further division can be traced in the dualism of north and south which underlay the Italian economy, caused by the differing areas of influence which the city-republics of northern Italy tended to create

consul from 1671 to 1702: 'se pure si pensasse che l'Inghilterra hà necessità dell'ogli, e però per necessità hà da venire a comprarlo con li denari; in ciò s'ingannano; perché l'Inghilterra non per altro ha bisogno dell'oglio, se non per le fabbriche de le pannine, le quali per non smaltirle ne Regno non le fabricano . . .'

[79] Abulafia, *The two Italies*, p. 40; Abulafia, 'Southern Italy', p. 379. See also G. Galasso, 'Social and political development in the eleventh and twelfth centuries' in *The Normans in Sicily and Southern Italy*, Lincei Lectures (Oxford: 1977).

[80] J. Marino, 'Economic idylls and pastoral realities: the "trickster economy" in the Kingdom of Naples', *Comparative Studies in Societies and History* 24/2 (1982), 213.

[81] Aymard, 'Commerce et consommation des draps', p. 127.

[82] 'Momenti e problemi di storia napoletana nell'età di Carlo V' in G. Galasso, *Mezzogiorno medievale e moderno* (Turin: 1965), pp. 167 ff.

within the south (for example, Venice in Puglia, Genoa in Sicily) and by the changing sequence of these influences over time (the Florentines, followed by the Catalans, followed by the Genoese); this fragmentation proved to be a further considerable obstacle to the development of the south, and, as we shall see, also contributed to the increasing role played by northern European countries in the organisation of Italian and Mediterranean trade. Rather than a stark contrast between the two parts of the country, Aymard prefers to see 'a stable relationship based on complementarity and on the mutual dependence of centre and periphery'.[83] It was a model of economic development in which the north played the role of leader, while the south laboured on in silence without any direct participation in the country's commercial exploitation of the continent.

Braudel has written that 'greatness consists in an asymmetrical arrangement of the economic order to the advantage of whichever country influences that order; such an asymmetry will continue to benefit that particular country in the more or less long term'.[84] When we examine the asymmetry which made northern Italy the leading commercial power in fifteenth- and sixteenth-century Europe, we need to ask therefore how much the periphery contributed to the ascendancy of the centre, and if this contribution, generated by force of circumstance from the asymmetry on a smaller scale which existed within Italy itself, was not perhaps the *conditio sine qua non* of the country's pre-eminence in this period. The question becomes essential when English ships begin to appear regularly in the ports of Italy and the roles of each participant in the economic order need to be redefined.

Braudel goes on to write that 'greatness implies an openness to the outside world; if this openness is diminished, the country's greatness disappears or goes into decline'.[85] It is possible to characterise the Italian crisis of the seventeenth century as the gradual introversion of the northern Italian bourgeoisie, judged by some historians to be 'the most blameworthy of the western bourgeois classes', a progressive closure to the world beyond Italy, and the failure of the model of economic development which was based on the complementary roles of north and south. The breakdown of this model led to

a progressive weakening of the economic and commercial ties which linked southern Italy to the cities in the north of the country. The latter first abandoned their reliance on the transport of corn from the south by sea, which proved too expensive and too hazardous, and began instead to cultivate their own grain. The same shift then occurs in the silk in-

[83] M. Aymard, 'La transizione del feudalismo al capitalismo' in *Storia d'Italia. Annali*, vol. I, *Dal feudalismo al capitalismo* (Turin: 1978), p. 1179.
[84] Braudel, 'L'Italia fuori d'Italia', p. 2112.   [85] Ibid., p. 2236.

dustry: in response to the growing popularity of the textile, the cultivation of mulberry trees was introduced into the farms and smallholdings of northern Italy. The fashion for acquiring feudal estates in the Kingdom of Naples also went into decline; in the second half of the sixteenth century, the Genoese sold off their securities on the tax revenues of the Neapolitan and Sicilian kingdoms, which they had bought during the Thirty Years War, and which now yielded nothing.[86]

The 'refeudalisation' of the south has been described as the sale at auction of a state to the highest bidder. It is at this point in time, when the northern cities were falling back on positions of retrenchment and economic conservatism and gaps began to appear in the age-old 'colonised' structures of the south that English ships were first seen in Mediterranean waters.

ENGLAND'S ENTRY INTO THE MEDITERRANEAN

The early years of England's participation in Mediterranean trade already show what was to prove an unfailing characteristic of English commercial activity: its capacity to adapt to the prevailing circumstances which it encountered as it expanded. Thus English merchants followed the systems in the two main areas of the Mediterranean, the eastern and the western, with Italy and its peninsula acting as the dividing line between the two. In the eastern Mediterranean, for so long the exclusive dominion of Venice, they traded as a monopoly through the Levant Company; in the west, on the other hand, where a number of maritime and commercial powers competed for dominance, they operated as small companies with a limited number of members and for brief periods only. The attempt to establish a Spanish Company in the Iberian peninsula had failed irremediably in 1607; the idea of an Italian company was never even mooted.[87] The Venice Company, established after the charter granted to Vellutelli, was, as we have seen, partly incorporated into the Levant Company, which left only the currants from Zante, Cephalonia and the Morea, all geographically speaking part of the eastern Mediterranean, within the protected area, while Puglian oil remained an article of free trade.[88] The capacity of English merchants to adapt to the circumstances they came across was not confined to the external organisation of trade: it

[86] Aymard, 'La transizione', pp. 1163, 1180.
[87] See P. Croft, The Spanish Company (London: 1973); E. R. Poyser, 'Anglo-Italian trade from the reign of Elizabeth to the French Revolution with a special reference to the port of Leghorn', M.Litt. thesis, University of Cambridge, 1951.
[88] Wood, A history of the Levant Company, pp. 19 ff.

was the guiding spirit of English commercial policy in the Mediterranean, and as such was a perfect expression of their business practice. It can be seen in the competitive methods employed by the English in the textile trade. The textiles that began to arrive in Italy on board English ships from the end of the sixteenth century onwards did not represent an increase in the volume of trade, but merely redirected the trade into other channels and extended the English role in it at the expense of foreign merchants.[89] It has also been observed that all the features of English manufactured exports to the Levant in the first half of the seventeenth century show that these were intended not to modify existing Italian production but to replace it outright.[90]

In order to understand the development of the English pattern of trade in the early stages of English commercial activity in the Mediterranean, it is instructive to follow the routes of one of the most sought-after spices of the time: pepper. In the sixteenth century there were two routes for the transportation of pepper: the first was controlled by the Venetians and was almost entirely overland, while the second was controlled by the Portuguese and went by sea. In the 1570s events conspired to disrupt both routes. The temporary closures of Antwerp, culminating in the sack of the Flemish port, created problems for ships sailing the Lisbon–Antwerp route, since Antwerp was the outlet for the markets of northern Europe. The route became even more hazardous after the Spanish annexation of Portugal, and the outbreak of hostilities between Spain and England, which meant that Portuguese ships were subject to frequent attacks from English privateers.[91] As a result, the overland route began to take more supplies of pepper as the sea route's popularity declined. Philip II's offer to Venice of a contract for the distribution of Portuguese pepper in Europe dates from this period.[92] Yet between 1570 and 1573 Venice was in its turn at war with the Turks.

With problems afflicting both the sea and land routes for the transportation of pepper, the way was clear for alternative solutions. In 1576–8, the Grand Duke of Tuscany devised an ambitious plan to obtain a global monopoly for the distribution of pepper, negotiating

---

[89] Clay, *Economic expansion and social change*, vol. ii, p. 117.

[90] R. T. Rapp, 'The unmaking of the Mediterranean trade hegemony: international trade rivalry and the commercial revolution', *The Journal of Economic History* 35/3 (1975), 521.

[91] PRO, SP98/1, 38–39, Grand Duke to Elizabeth, Florence, 29 Jan. 1590; SP98/1, 44, Cavalier Gianfigliazzi to Burghley, 31 Mar. 1591. Bongiovanni Gianfigliazzi, a Knight of Malta, was a prominent member of the Grand Duke's court. For Burghley, see note 17.

[92] Braudel, *La Méditerranée*, vol. i, pp. 506 ff.

both with the Portuguese and with the Sultan.[93] The French, on the other hand, were active in Aleppo from the beginning of the war between Venice and the Turks; their competition gave the Venetian consul even greater cause for concern than the decline in the imports of silk. English merchants had first ventured into the Levant in the first half of the sixteenth century under French protection, and this was still the case when William Harborne, on a mission from Staper and Osborne, the founders of the Levant Company, began to trade there in 1575; in 1580, this phase came to an end when Harborne obtained the agreement with the Sultan known as the 'Capitulations', which allowed the English free trade with Turkey.[94]

In the last quarter of the century the French, English and Dutch succeeded in carving out a significant space for themselves in the Levant trade, by buying goods with cash, thus causing prices to rise and creating problems for the Venetians. We have already seen that this was a proven technique used by newcomers to a market to destabilise the established traders. However, while the French continued to trade with this technique, the English and the Dutch soon began to exchange oriental products for cloth, lead, copper, tin, etc. Already by 1583 the English were paying only a quarter of the price of their purchases in money. Some payment in cash, which could vary from a fifth to a third of the total value of every transaction, remained essential even when the Levant Company was most successful.[95]

The English were faced with the problem, which they had inherited from the Italians, of gaining access to supplies of money to spend in the markets of the Levant. Until peace was concluded with Spain in 1604, Spain and Portugal, the principal sources of supply of Seville and Mexican pieces of eight, were not accessible to English merchants, who obtained them instead from the great commercial centres in northern Italy, Genoa, Livorno and Venice, where the currency arrived directly from Spain. From 1580 onwards, the Italian centres became thriving centres for the distribution of Spanish silver, much more so than Spain itself.[96]

English merchants acquired the currency they needed in the Italian ports mostly by selling their goods there: cloth, tin, lead, fish, as well as corn, which, as we have seen, could be purchased only with money.

[93] G. Laras, 'I Marrani di Livorno e l'Inquisizione' in *Atti del convegno 'Livorno e il Mediterraneo nell'età medicea* (Livorno: 1978), pp. 82–115.
[94] Wood, *A history of the Levant Company*, pp. 6–8.
[95] R. Davis, *Aleppo and Devonshire Square: English traders in the Levant in the eighteenth century* (London: 1967), pp. 196–7.
[96] Braudel, *La Méditerranée*, vol. 1, pp. 450–1.

These imported products were familiar in the Mediterranean markets, where they had been sold for centuries; from the first arrival of English ships in Livorno in 1573, England's role in this trade remained unchallenged.[97] The chartering of ships was also paid for in cash, and thus provided another way of obtaining pieces of eight in the Mediterranean, which, from Lepanto onwards, had been inundated with Spanish silver.[98]

Focusing for the moment on the port of Livorno alone, in 1601 we find Richard Gifford, half-pirate, half-merchant, seeking to hire out for the summer the ship under his command.[99] Some years later he reappears with the *Lyons*, financed by a number of prominent Englishmen for privateering activities against the Spanish. During the voyage, on learning of the peace settlement between Spain and England, Gifford changed his plans and sailed straight to Livorno to offer his services to the Grand Duke or hire out his ship for commercial purposes.[100] It appears from a list of debts which he was owed by the Grand Duke, who had called him expressly from England to work for him, that he had made a voyage to the Levant in 1610, costing 2,495 ducats; a further 400 ducats were owed to him for a return journey to Spain, carrying a cargo of Tuscan products on the *Greyhound*. Similarly, the *Prosperous*, another ship commanded by Gifford, had been sent to Messina, apparently with a cargo of gunpowder. Finally, 5,619 ducats was the advance on a sum, still outstanding, of 9,619 ducats spent by Gifford on a voyage to Algiers; the remaining 4,000 ducats were paid to him on his return to Livorno.[101]

The English ship *Triumph*, captured by Tuscan galleons in 1607, had been chartered at Sidon to carry a cargo consisting of cotton, currants, indigo and raw silk, to a total value of £8,000, to England. While the ship was still in the port, twenty Turks came on board, bound for Algiers with 10 tons of merchandise.[102] The ship *Thomas & William* was captured by the Tuscans shortly after the *Triumph*; it was on its way from Alexandria to Constantinople, chartered by a group of Turks

---

[97] Braudel and Romano, *Navires et marchandises*, p. 50.

[98] Braudel, *La Méditerranée*, vol. I, pp. 443 ff.

[99] PRO, SP98/1, 187, R. Gifford to Lord Buckhurst, Livorno, 28 June 1601. Thomas Sackville, first Earl of Dorset and Baron Buckhurst (1536–1608), poet, dramatist and Member of Parliament, was related to Elizabeth I on his mother's side. He was ennobled in 1557, and served as ambassador in France on numerous occasions. On the death of Burghley he was appointed Lord Treasurer and afterwards Lord High Steward.

[100] PRO, SP98/2, 93, R. Gifford to Cecil, Livorno, 13 Oct. 1604. The addressee was Robert Cecil, Earl of Salisbury; see note 17.

[101] PRO, SP98/2, 276, 'A true accompt of nineteen thousand nyne hundreth fifty and fowre ducketts of florence mony . . .' (1610).

[102] PRO, SP98/2, 119, 'The particulars of a letter from Zant . . .', 15 Sept. 1607.

whose goods on board had a value of 60,000 ducats. When it was captured, 160 Turks and Jews were found on board, including a 'Cadee', numerous merchants and prominent citizens. In the words of the informer: 'howsoever the owners wilbee great loosers, the ship stocke being lett out unto the Jewes as accustomed and unlesse our shipping may passe with better securitie our Turkish trade will goe to ruine shortlie'.[103] Such words reveal the importance of the carrying trade for English commercial activity in the Levant.

Tuscan attacks on English ships were in large part motivated by their need of vessels: in 1607 there were nine English ships, bought or captured, in the service of the Grand Duke.[104] The attacks were also a response to a long series of outrages perpetrated by the English from the end of the sixteenth century onwards which had proved harmful to Tuscan commercial interests. Privateering was in effect simply another way of acquiring the capital and precious metals needed to finance the Levant trade, and all too often was an excuse for piracy.[105] During the conflict with Spain the English claimed that they were justified in attacking Italian ships since these were transporting goods belonging to the enemy. On the basis of this argument, the Tuscans were vulnerable, as there was a community of Jewish merchants from Spain and Portugal, resident among them since the 1550s, who maintained close commercial links with their native countries. The Florentine ships were often captured on the routes between Livorno and Spain, frequently by English vessels coming from the port of Livorno, where they had been received with the greatest respect and courtesy.[106] In the case of the Tuscan ship *Gatto del Mare*, carrying goods from Lisbon to Livorno on behalf of the Ximenes family and captured by the English ship *Desiderio*, Elizabeth I had occasion to write to the Grand Duke. She pointed out that the Ximenes

> were by civil law regarded as subjects of the King of Spain, both by birth and status, since they continue to keep both their factors and their firms in those kingdoms, and pay for all public offices as subjects of the aforesaid King; for which reason they are evidently subject to reprisal ac-

[103] PRO, SP98/2, 120, letter of Humphrey Aldington, Livorno, 10 Oct. 1607.
[104] PRO, SP98/2, 259, 'The names of such English ships as the Duke of Florence hath present for his service, with a note of some others that he hath spoiled this realm of' (1608).
[105] See F. C. Lane, *Venice: a maritime republic* (Baltimore: 1973; 1977), p. 23.
[106] PRO, SP98/1, 24, Grand Duke to Elizabeth, Pisa, 4 Feb. 1590; SP98/1, 28, Grand Duke to Elizabeth, Florence, 7 Mar. 1590; SP98/1, 38, Grand Duke to Elizabeth, Florence, 29 Dec. 1590; SP98/1, 41, Grand Duke to Elizabeth, Florence, 1 Jan. 1591; SP98/1, 48, Grand Duke to Elizabeth, Florence, 8 May 1591; SP98/1, 50, Grand Duke to Elizabeth, Florence, 4 June 1591; SP98/1, 103, Grand Duke to Elizabeth, Florence, 27 June 1595.

cording to the right which is conceded to our vessels against those of the King of Spain under the articles of war.[107]

The *Gatto del Mare* was therefore carrying goods which belonged to subjects of the Spanish Crown; furthermore, the Queen continued, the Ximenes 'were known to be among the principal supporters of the Spanish fleet which in 1588 set out with hostile intent against the shores of England and merchandise belonging to subjects of the Spanish King is daily concealed under the cover of their name'.[108]

Thus at the turn of the century Elizabeth I and the Grand Duke of Tuscany found themselves engaged in a fierce contest of international law, to decide whether a merchant's place of origin or his place of residence was to be regarded as legally more important in determining his status. The Grand Duke eventually won this argument, preferring to protect the large number of Spanish residents in Tuscany, who were responsible for an extensive network of trading connections, rather than the handful of Florentine merchants working in Spain.[109]

The piratical attacks on ships carrying cargoes belonging to Tuscan subjects brought other benefits besides the obvious ones of plunder and the damage which was supposedly inflicted on the Spanish cause. These actions also discouraged the Florentines and the Jewish merchants who were resident in Tuscany from using Italian vessels, and damaged the Tuscan economy since, as the Grand Duke pointed out to Elizabeth, the marine insurers were all Florentine: in the last analysis, it was the Tuscans who paid the entire cost of the attacks.[110] It is also clear that an

---

[107] PRO, SP98/1,105, Elizabeth to the Grand Duke, 2 Sept. 1595. The Grand Duke at the time was Ferdinand I (1587–1609): 'per la legge civile essi essendo sempre suggetti per origine et per natura al Re di Spagna; tenendo del continovo in quei Regni e i loro fattori, et il nome loro, et pagando ogni carica publica come proprij suggetti di quello stesso Re; Per il che apertamente vengono ad essere sottoposti per ragioni di guerra alle lettere Nostre di rappresaglia concedute à i nostri vassalli contra di quei del Re di Spagna'.

[108] PRO, SP98/1, 107, Elizabeth to the Grand Duke, 2 Sept. 1595: 'ci sono scoperti esser stati de i principali aitanti della flotta di Spagna che nel anno ottanta otto hostilmente si spinse su le coste d'Inghilterra et che sotto questo lor nome le mercanzie dei sudditi di Spagna giornalmente sono colorite'.

[109] PRO, SP98/1, 248, Thomas Wilson to Robert Cecil, 14 Oct. 1601. Sir Thomas Wilson (1560?-1629), Member of Parliament, man of letters, Keeper of the Records at Whitehall, and founder of the State Paper Office, was knighted in 1618. He was closely connected to Cecil, and during the last years of Elizabeth's reign, was in constant employment as an informer. Deeply versed in Italian culture, he resided in the country from 1601 to 1602 in an attempt to discover the exact nature and scope of the plans being drawn up against England by the Papacy and Spain. See *Il commercio inglese nel Mediterraneo*, p. 32.

[110] PRO, SP98/1, 44, Cavalier Gianfigliazzi to Burghley, Florence, 31 Mar. 1591; SP98/1, 48, Grand Duke to Elizabeth, Florence, 8 May 1591; SP98/1, 50, Grand

increase in the misfortunes which befell Tuscan goods on the routes between Livorno and Spain would probably have caused the cost of insurance to rise, thus favouring, albeit indirectly, the chartering of English ships.

It must also be added, however, that English privateering in the Mediterranean was not wholly in the interests of English trade; it could also harm it, as on the occasion when Ruy Texera obtained a sequestration order on all the goods held by English merchants in Pisa and Livorno in reprisal for the English capture of a cargo of sugar belonging to him. The English merchants resident in Tuscany were quick to protest their entire innocence in the matter; later, when Richard Gifford was arrested by the Tuscans on a charge of piracy, they supported the Grand Duke's move: on both occasions, the Tuscan ruler 'could have done no less than he has done'.[111] Gifford's piracy in Algiers provoked a similar resentment among the merchants of the Levant Company, who accused him of damaging English commercial interests in the Levant by his actions.[112]

While the peace of 1604 seemed to bring a halt to the English attacks on Tuscan ships, the campaign of piracy waged against Venice continued. Once again, and with greater reason, English privateering had a double purpose: immediate gain and at the same time an indirect attack on England's most powerful competitor in the Mediterranean and, in particular, in the Levant. Historians regard the persistent piratical attacks on vessels of the Venetian fleet, together with shipwrecks and the subsequent rise in insurance premiums, as one of the causes which contributed to the decline of the Republic.[113] Venetian official records are full of complaints and fulminations directed against the English pirates who re-emerged in the Mediterranean whenever the season seemed favourable. The governor of Zante also complained in a letter to the Doge and the Senate that the pirates were accustomed to sailing in winter and in the worst of weathers, such was the mobility of the ships and the skill of their crews.[114] The Venetian consul in Lepanto added that they were allies of the Turks, and argued that all ports should be closed against

Duke to Elizabeth, Florence, 4 June 1591; SP98/1, 174, Grand Duke to Elizabeth, Florence, 17 Apr. 1601; SP98/1, 219, Grand Duke to Elizabeth, Pratolino, 6 Sept. 1601.

[111] PRO, SP98/1, 176, petition of the English merchants to the Grand Duke, 25 Apr. 1601; SP98/1, 203, Thomas Wilson to Lord Buckhurst, Pisa, 9 Aug. 1601.
[112] PRO, SP98/2, 115, Gifford to Salisbury, Livorno, 3 Dec. 1606.
[113] A. Tenenti, *Venezia e i Corsari* (Bari: 1961), pp. 136–44; N. Steensgard, *The Asian trade revolution in the seventeenth century* (Chicago: 1974), pp. 181, 192.
[114] CSP Venetian, 1603–1607, 6 Nov. 1603, pp. 109–10.

them.[115] The Venetian ambassador in London relayed the information that the piracy was organised by two followers of the pirate Ward, who had their headquarters in Ireland.[116]

With the reopening of the ports of Spain, Portugal, and southern Italy after 1604, using fair means or foul, England had achieved what it had set out to do. The Venetian agents were obliged to admit that the English were fast overtaking the Republic as the uncontested masters of the Levant trade; as early as 1607, some 'Turkey merchants' had already accumulated fortunes worth between 100,000 and 500,000 crowns.[117]

Round about 1600, a new change in the trade route of pepper and other spices was to have notable effects both on the nature of English trading and Italy's own role within the Mediterranean. In looking back on these early years of the century, Thomas Mun spoke of a 'revolution in trade';[118] the return of the pepper trade to the Atlantic sea route, sailed by Dutch and English ships, was indeed regarded as a 'revolution', not because of the restored sea route, which the Portuguese had continued to use throughout the sixteenth century, but because the former sellers in the Levant and in the Mediterranean countries and the former buyers in northern Europe had exchanged roles. Such a shift struck contemporary observers as far more remarkable than the change which had taken place in relations between northern and southern Europe in the closing decades of the sixteenth century.

From the 1570s onwards, a straightforward and comparatively painless process of substitution had occurred, with ships from northern Europe replacing those from the countries of the Mediterranean. The long-term consequences were serious, but, apart from the Venetians who saw their leading role in the carrying trade affected, the change did not strike contemporary observers as a revolution. Ships from northern Europe were a familiar sight in the Mediterranean, although their arrival was irregular; moreover, the advent of the new traders did not alter the underlying structure of European trade. The Mediterranean countries continued to buy kerseys, lead, tin and English fish, while the English continued to import spices from the Levant, currants and sweet wines from the Greek islands, and silks from the cities of Italy.

The 'revolution in trade' can be said to have begun in 1597, with the return to its home port of a Dutch ship which had left in 1594 as one of a fleet of ships bound for the Far East in search of a direct route to the spice-producing countries. The contact thus established continued to

---

[115] CSP Venetian, 1603–1607, 11 Feb. 1607, p. 445.
[116] CSP Venetian, 1607–1610, 4 Sept. 1608, p. 166.
[117] Wood, *A history of the Levant Company*, p. 37.
[118] Mun, *A discourse of trade*, p. 33.

develop until it was formally organised with the foundation of the East
India Company in 1600 and the Vereenigde Oostindische Compagnie
in 1602.

The effects of this development on the prevailing patterns of Mediterranean trade, however, began to be felt only from 1610 onwards. As
Braudel and Romano describe, in that year, two ships arrived in
Livorno: the *Nostra Signora di Pietà* 'from East India' and the *Nostra
Signora do Monte del Carmine* from Goa ('Gio de India'). The first was
carrying 4,170 'cantari' of pepper (a 'cantare' was equivalent to 150 lbs),
while the other had 4,000 'cantari' on board, together with indigo, cin-
namon, cloves, saffron, incense and canvas and other items.[119] In 1614,
Domenico Dominici, the Venetian resident in Florence, informed the
Signoria in the city that a cargo of pepper had arrived in Livorno from
London.[120] In 1615 the entire cargoes of two English ships, the *James*
and the *Clove*, were bought and largely re-exported to the Baltic, to
Constantinople, the Levant and to Naples.[121]

In 1625, the Turkish scholar, Omar Talib, made the following com-
ments on this reversal of roles in the spice trade:

> Now the Europeans have learnt to know the whole world; they send
> their ships everywhere and seize important ports. Formerly the goods of
> India, Sind and China used to come to Suez, and were distributed by
> Muslims to all the world. But now these goods are carried on Portu-
> guese, Dutch and English ships to Frangistan, and are spread all over the
> world from there. What they do not need themselves they bring to Is-
> tanbul and other Islamic lands, and sell it for five times the price, thus
> earning much money. For this reason gold and silver are becoming
> scarce in the lands of Islam.[122]

In 1621, Thomas Mun responded to complaints that the old route for
the spice trade via Aleppo had been lost by pointing out that England
had found a source of greater profits in the export of Levantine goods
from London to Italy, Turkey and other countries.[123] Thus the Mediterranean countries no longer sold pepper to northern Europe, but
bought it, together with other spices, as it arrived on Dutch or English
ships which carried it directly from Asia via the entrepôts of Amsterdam
and London.

The new trade route for pepper had many far-reaching consequences.

[119] Braudel and Romano, *Navires et marchandises*, pp. 67–8.
[120] CSP Venetian, 1613–15, 12 Apr. 1614, p. 112 and 12 July 1614, p. 148.
[121] Chaudhuri, *The English East India Company*, pp. 158–9.
[122] B. Lewis, 'Some reflections on the decline of the Ottoman empire', *Studia Islamica* 9
(1958), 118.
[123] Mun, *A discourse of trade*, pp. 32–3.

First and foremost, it removed one of the principal reasons for main-taining contact with the Levantine markets; as early as 1615, an anon-ymous Venetian observer identified the shift in the spice trade as the real and unavoidable cause of the decline in Venetian trade.[124]

Yet English ships did not abandon the Mediterranean route, and con-tinued to sail, with increasing frequency, as far as the Levant ports. Pepper and other spices were now added to their cargoes, while kerseys disappeared, to be replaced by broadcloths, which had nothing in common with the heavy and semi-finished cloths of that name which were produced for the northern European markets, the production of which had, besides, entered a phase of permanent decline. These new broadcloths were designed to combat the Venetian share of the market, since they counterfeited the Venetian woollens stamped with the lion of St Mark, although they were of inferior quality and cost less. By 1634, the Venetian republic was reduced to a 26 per cent share of the Levan-tine market, approximately the same as that of the French; the English had acquired a 40 per cent share, and the remaining 8 per cent was Dutch.[125]

The transformation of the Levant from a source of Oriental goods for export into a market for imported textiles led to the problem of what merchandise could be carried as cargo for the return journey. Raw silk was the only product which still travelled the caravan routes as opposed to the Atlantic routes. Table 1.1, with figures for the imports of raw materials into England in the seventeenth century, shows how increasing quantities of silk were imported, with the Levant as the prin-cipal source of supply throughout the century. However, this presup-posed a demand which the English silk industry had not yet succeeded in stimulating, at least in the first half of the century. Italy therefore functioned as a centre for the re-export and distribution of surplus raw silk from the Levant, unloaded from English ships in Livorno and directed to the European markets where there was a demand for silk.

In a similar way and over the same period of time, English merchants would offset the Italian ports against their trade in the Levant by using them both as alternative markets for the English textile exports which the markets of the eastern Mediterranean on occasion could not absorb and as centres for 'interloping', a form of smuggling designed to evade and infringe the Levant Company's monopoly.

[124] ASV, Collegio dei Cinque, Relazioni, 31, quoted in Steensgard, 'The Asian trade revolution', 184.
[125] CSP Venetian, 1632–6, 23 June 1634, pp. 236–7 and 15 July 1634, p. 246; see Rapp, 'The unmaking of the Mediterranean trade hegemony'. See below on broad-cloths, pp. 169ff.

Table 1.1 *Imports of raw materials into England in the seventeenth century* (£000)

| | 1622 | London (average) | | | England (average) |
		1634 and 1640	1663 and 1669	1699–1701	1699–1701
Silk	118	175	263	344	346
Dyestuffs	46	158[a]	146	203	226
Cotton	43	10	65	39	44
Potash	27	20	33	40	40
Hemp	22	22	86	116	194
Flax	13	12			
Oils	22	37	151	105	141
Timber	19	22	106	96	138
Textile yarns	19	45	83	169	232
Furs, skins and hides	12	26	55	40	57
Iron and steel	10	16	67	118	182
Wool	10	24	29	67	200
Pitch and tar	3	2	21	16	27
Others	38	48	153	114	209
Total	402	617	1,258	1,467	2,036

Note: [a] This figure includes large amounts of indigo destined for re-export.
Sources: Clay, *Economic expansion and social change: England 1500–1700*, vol. II, p. 157. Clay derives his figures from Millard, 'The import trade of London, 1600–1640', vol. III; Davis, 'English foreign trade, 1660–1700'; BL, Add. MSS 36785; PRO, Customs 3, 3–5. The figures have been rounded up to the nearest 1,000.

The statistical evidence gathered so far shows that in the mid seventeenth century the Mediterranean region was the principal market for English exports from the port of London.[126] The figures in Table 1.2 indicate that as early as 1640 the markets of southern Europe were almost equal in importance to those of the north. In addition to the demand for broadcloths in the Levant, which reached its maximum level from the 1650s onwards, this period also sees the growing popularity in the markets of the central and western Mediterranean of the 'new draperies', a group of products ranging from light worsteds to mixed fabrics, in which cotton or sometimes silk was used for the warp, while the weft was wool. The 'new draperies' were the most significant feature of English industrial development in the early Stuart period; they were adapted to the Mediterranean climate and were an appropriate response on the part of the English textile industry to the opportunities created by the new commercial contacts with the

[126] Rapp, 'The unmaking of the Mediterranean trade hegemony', 508.

Table 1.2 *Destinations of English domestic exports in the seventeenth century*
(percentages)

	Scotland and Ireland	North West Europe	Baltic, Scandinavia and Russia	Spain, Portugal and the Mediterranean	The Far East	America
London, 1640 All goods (English merchants only)		46.9		45.5		7.6
London, average of 1663 and 1669						
Woollens	0.4	31.7	5.5	56.5	1.3	4.6
All goods	1.8	36.6	4.4	47.8	1.4	8.0
London, average of 1699–1701						
Woollens	0.3	27.4	5.7	55.1	4.4	7.1
All goods	1.6	27.5	5.4	46.3	4.4	14.8
England, average of 1699–1701						
Woollens	0.9	44.5	6.2	39.4	2.9	6.1
All goods	3.9	41.9	5.8	33.5	2.8	12.1

Sources: Clay, *Economic expansion*, vol. II, table 11, p. 142. Clay derives his figures from Fisher, 'London's export trade in the early seventeenth century'; Gould, 'Cloth exports, 1600–1640'; Davis, 'English foreign trade, 1660–1700'.

region.[127] It was also a response, as will be seen, in line with the overall commercial policy of the English, which was to substitute, where possible, without radical innovation, in an attempt to undermine the Italian textile industry.[128]

From the 1620s onwards, the traditional pattern of English commerce in the Mediterranean underwent a realignment, with a shift away from imports and the development of a new focus on the export trade; it continued to develop in this direction for the rest of the century. The standard Mediterranean imports of wine, oil, salt, fruit, raw silk and silk yarn still arrived, and in increasing quantities, as tables 1.1, 1.3, and 1.4 demonstrate; the period also saw the emergence of two new imports to join these traditional ones: Spanish wool and Turkish cotton. However, the rate of growth in exports was more rapid; and in the second half of

[127] F. S. Fisher, 'London's export trade in the early seventeenth century', *The Economic History Review*, ser. 2, 3/2 (1950), 155, 158.
[128] D. C. Coleman, 'An innovation and its diffusion: the New Draperies', *The Economic History Review*, ser. 2, 22/3 (1969), 417–29; G. Pagano de Divitiis, 'Il Mezzogiorno e l'espansione commerciale inglese', 125–51.

Table 1.3 *Imports of manufactures into England in the seventeenth century*
(£000)

	1622	London (averages)			England (average)
		1634 and 1640	1663 and 1669	1699–1701	1699–1701
Linens and canvas	216	208	582	755	903
Mixed fabrics	101	48	32	44	44
Silks	80	89	183	164	164
Calicoes	1	26	182	367	367
Thread	36	43	141	74	79
Metal goods	11	14	73	55	72
Paper	11	14	47	31	32
Others	43	12	52	127	183
Total	499	454	1,292	1,617	1,844

Sources: Clay, *Economic expansion*, vol. II, p. 155. Clay derives his figures from Millard, 'The import trade'; Davis, 'English foreign trade'; BL, Add. MSS 36785; PRO, Customs 3, 3–5. The figures have been rounded up to the nearest 1,000.

Table 1.4 *Imports of foodstuffs, etc. into England in the seventeenth century*
(£000)

	1622	London (averages)			England (average)
		1634 and 1640	1663 and 1669	1699–1701	1699–1701
Wines	275	274	144[a]	467	546
Pepper	87	48	80	103	103
Sugar	82	106	292	526	630
Fruits	80	145	196	135	174
Tobacco	55	171[b]	70	161	249
Spices	32	35	34	24	27
Others	54	52	129	167	240
Total	665	831	945	1,583	1,969

Notes: [a] Imports of wine were unusually low in the 1660s.
[b] 'The 1604 customs valuation for tobacco was unrealistically high by 1640, thereby exaggerating the relative importance of tobacco imports at that date. By the 1660s a more appropriate valuation was in use, thus explaining the apparent drop in imports: no such drop in fact occurred' (see Clay, *Economic expansion*, vol. II, p. 168).
Sources: Clay, *Economic expansion*, vol. II, p. 156. Clay derives his figures from the sources used in table 1.3.

the century, these saw a significant increase with the re-export of goods coming in from the colonies and the East, thus extending that 'revolution in trade' which Thomas Mun had welcomed with the reappearance of the trade in pepper on the Atlantic route under the control of Dutch and English merchants. In 1600 the balance of trade was still quite clearly against the English, but that now began to change.

CHAPTER 2

THE SHIPS

THE CRISIS OF ITALIAN SHIPPING

The ease with which English ships were able to replace Italian and in particular Venetian vessels on the routes between northern Europe and the Mediterranean, and their gradual appropriation of the carrying trade within the Mediterranean, make it necessary to analyse the situation of Italian shipping both before and after the reappearance of the northern ships.

Recent historical thinking has tended to diminish the impact of the discovery of America on English commercial expansion in the seventeenth century.[1] Such a modified view may be true if we think of the New World as a market or as a source of raw materials, yet it remains undeniable that the newly discovered lands and maritime routes of the sixteenth century led to an unexpected broadening of European horizons, in which the countries of northern Europe occupied the key maritime positions, and which notably intensified the struggle for mastery of the seas. This development in turn gave rise to problems in navigational techniques and in the organisation of trading links.

In chapter 1 it was noted that one of the causes of Italian decline was the diversion of northern Italian capital away from commerce and industry into financial speculation and property investment. What lay behind this shift were the restricted possibilities for productive investment inherent in the structure of the region's economy. From the 1550s onwards, the new geographical discoveries encouraged the development of a new trading network, which extended far beyond the Mediterranean system; such a network required new navigational techniques and new types of ships, which the Italian merchant fleet had not

---

[1] See Rapp, 'The unmaking of the Mediterranean trade hegemony'; P. O'Brien, 'European economic development: the contribution of the periphery', *The Economic History Review*, ser. 2, 35/1 (1982), 1–18.

adopted. In short, Italian shipping was no longer competitive, and had ceased to possess the potential for growth. The Italians were therefore overtaken first by the Spanish and the Portuguese and then by the countries of northern Europe, although in the process they still proved capable of providing their rivals both with valuable ideas and with the men to fuel their success.[2]

In this connection, Texeira de Moto has shown how sailing ships were first perfected by the European countries with an Atlantic coastline and how nautical astronomy was introduced by the Portuguese at the end of the fifteenth century.[3] In the first half of the fifteenth century, the fleets of the Atlantic-seaboard countries added a square sail to their sailing ships in addition to the triangular lateen or 'Latin' sail, as used in the Mediterranean. With this sail, the two- or three-masted Portuguese caravels were able to sail to leeward as well as to windward, thus making the journey to the South Atlantic and back feasible. It was this development which enabled Bartolomeo Diaz to make his second voyage to South Africa, Columbus to sail as far as America, and Vasco da Gama to reach India in ships large enough to carry sufficient arms and provisions as well as a numerous crew. The Italians, on the contrary, remained tied to the seafaring techniques which were adapted to the geography and climate of the Mediterranean; they retained their rowing ships and did not introduce the technique of astronomical navigation until much later. Their navigation was essentially coastal and used dead-reckoning to plot the route, working from nautical maps unmarked with lines of latitude. The Dutch, on the contrary, were quick to adopt the Spanish and Portuguese discoveries, replacing the old 'portolanos' and 'roteiros' with new and improved nautical maps, such as those drawn up by Wagenaar and Blaeuw, who compiled entire atlases; while the English introduced new instruments of measurement, such as the back-staff, invented by John Davis, which could be used with one's back turned to the sun.[4]

The English resident in Tuscany was of the opinion that 'all the Italians are Dutch in their interests'.[5] This was especially true of the Florentine merchants, who, during the Second Dutch War (1665–7), all

[2] A. Texeira de Moto, 'L'art de naviguer en Méditerranée du XIIIe au XVIIe siècle et la création de la navigation astronomique dans les océans' in M. Mollat (ed.), Le navire et l'économie maritime du moyen-age au XVIIIe siècle principalement en Méditerranée (Paris: 1958), p. 140.

[3] Ibid.

[4] H. Kellenbenz, 'Technology in the age of the scientific revolution 1500–1700' in The Fontana economic history of Europe, p. 230. See C. M. Cipolla, Istruzione e sviluppo (Turin: 1971).

[5] PRO, SP98/5, Finch to Arlington, Florence, 7 July 1665.

supported the Dutch, since many had capital deposited in the banks of Amsterdam and probably owned shares in the Dutch East India Company.[6] In this sense we can say that a proportion of Italian capital, although technically invested in trade, nevertheless contributed to the new navigational techniques and commercial schemes being developed by the countries of northern Europe.

This can also be seen if we examine the specific sector of ship-building. In Venice. for example, after a period of depression in the industry, there was an increase in the privately financed construction of large merchant ships, which reached a peak in about 1560. The transition from galley to merchantman was essentially determined by economic criteria: the round ships cost less, once they were developed enough to offer greater mobility, on account of a more elaborate system of sails and rigging, and an acceptable margin of security, with their muskets, cannon and adequate manning.[7] While the period before 1570 was a prosperous one for the builders of large ships, the smaller vessels, the 'marciliane', used to carry foodstuffs within the Adriatic, were no longer built in Venice but outside the Republic's territory. From 1531 onwards protests had led to a series of prohibitions, and corresponding evasions. Until 1531 no foreigners were allowed to build ships in Venice, unless granted special permission; they were likewise forbidden to purchase or charter Venetian vessels, in the belief that the number of Venetian ships would serve to increase the Republic's volume of trade. In the fifteenth and sixteenth centuries, on the other hand, laws were issued which prohibited Venetians from building or buying ships elsewhere or transporting their goods on foreign vessels, on the contrary assumption that the volume of trade within the Republic could be exploited to increase the number of its ships.[8]

In 1590 these protectionist laws were revoked: from 1590 until 1599, fifteen ships constructed outside Venice were registered. By 1606, more than 50 per cent of the Venetian fleet consisted of foreign ships. In 1627, loans were made available to encourage the purchase of foreign ships; in 1693, 64 per cent of the four-masted ships in the service of the Republic had not been built in Venetian shipyards.[9]

---

[6] PRO, SP98/6, Finch to Arlington, Florence, 20 Oct. 1665.
[7] See F. C. Lane, 'Venetian shipping during the commercial revolution', *The American Historical Review* 38/2 (1933), 219–37. Lane maintains that while the cost of transportation on the galleys was double that for the Venetian merchant ships, the goods did not need to be insured. It is probable that the change in the nature of the cargoes carried had some effect on the transition from galleys to merchant ships; these years saw the Portuguese domination of the pepper and spice trade on the Atlantic routes, and its consequent disappearance from the Mediterranean and Levantine routes.
[8] Lane, *Venice: a maritime republic*, p. 378.   [9] Lane, 'Venetian shipping', 235–36.

A similar pattern of events can be traced in Genoa, despite the lack of firm evidence for a crisis in the shipping industry there. Unlike Venice or Marseilles, however, Genoa appeared to be a port which was 'more open to foreign shipping even before the definite onset of the crisis in merchant fleets'. The Genoese purchase of foreign ships, initially of Ragusan craft, is recorded as early as 1537; the Genoese went on to buy ships from Biscay, Italy and Flanders. From 1570 onwards, ships from the yards of northern Europe acquired an ever-increasing share of the market.[10]

The crisis of the Italian shipbuilding industry, which, from the 1570s onwards, was felt throughout the Mediterranean, gradually affected the construction of larger vessels. The various factors which contributed to the crisis led to one unavoidable outcome: the excessive costs of Italian ships meant that they could no longer compete with those from northern Europe. A Venetian document dating from 1581 states that costs had risen so sharply since 1573 that it was difficult to find anyone willing to undertake the construction of large ships.[11] An anonymous observer, writing at the beginning of the seventeenth century, complained that what once cost 25 ducats now cost 100, with the result that the great Venetian ships were no longer to be seen, while the *navilii minori* from France, England and Holland were ubiquitous.[12]

A decisive factor in the rise of shipbuilding costs was the increasing difficulty in the supply of the necessary raw material from the Mediterranean. There were two solutions to this problem of the lack of timber: the use of substitute material, which was evidently not a technical possibility in the seventeenth century, or the discovery of other sources of supply. The second solution caused a rise in the costs of production, since the only reliable source of timber was the Baltic, where transportation was almost entirely monopolised by the Dutch. The second solution thus had an inevitable corollary: the purchase of ships which had been built in northern European shipyards.[13] The step was a short one from the import of timber from northern Europe to the purchase of the ships themselves which were built there.

Yet the Dutch, from whom the Italians bought assiduously, had less timber than the Venetians. Their shipbuilding industry certainly benefited in part from its proximity to one of the main timber-producing

---

[10] Grendi, 'Traffico portuale', 613.

[11] ASV, Capitolari, II C 112, 4 Nov. 1581, quoted in G. Luzzatto, 'Per la storia delle costruzioni navali a Venezia nei secoli XV e XVI' in *Miscellanea di studi storici in onore di C. Manfroni* (Venice: 1925), p. 397.

[12] Museo Correr, Venice, Archivio Donà delle Rose, fs.8 ff., quoted in Braudel, *La Méditerranée*, vol. I, p. 286.

[13] D. Sella, 'European industries 1500–1700' in *The Fontana economic history of Europe*, p. 393.

areas, but its commercial attractiveness was the result of a coordinated approach which oversaw such elements as the transport of raw material, and in which costs were reduced to a minimum by using new types of craft, the use of new and advanced technology for the moving and sawing of logs, the building-up of vast deposits of material, the discipline and industry of the workforce, and, last but certainly not least, the abundance and comparatively low cost of available capital.[14]

The purchase of foreign ships failed to revitalise the Venetian merchant fleet. The English and the Dutch not only succeeded in building ships at lower cost, but also sailed them more efficiently; they began to take over a large part of Venice's incoming and outgoing traffic. Their vessels were lighter than the carracks favoured by the Republic, rarely exceeding 250 tons. The northerners were capable of sailing quickly and in little wind; Venetian crews found themselves unable to operate the foreign ships with the same efficiency and skill. Italian merchants started to entrust their cargoes to foreign ships, attracted by the lower charges for freight and the reduced insurance premiums.[15] The difficulties of Italian shipping were therefore not merely technological and confined to the shipbuilding industry; the entire network of the Italian carrying trade was affected.

The developing crisis in Italian shipping and transportation had been foreshadowed in the previous century with the expansion of the Ragusan fleet. The argosies, as the English called the Ragusan merchant ships, had come to dominate the Venetian and Genoese routes. The Dalmatian port of Ragusa, doubtless favoured by its proximity to the oak-forests of the Gargano, the spur-like peninsula on Italy's Adriatic coast, had succeeded in taking trade away from Venice within the Adriatic,[16] but the Ragusans' crowning success came in Genoa between 1564 and 1569, when 'the Ragusans [were] to be found on all the main Genoese shipping routes: to the East, to Sicily and Ibiza and the Castilian ports, with ships of large tonnage, very often financed or chartered by Genoese merchants'.[17]

In the last quarter of the sixteenth century and increasingly in the seventeenth, Italy came to depend on English and Dutch ships, not only for trading contacts with the ports of northern Europe but also for its own commerce within the Mediterranean.

---

[14] See V. Barbour, 'Dutch and English shipping in the seventeenth century', *The Economic History Review* 2 (1930), 261–90. It is interesting to note that the cost of labour was higher in Holland than in England, although this was not reflected in the final cost of the vessels.

[15] Lane, *Venice: a maritime republic*, p. 386; Grendi, 'Traffico portuale', 608.

[16] Lane, *Venice: a maritime republic*, p. 379.   [17] Grendi, 'Traffico portuale', 606.

THE NORTHERN EUROPEAN SHIPS

The last quarter of the sixteenth century saw an increase in Mediterranean commercial activity as, after the battle of Lepanto, the struggle between Christians and Turks died away, leaving the eastern Mediterranean under Turkish domination and the west controlled by the Spanish. Trade in the Mediterranean had received a particular stimulus from the return of the spice trade to the Levant and the use of the so-called 'Spanish road', the route taken by the Spanish silver which was destined for Flanders: this crossed the western Mediterranean from Barcelona to Genoa, and from there headed north beyond Monferrato and Savoy, the Alpine passes of the Mont Cenis and the Little Saint Bernard, normally via Milan, leaving a stream of precious metals in its wake.[18]

The reappearance of trading activity in the Mediterranean also owed something to the revival of contacts by sea with England, which had until then been maintained only irregularly by Venetian and Ragusan ships. In short, the revival of trade both on the routes between northern and southern Europe and within the Mediterranean led to a demand for merchant shipping which Italy, as we have seen, was in no position to satisfy. At the beginning of the 1570s, Venice was still at war with the Turks; signs of crisis in both the Republic's shipbuilding industry and its carrying trade were, in any case, already apparent. Genoa, on the other hand, was already accustomed to using foreign ships for its own trading; most of its capital, besides, was tied up in loans to the Spanish monarchy.

During the same period, England had begun to expand its fleet and was therefore responsive to the new demands from the Mediterranean. After almost a century of political stability and economic growth under the Tudors, the country had the appropriate resources with which to meet the new circumstances and the opportunities which they presented.[19]

This was the period of the rebellion in the Netherlands, which had started in 1566 with a series of local insurrections only to swell into a national uprising in 1572, followed by the 'Fury' or sacking of Antwerp in 1576 and the blockade of the River Scheldt in 1585. These developments forced the English to find an alternative source of supply for Mediterranean goods. The war between Venice and

[18] See G. Parker, *The army of Flanders and the Spanish Road, 1567–1659* (Cambridge: 1972).

[19] See R. Davis, *The rise of the English shipping industry in the seventeenth and eighteenth centuries* (Newton Abbot: 1962).

Turkey was another reason which made it imperative to establish direct contact by sea with the Mediterranean region. Contacts with the Baltic were in decline, since Holland was absorbed in its struggle against Spain; the English were able to exploit the opening thus created to establish contact with the port of Elbing, creating a link which survived even after the reappearance of the Dutch in the 1590s.

When the transcontinental European routes were reopened in the 1590s, England was firmly established in the Mediterranean. Even the onset of war with Spain did not seriously damage England's links with the region, since privateering, encouraged and supported by the government and the country's ruling classes, was already being waged in the years leading up to the war: together with the new trading contacts with the Levant, it had served to stimulate the development of the English fleet.

In 1560 England was low in the league of seafaring nations; although its navy was strong, its merchant fleet was insignificant compared to those of other European powers, vastly outnumbered by the fleets of Holland, Spain (including Portugal), Hamburg and Venice, and probably by those of Ragusa, Genoa and France as well.[20]

The great increase in the tonnage of the English merchant fleet takes place in the twenty years before the invasion of the Armada, set in motion perhaps by a growth in the coasting trade in coal and the fishing industry, although both these activities were almost exclusively reliant on small vessels.[21] A more significant cause is probably to be found in the growing interest in the Newfoundland cod trade; this continued to develop until the mid seventeenth century, giving English mariners essential experience of ocean-going navigation, and providing a further link in the development of the triangle connecting England, America and southern Europe. As with the Mediterranean market, from which it supplied a growing English demand, privateering once again acted as a stimulus, since it introduced the English to the new products originating from Asia or the New World.[22]

These new interests, together with the new contacts with the Levant, led to an increase in tonnage from a total of 67,000 in 1582 to 115,000 in 1629 (see table 2.1). The most notable increase is found in the ships of over 200 tons: these numbered 18 in 1582, slightly more than the 1572 figure; in 1629, there are more than 145.

The type of ship used in the English merchant fleet was substantially

[20] Davis, *The rise of the English shipping industry*, p. 2.
[21] See J. U. Nef, *The rise of the British coal industry* (London: 1932).
[22] K. R. Andrews, 'The economic aspects of Elizabethan privateering', Ph.D. thesis, University of London (1951), chapter 6.

Table 2.1 *The English merchant fleet, 1560–1702*

Year	Total tonnage	Number of ships 100–99 tons	Number of ships 200 tons and over
1560		more than 71	6
1572	50,000	72	14
1577		120	15
1582	67,000	155	18
1629	115,000	more than 178	more than 145
1640	150,000 approx.		
1660	200,000 approx.		
1686	340,000		
1702	323,000		

Source: Davis, *The rise of the English shipping industry* pp. 7, 10, 15. The estimates of tonnage for 1640 and 1660 are purely suppositions: Davis believes that his estimates are close to the actual figures.

different from its counterparts in the fleets of other northern European countries. These, in particular the Dutch, had concentrated on developing the type of vessel which would reduce the costs of transportation to a minimum while maximising the tonnage. The 'flyboat' or 'fluit' was built to carry bulky goods with a low unit value; it was defenceless and could operate competitively only under normal trading circumstances.[23]

While Holland was pre-eminent in the development of merchant shipping, England outdid all other countries in the design of warships. Built of English oak, which together with Biscay oak was regarded as the strongest timber available, English ships were celebrated for their solidity and durability.[24] Roger Coke wrote in 1675 that 'the Dutch build ships for all trades according to the best convenience; we only know how to build men of war, and our ships for other trades are of like figure, whether it be convenient or not'.[25]

The development of the merchant fleet in England was influenced by

[23] See Kellenbenz, 'Technology', p. 224; C. H. Wilson, *The Dutch Republic* (London: 1968).

[24] See N. Witsen, *Aeloude en Hedendaegsche Sheepsbouw en Bestier* (Amsterdam: 1671), pp. 179–80; D. Defoe, *Extracts from a plan of English commerce being a compleat prospect of the trade of this nation, as well as the home trade as the foreign, humbly offered to the consideration of the King and Parliament* (1728; 1730, 2nd edn) in J. R. McCulloch (ed.), *Select collection of scarce and valuable tracts on commerce* (London: 1859), p. 129; M. Oppenheim (ed.), *The naval tracts of Sir William Monson* (n.p.: 1902), vol. v, pp. 248–49.

[25] Quoted by R. Davis, *English merchant shipping and Anglo-Dutch rivalry in the seventeenth century* (London: 1975), p. 14.

native expertise in the construction of warships and thus developed in ways which were quite distinct from the fleets of other countries. This fundamental connection between the military and the mercantile functions of the English fleet was reinforced by other factors, such as Spanish control of the entrance to the Mediterranean in the period when England was establishing its trading interests there. Throughout this period relations between England and Spain alternated between latent hostility and outright war. A more important factor was privateering, which meant that English ships might have to confront not only Spanish, but also Portuguese and Dutch vessels in the Caribbean, along the coasts of Africa, and on the Atlantic routes as far as Brazil.

The English defensible ships were a smaller version of the warships.[26] According to Barbour, if it had not been for the fact that they flew the Royal Standard and were more heavily decorated, English warships would have been indistinguishable from the merchantmen in shape, rigging and sails, and the number of gunports.[27] In support of this view, it is not difficult to come across cases where a warship either passed itself off as a merchant ship or was mistaken for one, and vice versa. The *Kingfisher*, for example, built in 1676, had a carved bow which was assembled in such a way that it could easily be dismantled to deceive potential enemies.[28] In 1672, Captain Knevet of the *Algier* managed to evade the suspicions of a Dutch pirate ship by withdrawing the cannon and 'working his ship with much apparent awkwardness'.[29] There are also two cases where Dutch pirates boarded an English warship under the impression that it was a merchant vessel.[30]

The English merchant navy was seen as an integral part of the country's naval force, just as commerce was seen as a source of military strength. The concept of the protection of trade was unknown in England until the mid seventeenth century; it was assumed that all merchant ships which undertook long voyages were capable of defending themselves. The merchant fleet was in effect regarded as an auxiliary fleet of the Navy.[31]

---

[26] The term defensible ships is frequently used by Ralph Davis in *The rise of the English shipping industry*; I have adopted it because it conveys succinctly the idea of the armed English merchantman, capable of defending itself on its own. See also Barbour, 'Dutch and English shipping'.

[27] Ibid., 263.

[28] L. G. Carr, *Old ships' figure-heads and sterns* (London: 1925), p. 22.

[29] *The diary of Henry Teonge, Chaplain on board His Majesty's ships Assistance, Bristol, and Royal Oak, anno 1675 to 1679* . . . (London: 1825), p. 5.

[30] CSP Domestic, 1672–73, 26 Oct. 1672, p. 85; PRO, SP Domestic/332, 318, Philip Lanyon to James Hickes, Plymouth, 26 Jan. 1673.

[31] J. S. Corbett, *England in the Mediterranean* (London: 1904), vol. I, p. 78.

This explains why English merchant ships, which were built like small warships, were unable to compete with Dutch ships, both in terms of construction and operating costs; in normal commercial conditions, the cost of Dutch freighters was always more advantageous. However, conditions in the Mediterranean throughout the seventeenth century were far from normal: there was warfare between the European states, and, in the absence of warfare, continuous piracy. The relative operating costs of vessels were not therefore the determining factor in a merchant's choice of what type or nationality of ship to use, since the closely connected costs of insurance and of defence had to be added on.[32] The Venetians themselves acknowledged that it was more cost-effective to charter an English ship, even if its running costs were 10 per cent higher than those of its Venetian equivalent, since these higher costs were compensated for by notably reduced insurance premiums.[33]

There was another factor which encouraged the use of English defensible ships. A dominant feature of Mediterranean trade was what Sir George Downing called 'rich trades', that is, the trade in valuable commodities of little bulk or weight, for which the cost of transportation was not a vital consideration.[34]

According to Braudel, the return of English ships to the Mediterranean from the 1570s onwards was due in part to the growing demand for the lead and tin which they carried; they came, however, principally because they were responding to the direct invitation of the Tuscan Grand Duke and the encouragement of men like Orazio Pallavicino.[35] It could be said that the Tuscans showed unusual political foresight, which was certainly not shared by either the Venetians or the Genoese, yet what led them to make their choice was their awareness of the inadequacies of the Italian fleet, in terms of its size, quality and costs, as revealed by the increased volume of Mediterranean trade. The first to foresee future developments were the Italian merchants resident in England, who were the men in the best position at the time to under-

---

[32] Davis, 'England and the Mediterranean', p. 127.

[33] CSP Venetian, 1626–8, 2 Oct. 1627, pp. 399–400.

[34] PRO, SP84/168, 219–220, Sir George Downing to Henry Bennet, The Hague, 25 Dec. 1663; L. A. Harper, The English navigation laws (New York: 1939), p. 286; see also Israel, 'Dutch primacy'. Sir George Downing (1623?-84), soldier, diplomat and politician, moved with his parents to New England in 1638, where he completed his education at Harvard College, from which he was only the second person to graduate. In 1645, after a spell as ship's chaplain in the East Indies, he returned to England. He sat in both Parliaments under the Protectorate, supporting an anti-Dutch policy. In 1657 he was appointed English resident in The Hague, and continued to hold the post after the Restoration, when he played an active part in the capture of the regicides who had escaped to Holland.

[35] Braudel, La Méditerranée, vol. I, pp. 560–1. See above, p. 5.

stand the changing circumstances in both northern Europe and the Mediterranean.

The events of 1590–1 also played a role. These were years in which the demand for corn in the Mediterranean was high. Ferdinand I of Tuscany extended another direct invitation to England, Holland, Marseilles and Turkey, Genoa opened its port to northern European ships, and Venice lifted its ban on the registration of ships built abroad.

Braudel also claims that the return of the English was dependent on the renewed prosperity of the Italians, who wished to delegate activities which were seen as 'proletarian'.[36] It is more probable, however, that, given the evident shortcomings of their own merchant fleets, the Italians were forced to relinquish the responsibility for shipping to the northern Europeans. They may also have wanted to do this, at least in part, since the English and the Dutch ships were both more advanced and more secure, and offered a more efficient and economic service.

THE DEFENSIBLE SHIPS AND THE SYSTEM OF PROTECTION

We have seen how the demand for English merchant ships grew strongly in the wake of the crisis in the Italian shipping industry and the increase in Mediterranean trade in the last quarter of the sixteenth century. The defensible ships were particularly suited to the endemic warfare which prevailed in the Mediterranean; they were also appropriate for the type of merchandise transported, products of high unit-value, compact yet light in weight. We have also seen that Tuscan attacks on English ships were partly in retaliation for the piracy practised by some of these ships and partly a result of the urgent need for vessels which affected all the Italian ports, but must have been particularly acute in the new port of Livorno.[37]

Two opposed factors, although both specific to Livorno, also help to explain the popularity of the defensible ships in the Tuscan port: the presence of the 'Cavalieri di Santo Stefano', who engaged in privateering activities against the Turks, and the Jewish mercantile community, of largely Spanish, Portuguese and Levantine extraction, who maintained close relations with all the Mediterranean ports, but especially with those on the Turkish and North African coasts where similar Jewish communities were to be found. The first group was untiring in its struggle against the infidel, while the second maintained a thriving

[36] Ibid.
[37] In Livorno the shipmasters and sailors benefited from a variety of indemnities, exemptions and privileges (PRO, SP98/1, 42v–43, 'First invitation of strangers to Leghorn', 13 Feb. 1591).

commercial network which made them a natural target for the carrying trade and piracy alike. One further reason for the success of the defensible ships in Tuscany may be found in the fact that, whereas Venice and Genoa had long had close trading links with the Low Countries, with the natural consequence that they preferred to charter or to buy Dutch ships,[38] Tuscany had ties to England which dated back to the establishment of a colony of English merchants in about 1485, the first such foreign colony in the Mediterranean. In 1490, the two governments had discussed the possibility of organising the distribution of English wool for the entire Mediterranean area through Livorno alone; this was also the period which saw the failure of Tuscany's last attempt to create its own merchant fleet.[39]

The Grand Duke, therefore, needed English ships both for privateering and commercial purposes. As we have seen, Richard Gifford was summoned to Livorno by the Grand Duke, and employed his time and his ships both in trading and in attacks on the Algerian fleet.[40] When the Levant Company protested, fearing reprisals against its own merchants, the Grand Duke promised to stop using the English ships which called at Livorno for his crusade against the Turks.[41]

Only a year later, however, he reneged on his promise, with the sequestration of three English ships: the 200 ton *William & Thomas* from London, the 200 ton *Matthews* from Plymouth and the 180 ton *Triumph* from London.[42] The last, like the 300 ton *Mayflower*, was sent on privateering expeditions, while the 300 ton *Royal Exchange* was sent by the 'Cavalieri di Santo Stefano' against the Turks, with a crew consisting of

[38] On the use of Dutch ships in Venice, see Lane, *Venetian shipping*, p. 235; Braudel, *La Méditerranée*, vol. 1, pp. 195–6; H. Kellenbenz, 'Le déclin de Venise et les relations de Venise avec les marchés au Nord des Alpes' in H. Kellenbenz, *Decadenza economica veneziana nel secolo XVII* (Venice: 1961). Dutch influence proved long-lasting: in 1665 the English resident in Florence wrote: 'I find also that at Venice almost all English business is either in Italian or in Dutch hands . . .' (PRO, SP98/5, letter from Sir John Finch, 13 June 1665). On Genoa, see Grendi, 'I nordici', 40; Barbour, 'Dutch and English merchant shipping', 240.

[39] Ruddock, *Italian merchants and shipping* p. 209; see above, chapter 1, note 3.

[40] PRO, SP98/2, 115, Gifford to Salisbury, Livorno, 3 Dec. 1606; SP98/2, 162, Grand Duke to Salisbury, Ambrogiana, 1 Dec. 1606; SP98/2, 276, 'A true accompt . . .'

[41] PRO, SP98/2, 115; in reprisal for Gifford's attack all the English merchants in Algiers were taken prisoner and forced to pay $2,000 or 'reals of eight' before being ejected from the city (SP98/2, 253, 'A memorial of the injuries which the Great Duke hath caused to be done to the English nation, since his Majestyes entrance to the crowne of England with exceeding dishonour of his Majesty if soe it be lawefull to say'); SP98/2, 104, Grand Duke to James I, Florence, 20 May 1606.

[42] PRO, SP98/2, 112, and SP98/2, 259 (1608): two copies of the same text entitled 'The names of such English ships . . .'

Italian and English sailors; its eventual fate was to run aground and sink in the port of Livorno itself.[43]

Four years earlier, in about 1604, Tuscany had purchased four English ships: the 200 ton *Prosperous* from the merchant Thomas Alibaster, the 300 ton *Dragon* from Sir John Ferne, the *Little Exchange*, a Bristol-built ship of 140 tons, probably belonging to a certain White of 'Ratleife', and a fourth, of which the name and the tonnage are unknown, but which was purchased together with its cargo.[44]

The Grand Duke's sequestration of English ships 'was all the more surprising since such conduct was unheard of during the reign of the late Queen';[45] it was connected to an intensification of privateering after the conclusion of the peace with Spain, which had left many mariners inactive, and to the greater skill of the Barbary fleets, which were now supplied with Dutch and English ships manned by crews who had been trained by privateers from northern Europe. The enhanced supply of English ships after 1604 perhaps provided a further incentive for the Grand Duke's acquisitions: the Venetian ambassador in London observed that, after the conclusion of peace with Spain, there was a rush to sell the larger ships.[46]

One further piece of evidence for the Grand Duke's interest in English ships can be found in the hospitality which he extended to Robert Dudley, who was given all the technical and financial assistance he needed for his naval studies and shipbuilding projects.[47] In 1611 we

---

[43]   PRO, SP98/2, 251, 'Copy of petition shown by Jonas Aldrich to Granduke' (1608); SP98/2, 112 and 259.

[44]   PRO, SP98/2, 112 and 259.

[45]   PRO, SP98/2, 145, 'Stefano Lesieur Cav.re mandato dalla Maestà del Potentissimo Re della Gran Britania a V. A. S. Propone in nome di S. Mta i punti susseguenti et desidera la sua dichiarazione sopra di essi', 11 June 1608.

[46]   CSP Venetian, 1603–1607, 30 June 1604, p. 164.

[47]   See P. F. Kirby, 'Robert Dudley e le navi granducali' in *Atti del convegno 'Gli Inglesi a Livorno e all'Isola d'Elba'* (Livorno: 1980), pp. 35–40. Robert Dudley was the illegitimate son of Sir Robert Dudley, Earl of Leicester and favourite of Elizabeth I. Having failed to prove his legitimacy, he converted to Catholicism and fled to Italy. At Oxford, Dudley devoted his time to the study of shipbuilding and naval engineering, with Sir Thomas Chaloner. After leaving university, he had a small fleet of ships built, with which he sailed to the West Indies, Trinidad, and as far as the mouth of the Orinoko; on the voyage back, he sank nine Spanish ships. In 1596, he was appointed commander of the *Nonpareil*, and took part in the siege of Cadiz; he was afterwards knighted. Besides being a navigator, he was a designer, shipbuilder and skilful cartographer. His main work, *L'arcano del mare*, was published in a great 2-volume folio in Florence in 1646, and in a second posthumous edition in 1661 (see M. Pinna, 'Sulle carte nautiche prodotte a Livorno nei secoli XVI e XVII' in *Atti del convegno 'Livorno e il Mediterraneo . . .'*, pp. 139–45; G. Guarnieri, *Livorno medicea* (Livorno: 1970), pp. 50 ff.).

find Dudley in Livorno working on the design of a 300 ton ship for Cosimo II, probably a 'galezabra', a ship carrying powerful artillery and particularly effective in combat up wind.[48] In 1608, he launched his first ship built for Cosimo, the *San Giovanni Battista*, armed with sixty-four great cannon; Dudley himself described the ship as 'a rare and sturdy sailing-vessel, of great fame, and the terror of the Turkish fleet'. He went on to build a 'galerone' or 'galeratone', also provided with oars, for the Grand Duke, as well as a 'galeratina', which was named the *San Cosimo* in honour of the Grand Duke.[49]

Dudley and the English defensible ships, therefore, were meeting an Italian demand for armed ships fostered by a wave of crusader-like enthusiasm. The struggle against the Turks and the privateers was waged by the 'Cavalieri di Santo Stefano', the Knights of Malta and the Spanish navy, which included Neapolitan and Sicilian galleys. The Spanish viceroyalty of southern Italy thus played an active role both in the hostilities and in the transportation of arms and munitions on behalf of Spain. The need for armed merchant ships was particularly acute in Naples, under the viceroy Ossuna, who was familiar with the English defensible ships and greatly admired their construction, equipped as they were with the most up-to-date military technology of the period.[50]

During a period of conflict between Naples and Venice (1617–18), Ossuna asked the Spanish ambassador in London, Gondomar, to charter eight English ships in his own name, and besought James I not to deny him what he had already granted the Venetians.[51] On receiving a negative reply, the Viceroy sent Henry Gardiner, the Naples-based factor for two London merchants, Richard Fishborne and John Browne, to England, in order to procure ships and munitions which could be used against the Venetians.[52] The result of Gardiner's mission is not known; what is evident is that Ossuna, like the Tuscan Grand Duke, was prepared to use all the means available to him in his efforts to procure English ships. While he was trying to persuade the English king to sell him defensible ships, Ossuna also resorted to what Cosimo II had called 'the common practice among rulers, when the need arises, to avail

[48] PRO, SP98/2, 280, letter written by H. Locke, Florence, 15 June 1611.
[49] Kirby, 'Robert Dudley', pp. 36–8. The Grand Duke of the time was Cosimo II (1609–20); CSP Venetian, 1610–13, 7 July 1612, p. 389; 14 July 1612, p. 393: 'raro e forte veliero di grande riputazione, terrore dei Turchi sul mare'.
[50] Corbett, *England in the Mediterranean*, vol. 1, pp. 21 ff.
[51] Ibid., pp. 54–61. Venice had chartered, in addition to twelve Dutch warships, seven English merchant ships, together with a further two, probably belonging to the Levant Company, which were already in the Mediterranean.
[52] PRO, SP93/1, 74, Alexander Rose to Sir Thomas Lake, 27 Feb. 1618.

themselves of the foreign vessels and men which happen to be found in their territory'.[53]

In June 1617, Ossuna forced the *William & Ralph*, anchored in Naples on its way to Gallipoli, to take on board soldiers and provisions bound for the Gulf of Venice, and to bring back other cargoes from Barletta and Manfredonia to Naples. The captain of the ship, under the threat of being sent to the galleys, was forced to sign a charter-party for 1,650 crowns, with an additional 400 crowns for a further month of enforced detention in Naples; of these, only 455 crowns were ever paid by the Viceroy. Moreover, six English sailors on the ship were forced under threat to serve in the Neapolitan fleet, although two managed to escape by jumping into the sea. Thomas Trentfield, the captain of the *Delight*, belonging to the London merchants William and Ralph Freeman, was similarly faced with an enforced choice of either selling his ship to Ossuna or entering the Viceroy's service in the war against Venice.[54]

The incident with the six sailors from the *William & Ralph* highlights another common need in the Italian ports during the seventeenth century: the need for sailors. Livorno made every effort to attract all kinds of mariners. In Venice too there was a shortage of sailors to man the ships, which proved to be a severe limitation on the Republic's maritime power. Even as early as the Battle of Lepanto, the crews of the Venetian galleys were so undermanned that complements of Spanish soldiers had to be shipped on board in order to make up their numbers.[55]

According to a document dating probably from the mid seventeenth century, the thirty-six galleys which comprised the Neapolitan fleet were anchored in harbour, without soldiers and often lacking half their crews.[56] In 1675, George Davies, the English consul in Naples, discovered from the Admiral of the Spanish fleet, the Prince of Montesarchio, that no fewer than fifty out of seventy sailors in the fleet were native Englishmen.[57] Davies later complained to the Admiral that men from Spanish warships were going aboard the English ships anchored in Naples and demanding the documents of sailors who had fled their ships to join the service of the Spanish king.[58]

[53] PRO, SP98/2, 147v.,'Risposta fatta alli punti proposti dal Mandato della M.tà del Re della Gran Bretagna all'A. S. del Gran Duca di Toscana' (1609): 'l'uso comune dei principi in caso di necessità [di] valersi di vasseli e uomini di altre nazioni che si trovano sul loro territorio'.
[54] PRO, SP93/1, 76, 'Richard Goodlake master of the Shipp named the William and Ralph of London doe hereby testifie for the truth', 3 Mar. 1618.
[55] Lane, *Venice: a maritime republic*, p. 364.
[56] PRO, SP93/1, 130, 'Sommario della relazione del Regno di Napoli', s. d.
[57] PRO, SP93/2, 23, dispatch from the consul, Davies, Naples, 11 June 1675.
[58] PRO, SP93/2, 36, George Davies to Williamson, Naples, 30 July 1675.

A crew which was largely made up of Englishmen might also mean that a ship could pass itself off as English, at a time when the Royal Standard was widely respected in the Mediterranean. In order to put a stop to this practice, which led to the continuing loss of English sailors and damaged English maritime interests, in 1675 the Secretary of State, Henry Coventry, sent a circular letter to all the English residents, consuls and factors in the Mediterranean area, informing them of the instructions that had been issued to the captains of warships to force all Englishmen found serving on foreign ships to enter the service of His Majesty.[59] It was a question both of numbers and of skill. As we have seen, Venice did not solve the problem of its lack of ships simply by buying them abroad; the defensible ships were the sturdiest and the most technologically advanced of the armed ships of the time, and skilled crews were needed to sail them. It will be recalled that the governor of Zante was astonished not only by the agility of English ships, but also by the ability of their crews who were accustomed to sailing even in the middle of winter.[60]

If we discount textile manufacturing, shipbuilding was the most advanced industry in seventeenth-century England, and the men who worked in the shipyards were regarded by contemporaries as highly skilled and specialised. English sailors were thus much sought after throughout the seventeenth century, brought on board the ships of other nations by force, through deception, or lured with the promise of better pay. Antonio Bogus is a good example of this enthusiasm for English crews: he was an Armenian merchant based in Livorno, and the owner of numerous ships sailing under a variety of national flags; according to Chellingworth, the local consul, Bogus made persistent attempts to deceive English sailors into working for him, but failed to get sufficient numbers of them to man his ships, since most were fighting in the war against Holland.[61]

Somewhat later, we find Finch writing to the Secretary of State to inform him that nineteen sailors had escaped from the frigate *Mary Rose* as soon as it had arrived in Genoa; three had gone on to Livorno to seek

[59] PRO, SP104/185, 25, 'Mr Secretary's letter to the severall Residents, Consuls and Agents upon the coasts of the Mediterranean seas', Whitehall, 20 Dec. 1675. Henry Coventry (1619–86) worked as a Royalist agent in Germany and Denmark during the exile of Charles II. From 1664 to 1666 he served as ambassador to Sweden. He was appointed Secretary of State for the Northern Department in 1672; in 1674 he was transferred to the Southern Department, where he remained until 1680. See *Il commercio inglese nel Mediterraneo dal '500 al '700*, pp. 34–6, 333 ff.

[60] CSP Venetian, 1603–1607, 6 Nov. 1603, pp. 109–10.

[61] PRO, SP98/7, Chellingworth to Arlington, Livorno, 16 Aug. 1666. See below, pp. 119–20.

work on foreign ships. The English resident in the port had imprisoned them until they could be put on a ship bound for England, where their desertion would be suitably punished.[62]

During the Second Dutch War, all English sailors serving on foreign ships were ordered to make their way to Livorno, where Sir John Lawson would muster them, since he was expected to have to call at the Tuscan port for reprovisioning.[63] It is interesting to note that the ensuing shortage of men, after the order had been relayed through the English consuls in the various Mediterranean ports, prevented the French fleet from setting sail from Toulon.[64]

The availability of skilled sailors and navigators was certainly one of the strengths of the English naval system. In this connection, Finch wrote to Arlington in April 1667:

> my Lord with unspeakable confort I tell your Lordship that the Trade his Majesty has carryd' on for his Subjects during the warr hath put terrour into all his Ennemyes, who from hence argue the Impossibility of the want of mony for his service and the dreadfulnesse of that Power, which can spare mariners enough to carry on a Generall Trade and yet at the same time Equippe a fleet to contrast with three Ennemyes . . .[65]

The coasting trade in coal and the fishing industry were schools 'for breeding mariners', in the sense that they provided useful training for English sailors; it was above all the Newfoundland fishing industry which accustomed men to ocean-going voyages, just as it had encouraged the development of English shipbuilding techniques.[66] Both the vessels used for the transportation of Newcastle coal, considered to be the largest employer of sailors among the different trades, and those used for fishing, which could employ the time spent on the outward voyage

---

[62] PRO, SP98/9, Finch to Arlington, Livorno, 2 Apr. 1668.

[63] PRO, SP98/6, Finch to Arlington, Livorno, 8 Mar. 1666; 12 Apr. 1666; 3 May 1666. Sir John Lawson (?–1665), an admiral of Anabaptist faith and republican sympathies, went into retirement until 1659, when Parliament called upon his services. He was on several occasions in command of the Mediterranean squadron from 1661 to 1664.

[64] PRO, SP98/6, Finch to Williamson, Livorno, 4 May 1666.

[65] PRO, SP98/8, Finch to Williamson, 11 Apr. 1667.

[66] 'Sir Thomas Roe's speech on the decay of trade' (1641) in J. Thirsk and J. P. Cooper (eds.), *17th century economic documents* (Oxford: 1972), p. 44; H. Robinson, 'Briefe consideration concerning the advancement of trade and navigation' in Thirsk and Cooper, *17th century economic documents*, p. 57. See also Davis, 'The rise of the English shipping industry', 114–15. There was a considerable increase in trade with Newfoundland from 1575 and throughout the first half of the seventeenth century; the number of ships involved rose from 30 in 1574 to 200 in the first decade of the new century, and 300 in the 1630s (H. A. Innis, *The cod fisheries* (Toronto: 1954), pp. 31, 69–70).

for training, accepted 'landmen' in order to teach them seamanship. On the Mediterranean routes, on the other hand, only experienced sailors were taken on: a contemporary observer wrote that 'in the Shippes that voyage southward or otherwise farre out of the Kingdome, there is no Owner, or Maister, that will ordinarili entertaine any Land-men, be he never so willing, as being bound by the Charter-Partie to the Merchant, as they say, not to carry but sufficient Men, as such as know their Labour . . .'[67]

The defensible ships remained the outstanding feature of the English merchant fleet throughout the seventeenth century. The English did not forget that the Spanish Armada had been defeated in 1588 thanks to the great merchant vessels, built for battle as well as trade, and were not slow to recall that they might be needed again.[68] Vessels of all tonnages, from 50 tons upwards, were therefore built like small warships, especially in the earlier part of the century: of robust structure and with sturdy masts, they were equipped with men and cannon so that they were suitable both for trade and for privateering. They could also be incorporated quickly, if the need arose, into the navy.

In the mid seventeenth century, however, a radical change in the concept of defence led to a general reorganisation of the country's naval system; this in turn affected trade in the Mediterranean in general and with Italy in particular. In the years from 1650 to 1665, in the period between the First and Second Dutch Wars, a clearer distinction began to be drawn between the roles of merchant ships and warships. The first were still built to be powerful, but they were now confined to commerce; although they were occasionally called upon to serve as an auxiliary force, they were no longer considered to be an integral part of the English navy or military fleet. Warships, on the other hand, were now seen as a permanent component of the country's military strength: they were built, equipped and manned only for military purposes. They were also responsible for the protection of merchant vessels if these were attacked by enemy ships or privateers.[69] A series of parliamentary measures, beginning with the 1651 Navigation Acts, provided a legal framework for this new relationship between the mercantile and military fleets.[70]

---

[67] 'The trades increase' (1615) in The Harleian miscellany, or, a Collection of scarce, curious, and entertaining pamphlets and tracts . . . (London: 1745), vol. IV, pp. 202–20.
[68] See Baumann, The Merchant Adventurers.
[69] Corbett, England in the Mediterranean, vol. I, pp. 225–6.
[70] See Harper, The English navigation laws, and Davis, The rise of the English shipping industry, chapter 14. The Navigation Acts of 1651 were renewed and enlarged in 1660; the Act of Frauds and the Staple Act were added in 1662 and 1663. Unlike the 1651 Act, the 1660 measure was principally concerned with exceptions: the transport of all

This change, which served to clarify the two roles, was largely a response to the intense competition from the Dutch in the carrying trade. Finch wrote to Arlington:

> Tis within my memory, that in the Mediterranean the trade of foreigners, by carrying theyr commodityes from Port to Port within the Streights, and without as far as Lisbone only, did maintain between 20 and 30 stout ships, without touching England, which did not only make considerable returns of mony into England, not only render our Trade flourishing and secure; but what is more His Majesty had a considerable strength maintaind by Strangers. My Lord wee have not at Present one, the reason is, the Dutch observing that all the forreigners gave greater freight to our ships then theirs, by reason of the goodnesse of our Vessells, They, partly for their own Security against the Barbary coast, partly to invite forreigners to load on theyr vessells, sent out a yearly Convoy to Protect theyr Ships, which takes up all the Spanish mony and fine goods from Spayn for Italy, from Italy for the Levant, and again from the Levant for Italy, and from Italy for Spayn; and in this Trade they employ their men of Warr which I apprehend facilitates their Expense . . . [71]

In addition to the threat from Dutch competition, another force for change, especially in the 1670s, was the growing recognition in England of the significance of Mediterranean trade, and of the need to reorganise English shipping in response; the Mediterranean countries were already of paramount importance for the English textile industry, both as a source of raw materials and as a market for the industry's finished products.[72]

The need for reorganisation was initially felt during the First Dutch War, when, for example, the Council of State of the Commonwealth issued the English consul in Livorno with a requisition order, dated 13 September 1652, for all the English vessels to be found in Italian ports. The commissions (for arms) sent out from London were, however, ignored by the captains of the *Samson*, the *Mary* and the *Levant Merchant*, at anchor in the Tuscan port. After Longland had repeated, to no avail, the government's 'invitation' in the presence of Captain Badiley and Captain Apleton, who had escorted the merchant ships to Livorno, he read the commissions aloud to the assembled crews of the three ships

goods was free, except for certain European products, which could be transported either by English ships or by ships belonging to the producing country, on payment of a levy known as the 'alien duty'. The Act of Frauds eliminated the indirect importation of goods via Holland, while the Staple Act regulated trade with the colonies, which were obliged to give up direct trading relations with Europe: England was to be the intermediary for all trade between the two areas.

[71] PRO, SP98/8, Finch to Arlington, 13 June 1667.
[72] See Rapp, 'The unmaking of the Mediterranean trade hegemony', 502 and table 2.

and then had them affixed by a notary to the mainmasts. An agreement was finally reached: the commanders agreed to enter the service of the Commonwealth with their ships and their men, after the sailors' pay was fixed at a monthly rate of £3 and 15 shillings.[73]

The government met with similar objections from the English ships anchored in Venice, where the crews required an advance of three months' pay as a condition for their acceptance.[74] Large sums of capital were needed, therefore, to arm the dozen or so commissioned ships; 1,000 men had to be sent out to Livorno to provide the three ships there with adequate crews;[75] finally, the ships had to be allowed to carry their cargoes to their intended destinations before they entered into military service. The potential use of merchant ships for military purposes was a serious obstacle to trade, while, conversely, their commercial undertakings meant that it was a slow and costly process to commission them when they were needed. Captain Badiley commented that

> it could not bee thought their was to bee Found in these seas a 1/3d part off the nomber off Shippeing, emptie and voyd of imployment but it must needs bee meant, their honers intent was, as well to imprest Laden Shipps as others upon occasion and it seemes to be necessary, because particuler Letters that Came lately out off England: makes it something dubious wheither their can bee Spaired a fleet or great Squadron at this tyme, for our Succour, in regard the hollander hath a great fleet comeing Forth . . .[76]

Fifteen years later, during the Second Dutch War (1665–7), the situation had completely changed: the Navy did not need to call on the help of the merchant ships, but, on the contrary, was able to provide them with uninterrupted protection by convoy; with the assistance of the 'Mediterranean fleet', the constant presence of a deterrent force was assured. This double function of attack and defence, first experimented with in these years, was to become the basis for the new system of protection for England's merchant ships in the Mediterranean.

[73] PRO, SP98/3, 256, Longland to the Council of State, Livorno, 29 Nov. 1652. Charles Longland, a merchant resident in Livorno, was appointed consul under the Protectorate. After the Restoration, he remained in Livorno as a merchant.
[74] PRO, SP98/3, 274, Longland to the Committee of the Navy, Livorno, 20 Dec. 1652. There was already a custom of giving sailors 'advance money', which was normally equivalent to a month's pay (see Davis, The rise of the English shipping industry, p. 143).
[75] PRO, SP98/3, 274, Longland to the Committee of the Navy, Livorno, 20 Dec. 1652; SP98/3, 256, Longland to the Council of State, Livorno, 29 Nov. 1652.
[76] PRO, SP98/3, 264, letter from R. Badiley, Livorno, 18 Feb. 1652.

THE PROTECTIVE SYSTEM AND TRADING ZONES

What had been the single nature of the English fleet thus evolved, from the 1650s onwards, into two distinct functions, the military and the mercantile, with the first taking responsibility for the protection of the second.

Within the Mediterranean this process underwent further refinement: a bipartite system was developed in which there were convoys assigned to the merchant ships on the most hazardous routes and naval squadrons on general patrol which were ready to attack or defend as the need arose. A period of approximately twenty-five years, from 1650 to 1675, was to elapse, however, before this system was fully in place.

The first convoys appeared in Livorno in 1651.[77] The route described by Captain Edward Hall in his logbook already resembles those most commonly found in later years, when the protection of the Mediterranean merchant fleet had become a highly organised affair.[78] The *Triumph*, commanded by Hall, together with other warships, left London for the Mediterranean ports: they first put in at Portsmouth, and then followed a route which took them to Lisbon, Cadiz, Alicante, Genoa, Livorno, Naples, Messina and Zante, from where they set off on the return journey. They patrolled the areas they sailed through, left the merchant ships they were escorting at their destinations, picked up others which needed protection, sent off single warships to accompany individual merchant ships which needed to deviate from the principal route, fixed *rendezvous* in agreed ports and on agreed dates – all according to a pre-arranged programme which was nevertheless flexible enough to allow for variation.[79]

At the beginning of the 1660s it was still evident that the new system of protection was not completely operational. In 1663, for example,

[77] The first English convoy dates back to 1649, when it was decided that ships sailing in dangerous seas needed to be accompanied (M. Oppenheim, *A history of the administration of the Royal Navy and of merchant shipping in relation to the Navy* (London: 1896), p. 313). Several laws were passed confirming this provision, in 1650, 1659, 1660; finally, in 1662, the system was properly established under the supervision of the Duke of York. In 1650, for the first time, the Levant Company asked for protection for its ships (Wood, *A history of the Levant Company*, pp. 212–13). The Duke of York's reforms also oversaw the introduction of passes, a system which continued to develop over the following decades (see PRO, SP98/4, 250, Read to Bennet, 1663; SP98/4, 274, Kent to Williamson, Livorno, 23 Nov. 1663).

[78] PRO, SP98/3, 208, 'Il caso del cap. Balle' (1652). Balle is a misspelling of Hall; he was 'Rear Admirall of the Parliamentary Fleet and Commander in chiefe of that Squadron thereof then sent out for Convoy into the Mediterranean Seas'.

[79] PRO, SP98/3, 224–5, 'A journall kept by me Edward Hall aboard the Triumph', 14 Feb. 1651–16 July 1652.

several English ships were captured by the Algerians, despite the peace treaty which had recently been signed and ratified.[80] In January 1665 Morgan Read, the consul in Livorno, suggested that local merchant ships might be armed and go out to meet arriving ships and escort them into the port. Read believed that such an arrangement was essential and urged the Turkey Company, which had particular trading interests with ports along the coast of North Africa, to present a petition to the King on the matter, proposing a plan for the security of the merchant ships.[81]

In addition to the advantages which the merchant ships derived from the protective presence of the convoys, it was also clear that there was a close connection between the squadrons of naval ships and the carrying trade as a whole. Writing in February 1666 during the Second Dutch War, the English resident Finch remarked that the appointment of the Duke of Albemarle as Commander-in-Chief of the English Navy had shaken Italian confidence in a Dutch victory and caused them instead to hail the English king as sovereign over the seas.[82] At the same time, while Sir Jeremy Smith was anchored in the port of Tangiers with eight warships, the consul Chellingworth noted that the demand for English ships was such that their prices had tripled, much to the advantage of their crews.[83] Thomas Dethick's more sober estimate was that the cost of freight had doubled as a result of the scarcity of ships in Italian waters.[84]

The proposal which Finch put forward, about a year later, was to have a naval squadron of four to six warships permanently stationed in the Mediterranean. One advantage of the plan was that reprovisioning could be carried out in Villafranca, which had recently been declared a free port, at a much lower cost than in England. Although Finch conceded that the overall cost might at first sight appear excessive, he main-

---

[80] The peace treaties negotiated by Sir John Lawson with Algiers, Tripoli and Tunis in June 1662 (see PRO, SP98/4, 150, Kent to Nicholas, Livorno, 26 June 1662) were ratified in October/November of the same year (see PRO, SP104/172, 15–53).

[81] PRO, SP98/5, Read to Bennet, Livorno, 16 Jan. 1665. Morgan Read was the English consul in Livorno from 1660 to 1665.

[82] PRO, SP98/6, Finch to Arlington, 8 Feb. 1666. George Monck, 1st Duke of Albemarle (1608–70), served under Charles I and Cromwell. In 1652 he was appointed General of the Fleet, together with Blake and Deane, and despite his complete lack of naval experience, succeeded in establishing the order and discipline in the force which were to prove the foundation for its future successes. He supported the return of Charles II. In 1665 he was again entrusted with command of the fleet, which met with heavy defeats at the hands of the Dutch.

[83] PRO, SP98/6, Chellingworth to Arlington, Livorno, 8 Feb. 1666. Sir Jeremy Smith (?-1675) was sent to the Mediterranean in 1665 as the commander of a small naval squadron. On his return he was made an Admiral and given a knighthood.

[84] PRO, SP98/6, Dethick to Williamson, Livorno, 22 Feb. 1666.

tained that, if the project were well managed, its benefits would be so apparent that private capital would soon be forthcoming. Such a project would succeed in winning back control of the Mediterranean carrying trade from the Dutch, who had succeeded in gaining the upper hand with the organisation of an annual convoy. Both the Genoese and the Venetians were also building fleets for the same purpose, financed by private capital. In order to win back control of transportation in the Mediterranean, the only solution was the maintenance of a convoy over an extended period of time. Merchants would see a reduction in insurance premiums; the Barbary pirates, who in the last five or six years had caused great loss of revenue and ships, could be kept at bay, and Italian rulers would realise that the English were capable of responding to any attack made on them without incurring extra expense.[85]

A few months later the English resident passed on the information that the Algerians were being freely allowed to take refuge in the ports on the coast of Provence in order to repair their ships; he also mentioned that Toulon had become a free port for them and that the French were urging them to renege on the peace treaty they had signed with England. The situation was made worse by the fact that the Dutch had armed their ships which traded with Spain to avoid sequestration by the French searching for Spanish goods. English merchants were of the opinion that if warships were not sent soon to the Mediterranean, the peace with the Algerians would not last much longer; the mere presence of the English frigates, however, would thwart the French ambition to remain the only country which enjoyed peaceful relations with the Barbary states.[86] In March 1668 the warship Mary Rose arrived in Livorno from Spain and Genoa, carrying an immense amount of bullion; Finch observed that if two or three frigates had been in Tangiers to accompany the Mary Rose, they could have earned a huge sum protecting the transportation of Spanish pieces of eight to Genoa and Livorno, since the Genoese convoys no longer dared to sail out of port for fear of the French. Finch ended by saying that once the English had reclaimed control of this important activity, they should make every effort to retain it.[87]

It was increasingly clear that Mediterranean trade was bound up with the problem of the protection of the carrying trade, which was not only essential to guard the ships from attack by pirates or enemy countries, but also made trade more competitive by reducing insurance premiums.

---

[85] PRO, SP98/8, Finch to Arlington, Florence, 13 June 1667.
[86] PRO, SP98/8, Finch to Arlington, Florence, 22 Nov. 1667; Dethick to Williamson, Livorno, 28 Nov. 1667.
[87] PRO, SP98/9, Finch to Arlington, Livorno, 19 Mar. 1668.

Competition in the carrying trade was twofold: there were the 'rich trades', the transportation of valuable commodities, which was highly profitable, but also dangerous, since these were the ships targeted by the Algerian and European pirates at loose in the Mediterranean; and there was the remaining trade.[88] The network of 'rich trades' covered the whole Mediterranean. In the west it was organised round the transportation of grain to Spain and Portugal, for this was paid for in silver, and of Spanish silver to Genoa, from where it was destined for Milan or the Low Countries. In the eastern Mediterranean, a proportion of this bullion made its way towards the Levant to finance European trade there. On the return route, the ships carried raw silk from Persia, galls, cotton, goathair and other goods, destined for the most part, together with Spanish wool, for the textile industries of the west. Within this network, Italy, and the port of Livorno in particular, functioned as a centre for the distribution and exchange of silver pieces of eight and Levantine merchandise.

There were other more restricted networks of trade routes which intersected with this main system: the transportation of sugar from Lisbon, for example, or of agricultural products from southern Italy to the cities in the north of the country, or the trade in flax, skins, senna, wax, etc. from the North African ports.

Because of the value and the risks of Mediterranean trade, in which only a relatively small number of ships was involved (figure 1), the organisation of a system of protection required special attention. If we trace the routes taken by various convoys in a period of comparative peace for England, the years from 1674 to 1688, we find a concentration of ships sailing from Yarmouth on the east coast, across the Channel, down the coast of Portugal and through the Straits of Gibraltar, as far as the shores of the eastern Mediterranean (figure 2). The most heavily protected part of this route was the passage between Cadiz and Livorno, two ports which were vitally important both as trading centres and as key positions in the English system of maritime protection. The dangers of sailing in Mediterranean waters were increased by the land-locked nature of the sea itself (the *mare clausum* of the Romans), which meant that there were few alternatives to the fixed routes followed by the merchant ships. In addition to the predictability of their itineraries, the appearance of English ships in the Mediterranean, with their cargoes largely made up of fish, was seasonal; these regular patterns of time and place made them vulnerable to discovery and attack by pirates or enemy forces.

[88] PRO, SP98/6, Finch to Arlington, 1 Mar. 1666.

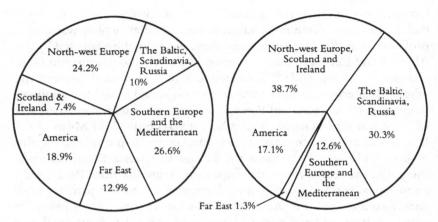

Figure 1   Proportions of English imports by value (average 1699–1701) and of shipping tonnage used for English imports (including English and foreign ships, 1686)

Sources: Clay, *Economic expansion*, II, p. 167; the figures in the left-hand chart are based on the information given in table 1.1; those of the right-hand chart are taken from Davis, *The rise of the English shipping industry*, p. 200.

In the 1670s the Mediterranean region was the leading market for the products of the English woollen textiles industry, sent out from the Port of London, and at the same time its principal source of the raw materials which were indispensable for the manufacture of broadcloths and the 'new draperies' – Spanish wool, olive oil from Puglia, silk yarn from Sicily and Naples, Levantine galls, alum from the Papal State, cotton and mohair. The English operated a 'system of deterrence' in the Mediterranean, based on their capacity, in the event of attack, to counter-attack and inflict serious damage on the adversary.[89] In this way, England succeeded not only in intimidating its enemies but also in obliging its friends to extend their favours. During the outbreak of plague in London in 1666, the Viceroy of Naples, Cardinal d'Aragona, prohibited English ships from loading supplies of olive oil in Gallipoli. At the same time, and probably as a result of the presence of the English fleet in the Mediterranean, Finch managed to extract a concession that English ships, including one, *The Brothers*, which had been refused entrance by Naples, could unload their cargoes of fish in Livorno, despite the port's severe public hygiene regulations.[90] The following year a commercial

[89] See E. Luttwak, *The Pentagon and the art of war* (New York: 1984).
[90] PRO, SP98/6, Finch to Arlington, 1 Mar. 1666; Finch to Arlington, Pisa, 8 Feb. 1666. See below, pp. 109 and 164.

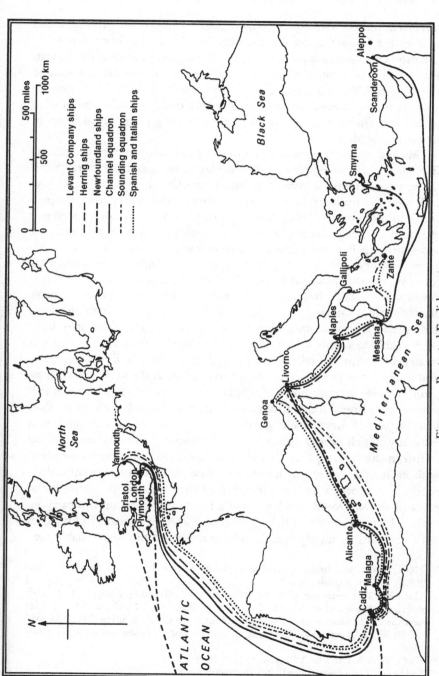

Figure 2 Protected English routes

Sources: S. Hornstein, 'The development of the English Navy in peacetime', Ph.D. thesis, University of Utrecht (1985).

treaty was signed with Spain, which granted important privileges and facilities for English ships and merchandise in all the Spanish ports.[91] The protection provided by the English naval fleet in the Mediterranean was gradually becoming more regular and more consistent. The double aspect of the English naval presence in the area – the convoys for defence, the squadrons for attack – was fully operational by the time of the Second Dutch War and succeeded in limiting commercial losses in the eastern Mediterranean.

This new system represented a considerable advance over the defensible ships: there were economic advantages, because the centralisation of the system reduced costs;[92] political benefits, in that the state now took over the responsibility for defence from individuals; and organisational improvements, since the regularity of the defensive presence increased not only the security but also the reliability of the carrying trade, making it more attractive and accessible. The system was also more advanced than the Dutch system of annual Mediterranean convoys, in which the times of sailing and the routes which were followed were notably inflexible.[93] However, grouping together so many merchant ships carrying similar merchandise and conveying them to the same places led to an abrupt saturation of the market, which may have been unable to supply demand before the ships' arrival. Such a situation created losses for the sellers, who found themselves in direct competition with each other in an oversupplied market; at the same time buyers could not rely on continuity of supply. In Livorno in 1667 so much fish arrived from England that profits were affected: 8,000 barrels rather than 110,000 would have made greater profits. The need was felt for a company which would concern itself exclusively with the distribution of fish in the Italian ports. At the time, however, merchants competed with each other to reach the markets first in order to maximise their profits.[94] A more rational organisation of the distribution system in the ports of arrival would also have had a beneficial effect on the carrying trade. The convoy system helped to ensure a secure service, but it led to stark contrasts in supply which only exacerbated the unavoidably sea-

---

[91] PRO, SP103/66, *Articles of peace, commerce & alliance between the Crowns of Great Britain & Spain concluded in a Treaty at Madrid the 13/23 of May, in the year of our Lord God 1667*. This treaty included the 'Royal cedulas' granted by Philip IV to English merchants living and working in Andalusia, 19 Mar. 1645. To obtain this dispensation the English had offered the Spanish king 2,500 ducats in silver (PRO, SP103/ 66, *Royal cedulas granted by the King of Spain to the English residing and trading in Andalusia*).

[92] PRO, SP98/8, Finch to Arlington, 13 June 1667.

[93] See Israel, 'The phases of the Dutch *staatvaart*', 23.

[94] PRO, SP98/8, Finch to Arlington, Livorno, 11 Apr. 1667. See below, p. 162.

sonal nature of English maritime trade in the Mediterranean. On the other hand, such lack of flexibility was much less of a handicap in the transportation of bullion or luxury commodities, the so-called 'trade of foreigners', and the commercial sector which aroused most international rivalry.[95]

Annual convoys not only followed a rigid timetable but also a fixed itinerary. The protection of a specific route, however complex it might be, necessarily neglected the other routes. Even if several routes were covered, gaps would always remain. In the case of the Mediterranean, since only some routes could be protected, the effort was made to protect the richest and most important, starting with the Spain–Italy–Levant route, which carried the 'Spanish trade' and the 'Levant trade', controlled, in turns, by the Genoese until 1630,[96] the English until 1647, the Dutch until 1665, and then again by the Genoese during the Second Dutch War.[97]

The system of protection organised by the English in the second half of the seventeenth century was based on convoys, which accompanied the merchant ships regularly on the principal routes, and on naval squadrons, generally composed of four or six frigates, which served as a deterrent and could on occasion provide an escort; the system gave rise to a series of protected zones, which included the whole of the western and central Mediterranean, and part of the east (figure 2). The gradual abandonment of the concepts of independent protection and of protection only on certain routes in favour of a system of control covering an entire network or area of trade was a significant step towards the establishment of English commercial hegemony in the Mediterranean.

PROTECTED ZONES AND THE CARRYING TRADE

The first positive effects of the new system of protection can be seen in 1666, when England was at war with Holland. The demand for English ships in the port of Livorno was so high that prices doubled and even tripled. The western Mediterranean had become so safe to sail in that Sir Jeremy Smith's frigates were able to leave the ships they were accompanying at Tangiers to continue their journey without them, and

---

[95] PRO, SP98/8, Finch to Arlington, Florence, 13 June 1667. See also Israel, 'The phases of the Dutch *staatvaart*', and *Dutch primacy*.

[96] In this phase Dutch participation was limited to the use of their ships; trade itself remained under the control of Italian merchants.

[97] PRO, SP98/8, Finch to Arlington, Livorno, 25 Apr. 1667. According to Finch, it was only the absence of the English in this period which gave the Genoese room to act.

other 'fish ships' continued to make the journey without the protection of a convoy. The prevailing situation struck contemporary observers, and, in particular, the contrast with the complete absence of Dutch ships; Thomas Dethick asserted that these would not reappear until the end of the war, leaving the English the masters of the Mediterranean.[98] Finch declared, doubtless with some exaggeration:

> Wee have to his Majesties immortall glory and Confusion of the Dutch 12 English vessells in Port; and the Dutch not one all this year from Holland; and though there are few of ours of defense; yet they came without Convoy, and meet neither Dutch nor French, the very name of his Majesties Frigatts having frighted them all into Tolon.[99]

This trouble-free situation continued into 1667, with the result that even those who supported the Netherlands began to acknowledge England's supremacy of the oceans.[100]

The reduction in the costs of defence for merchant ships was most obvious in the reduction of their crews: this was certainly not the result of any technological improvements in the ships themselves, but can be ascribed to the diminished threat of danger to English ships. There was no corresponding reduction in the ships' armed defences: the English merchant fleet continued to use the defensible ships, manned by smaller crews.[101] It was frequently observed in Livorno that the English ships which arrived in the port were completely unprepared for attack.[102] The consul Morgan Read wrote in 1665:

> The masters of severall shipes come to thos parts from England and nowe goeing to Galipoly in Apuglia to Load Oyles and to Zante to Load Currants for their Returns unto London and other parts of England and Being about twenty sayle of shipes tho some of good Burthen yet slightly manned, as they say, occasioned by the Proximity (of) England . . .[103]

Another consequence of the new system of protection was the reduced tonnage of English ships sailing in the Mediterranean. This

---

[98] PRO, SP98/6, Dethick to Williamson, Livorno, 1 Mar. 1666.

[99] PRO, SP98/6, Finch to Arlington, 1 Mar. 1666.

[100] PRO, SP98/8, Finch to Arlington, Livorno, 31 Jan. 1667.

[101] Davis, *The rise of the English shipping industry*, pp. 58–9. The English government passed a law obliging all ships over 200 tons sailing in the Mediterranean to carry a minimum of 16 cannon and 32 crew, subject to penalty (Charles II, c. 12,2 and 3). In 1668 the Levant Company stipulated that its ships were to have at least 15 crew for every 100 tons (Wood, *A history of the Levant Company*, p. 211). Both directives proved futile: crews of this size were more suited to the ships of the 1620s and 1630s than the Restoration period.

[102] PRO, SP98/8, Finch to Arlington, Livorno, 24 Jan. 1667 and 31 Jan. 1667.

[103] PRO, SP98/5, Read to Bennet, Livorno, 14 Feb. 1665.

reduction in tonnage was part of an overall trend affecting the entire English merchant fleet from the 1670s onwards. Three-quarters of the English ships working the Bordeaux route for cargoes of wine and brandy in 1664 were ketches and similar small vessels.[104] A memorandum informs us that the average tonnage of the ships bound for France from London between 29 September 1669 and the same date a year later, excluding those sailing empty, was 54.2 tons, while those setting out from other English ports during the same period, this time including the empty ships, had an average tonnage of 36.5.[105]

The increase in the number of small vessels of reduced tonnage also reflects a tendency in the shipbuilding industry as a whole from the 1640s to the end of the century. In 1676 a correspondent of the then Secretary of State Williamson wrote from Deal that the tonnage of the majority of ships built in the previous three years had been between 60 and 120 tons, notably smaller than the ships built in the preceding twenty years and earlier.[106] By the end of the century the average tonnage of English merchant ships was about 100 tons.[107]

In the Mediterranean, ships of smaller tonnage and limited defences were unusual before the 1660s, but their numbers steadily grew. Ralph Davis notes a sharp drop in the average tonnage of the English ships trading with Spain in the quarter century from 1650 to 1675.[108] The same phenomenon can be found in all the Italian ports; heavy tonnage vessels continued to sail the Levant routes, although even in the eastern Mediterranean smaller ships began to appear more regularly – the 150 ton *William & Elizabeth*, for example, or the 200 ton *Virgin*.[109]

The tendency can be seen more clearly in table 2.2, which contains the relevant figures for a group of English merchant ships sailing the route between Livorno, Puglia and Zante in 1666. Their tonnage ranges from 80 to 350 tons: of these 50 per cent have a tonnage in excess of 200 tons, and 50 per cent below this figure. Further evidence of this change can be found in contemporary documents, where there are continual references to the presence of 'small ships' in Italian waters. In March

[104] PRO, SP78/118, 264–5 [Sir David Inglish] to Bennet [Bordeaux, 13 June 1664].
[105] PRO, 30/24, Shaftesbury Papers, Supplementary, bundle 7/602, 'An abstract of what English shipps & vessells were bound out for France, and what French shipps & vessells arrived in any port of England between ye 29 day of September & ye 29 day of September 1670.'
[106] CSP Domestic, 1676–7, 28 Aug. 1676, p. 300.
[107] R. G. Albion, *Forests and sea power: the timber problem of the Royal Navy, 1652–1862* . . . (Cambridge, Mass.: 1926), p. 116.
[108] Davis, *The rise of the English shipping industry*, p. 60 n.
[109] PRO, SP98/9, Livorno, 20 Feb. 1668; see D. C. Coleman, *Sir John Banks, baronet and businessman* (Westport, Conn.: 1975), p. 25.

Table 2.2 English merchant ships sailing from Livorno, 9 July 1666

Ship	Captain	Port of embarkation	Tonnage	Cannon	Crew	Tonnage/cannon[a]	Tonnage/crew	Crew/cannon
A. Cargoes of olive oil								
Daniel & Roger	P. Couze		200	16	24	12.5	8.33	1.5
Margrett & Elisabeth	E. Tiddeman		160	14	30	11.43	5.33	2.14
Three Sisters	M. Symonds		120	10	20	12	6	2
Delight[b]	H. Galsworthy	Plymouth	100	8	16	12.5	6.25	2
Returne	T. Wallis		120	10	22	12	5.45	2.2
Endeavour	J. Hardringham		140	12	24	11.7	5.83	2
George & Martha[c]	E. Bloome		220	14	30	15.71	7.33	2.14
Amity[b]	R. Alderman	Plymouth	100	12	26	8.33	3.85	2.16
Gift[b]	J. Smyther	Bristol	80	10	20	8	4	2
Totals			1,240	106	206			
Averages			137.77	11.77	22.88	11.56	5.72	2.01
B. Cargoes of currants								
The Brothers Friendships	W. Hackett	via Alicante	350	26	40	13.46	8.75	1.54
Rose-Bush[b]	H. Hunt		300	28	50	10.71	6	1.79
Tunis Merchant	W. Baker		350	24	50	14.58	7	2.08
The Brothers[b]	T. Harvey		200	20	40	10	5	2
Elisabeth	R. Browne		160	14	30	11.42	5.3	2.14
Wellcome	H. Mudd		300	24	44	12.5	6.8	1.83
Leicester	T. Clapp		250	20	40	12.5	6.25	2
Totals			1,950	156	294			
Averages			278.57	22.28	42	12.16	6.44	1.9

Notes: [a] The ratios of the last three columns (tonnage/cannon, tonnage/crew, crew/cannon) have been calculated on the basis of the figures in the first three columns.

[b] These merchant ships had arrived in Livorno with cargoes of pilchards.

[c] The *George & Martha* was carrying a cargo of lead and pepper.

Source: PRO, SP98/7: 'Arryved in this Port severall merchant shipps as followeth belonging to the Subjecys of this sacred Majesty of Great Brittaine whome God preserve, Laden in parts from the Levant, all Bound homewards having devised themselves in three Squadrons – Constituted by mutuall Consent . . .', Livorno, 9 July 1666.

1666, for example, the English consul in Livorno writes that there are twelve 'small ships' in port, all belonging to the English, most carrying fish, bound for Gallipoli and Zante and awaiting an escorting convoy. He added that there were also two 'small English merchantmen': the 80 ton *Friendship* en route for England from the port of Ancona with a cargo of hemp and sulphur, and the 100 ton *Dexterity* bound for Gallipoli to collect a cargo of oil.[110]

A further example comes from April 1667, when four English ships left Livorno for London after having loaded their cargoes: the *Samuel & Jonathan*, the *Lucas*, the *Friendship* and a small pink of 45 tons. The following month saw two 'small English ships' calling in at Livorno on their way home from Gallipoli with a cargo of olive oil. In June, the *Diligence*, a ship belonging to the London merchant John Gould, was captured by a French boat. It was a 'small English vessell' of 50 tons, with a crew consisting of six men and a boy; it had been separated from its convoy by rough weather off Messina. At the same time, the only ship anchored in Livorno was 'a small English pinke' bound for Zante. Another arrival in Livorno in 1667 was the 80 ton *Charles* with a cargo of sugar: it had come from Barbados via Tangiers and Malaga, in an attempt, which was immediately quashed by the English authorities, to establish direct trading relations with the Mediterranean. In October it was followed by a further two 'small vessells' sailing from Jamaica with a cargo of cocoa.[111]

The small ships from England also frequented the southern Tyrrhenian. In 1675, the consul in Naples, Davies, wrote about a 'Small English Pinke with Newfoundland fish', which had been detained by the Viceroy, and another two 'small vessells as they supposed Herring ships', which appeared to have taken part in the attack on Messina along with the French fleet. In the same year, a 'small English vessell', the *Affrican Pinke* called at Naples, carrying all the goods of English merchants resident in Sicily, who feared an outbreak of hostilities between the French and the Messinese.[112]

The use of small vessels for the shipment of valuable commodities was not without its risks. In 1669 Finch reported that, despite the treaty, the Algerians were constantly tempted to attack them.[113]

---

[110] PRO, SP98/6, Chellingworth to Arlington, Livorno, 8 Mar. 1666, 31 May 1666.

[111] PRO, SP98/8, Chellingworth to Arlington, Pisa, 24 Apr. 1667; Livorno, 2 May 1667, 1 June 1667, 8 Aug. 1667, 3 Oct. 1667; Finch to Arlington, Florence, 1 Nov. 1667. See below, pp. 180.

[112] PRO, SP93/2, 5, dispatch from Consul Davies, Naples, 9 Apr. 1675; SP93/2, 32, dispatch from Consul Davies, Naples, 16 July 1675.

[113] Bodleian Library, Rawlinson MSS, A 478, f. 1, Finch to Arlington, 8 Mar. 1669 (copy).

Among the 'small vessels' which frequented Italian ports, a difference in destination corresponding to tonnage can be observed. In Livorno, it was for the most part the 'fish ships' which arrived: once their cargoes were unloaded, they can be divided into two categories: those sailing on to Puglia, above all to Gallipoli, to collect supplies of olive oil, and those continuing their journey to Zante, or less frequently to the Morea, to collect currants for the London market. Table 2.2 reveals a distinction between the 'oil ships' and the 'currant ships', the average tonnage of the first being about half that of the second group. Similarly, the size of the crew and the number of cannon on the ships bound for Puglia were half those found on the 'currant ships'. We can find other evidence for this distinction in contemporary documents. A letter to the Secretary of State from the consul in Livorno, Charles Chellingworth, lists the following ships anchored in Livorno in February 1668: the 300 ton *Thomas & Francis*, with 20 cannon and 36 men on board, bound for Naples and Scanderoon; the 300 ton *Hamburgh Merchant* bound for the Morea; the 150 ton *William & Elizabeth*, with 8 cannon and 12 crew, *en route* for Scanderoon; the 150 ton *Ingram*, which had taken on a cargo of precious goods with a value of 200,000 pieces of eight for London; finally, the *Genoa Merchant*, described as a 'small ship', bound for Gallipoli.[114]

In Finch's view, the establishment of a company for the distribution of fish in the Italian market would be beneficial for English maritime trade in Italian waters, precisely because it was the 'smallest vessels' which were engaged in this trade.[115] The 'small ships' were advantageous in several ways for the English merchant fleet. First and foremost, it was easier to put up the capital to build, purchase and equip them; they were more economical to run; they encouraged the sharing of risk; they were quicker to load and unload; it was easier to anchor in minor ports or close to shoals; finally, they obviated the problem of having to sail in ballast, without a full cargo. The 'small ships' were particularly suited for the transportation of fish, the key English import in the Italian market: smaller cargoes avoided saturating the market in Livorno and made for a more equitable distribution. The consignments which were destined for other places in Italy, in particular in the south, could be transported directly, eliminating the need to transfer them to the local ships which served the ports along the coast. The same was true for the two principal exports of olive oil and currants. In short, the returns on capital invested in maritime transport were both larger and more immediate.

---

[114] PRO, SP98/9, Chellingworth to Arlington, Livorno, 20 Feb. 1668.
[115] PRO, SP98/8, Finch to Arlington, Livorno, 18 Apr. 1667.

This, however, did not lead to an increased number of voyages: the seasonal nature of both imports and exports in the Italian market made this impossible. Longer periods of inactivity, the natural consequence of more efficient seasonal trading, must have encouraged an increase in the English carrying trade in the central Mediterranean.

Two factors, therefore, contributed to the increased presence of 'small ships' in Italian waters: first, the enhanced efficiency of the English system of protection, and second, the existence of a secure network of bases in the Mediterranean on which the merchant ships could rely when they were in need of provisions, repairs, finance, shelter, news or other assistance.

Braudel has written that an increase in the number of small vessels is generally an indication of a great expansion in the volume of trade.[116] The English 'small ships' are indeed the most striking indication of such a growth in trade between England and Italy: from the 1670s onwards, two connected developments in this expansion of the market, both relating to southern Italy, can be observed. First, there was throughout the seventeenth century and later a steady increase in the export of English goods, transported on English ships on behalf of English merchants, for the Italian markets; this increase was matched by imports into England of Italian agricultural products, above all of raw materials for the English textile industry; these trends indicate that the English were developing a policy whereby they would gain commercial control of the Italian market. A similar policy was being followed by the Dutch, and it marks the beginning of the absolute crisis in Italian commerce, that is, the loss of its control over its own trade.[117] Secondly, the same period sees a remarkable increase in the chartering of English ships within the Mediterranean as a whole and in Italy in particular, by Italian merchants and by the Jewish and Armenian merchants resident in Livorno.[118]

At the same time a gradual change was taking place in freight and in trade whereby English ships and merchants replaced their Italian equivalents in such sectors as the transport of Sicilian corn to Spain, of Puglian corn to Genoa, and even the transport of grain and oil for the Mediterranean domestic markets. This strategy of gradual encroach-

---

[116] Braudel, *La Méditerranée*, vol. I, pp. 273–4.

[117] See Israel, 'The phases of the Dutch *staatvaart*', and *Dutch primacy*.

[118] Thomas Dethick wrote in December 1667: '. . .The "Dover Merchant" departed on the 17th inst. for Zant & a Catch for Gallippolli, 2 other English ships are ffreighted by Strangers for Lisbone, soe that wee alreadie finde the good effects of peace for our trade & employment of shipping. . .' (PRO, SP98/8, Dethick to Williamson, Livorno, 19 Dec. 1667).

ment on the network of food supply within the western Mediterranean was evident during the siege of Messina, when England, which had remained neutral in the conflict, took control of the entire commercial network. The persistent French sequestrations of English ships reveal the extent to which the corn trade had been monopolised by the English. In 1667 the *Dolphin* was carrying a cargo of corn from Puglia to Genoa for an English merchant in the city, Richard Shucksbrough, when it was captured by the French and taken to Messina.[119] In January of the following year, a further seven English ships were captured and escorted to the Sicilian port. Only one was carrying a cargo of olive oil from Brindisi to London for John Gould; the other six were transporting corn, barley and biscuits. One of these, the *Lion*, was sailing to Seville or Cadiz for George Davies, the English consul in Naples; the others were headed for the Ligurian coast. The destination of two of them, the *Eagle* and the *Industry*, was Oneglia; the first had been chartered by an English company in Livorno, Newport & Littleton, while the second, carrying a passport in the name of the Duchess of Savoy, was working on behalf of Augustin Pery. Finally the *Crown*, the *Resolution* and the *Genoa Merchant* had been commissioned by English merchants resident in Naples, Livorno and Genoa to sail to Genoa.[120]

The hypothesis that there was also an expansion in trading and freightage for English ships in southern Italy is based on other considerations. Until the Restoration of Charles II, the Naples consulate covered the whole of mainland Italy south of Naples; the post of consul was not a royal appointment, and, like the post in Civitavecchia, was normally not filled by Englishmen, who, Finch observes, tended to regard such posts as being beneath them.[121] From the 1640s the post was held by Francis Brown, an English Catholic married to an Italian and a member of the household of a Neapolitan noble family.[122] He left the post during the Protectorate; on returning to it in 1660, the port of Gallipoli was excluded from the territory for which he was responsible.[123] The

---

[119] PRO, SP93/2, 216, dispatch from the English consul, Samuel Stanier, Messina, 17 July 1677.

[120] PRO, SP93/2, 245, 'Relazione del marchese d'Oppede, capo della giustizia, polizia e finanza delle armate terrestri e navali in Sicilia', Messina, 16 Jan. 1678.

[121] The post of consul at Civitavecchia had previously been held by an Italian; and the post in Naples by a Ragusan (PRO, SP98/9, Finch to Arlington, 9 Apr. 1668). See H. G. Koenigsberger, 'English merchants in Naples and Sicily in the seventeenth century', *The English Historical Review* 62 (1947), 302–66.

[122] PRO, SP98/9, Finch to Arlington, Livorno, 6 Feb. 1668.

[123] PRO, SP93/1, 183, 'Petizione alla Sacra Maestà dai suoi fedeli sudditi i Mercanti di Napoli per avere un console', Naples, 1664.

resident English merchants in Italy had asked for a consul to be appointed with sole responsibility for the Puglian port, given the large number of ships which arrived there each year to collect cargoes of olive oil; the only contact hitherto had been a local cooper. In 1664, on the recommendation of Joseph Kent, William Locke was appointed to the new post, to be succeeded the following year by Charles Chellingworth.[124] Shortly afterwards, John Byam, a Protestant merchant resident in Rome, was appointed consul at Civitavecchia. In Sicily the post of consul was sought after by Martin Wilkinson, who was even prepared to pay £100 in order to obtain it, a ploy no-one before had thought necessary for such posts in southern ports.[125] Wilkinson clearly thought that his offer made good business sense, since 'consulage', the dues which the local consul received for his services, was incurred by each ship which arrived in the port.

Two items of contemporary evidence confirm the idea that the appointment of an English consul reflected the increased commercial and strategic importance of a port. On the death of Morgan Read, the consul in Livorno, the majority of English merchants living in the town petitioned the resident to appoint Read's Italian widow and her brothers. Finch wrote to the Secretary of State expressing his regret that he could not accede to the general wish since he thought an Englishman more appropriate for the post at such an important time: the King's commands and the responsibility for seeing them enacted should be entrusted to one of his subjects who could be punished for negligence or betrayal. Furthermore, he thought it inadvisable that Italians should receive information on the cargoes, weapons, routes and departure times of the English ships which called at Livorno.[126]

Finch advanced the same argument when a similar situation arose in Venice. Aloisio Morelli, a Venetian who had been in partnership with an English merchant and spoke fluent English, had been proposed for the vacant post. While Finch acknowledged his ability and trustworthiness, he nevertheless regarded his nationality as an insurmountable obstacle; moreover, he was married to a Dutch woman. In writing to

[124] PRO, SP93/1, 149, Kent to Williamson, Naples, 13 May 1664; SP104/174B, 31, letter from Charles II to William Locke appointing him English consul in Gallipoli, 1 May 1664; SP104/174A, 71, letter from Charles II to Cardinal d'Aragona, the Viceroy of Naples, appointing Charles Chellingworth consul, 17 Apr. 1665; SP104/174A, 72, letter from Charles II to Charles Chellingworth appointing him English consul in Gallipoli, 12 Apr. 1665. See above, p. 16, note 57. In reality, Joseph Kent, the English consul in Livorno, was temporarily substituted by Charles Chellingworth, who took up his post in Gallipoli only in 1675.

[125] PRO, SP98/8, Dethick to Williamson, Livorno, 21 Nov. 1667.

[126] PRO, SP98/5, Finch to the Secretary of State, Florence, 13 June 1665.

Arlington, Finch declared; 'I doe not thinke him fitt to act the English Interest there, which is in competition onely with Italians and Dutch, and besides I know he must not speak for the English Interest when his own Lords will have him, being theyr Subiect; to be Silent.'[127]

It was estimated that the consul in Civitavecchia earned £5 a year in 'consulage', while at Naples this figure rose to between £10 and £15.[128] If we calculate that the 'consulage' at Livorno was worth 10 pieces of eight, equivalent to a little over £2 for each vessel, and assume that the 'consulage' was proportionally less for the less significant ports in the south, Finch's figure would suggest the arrival of no more than seven ships in the port of Naples at the beginning of the 1660s.[129] This figure however does not comprise all the trade which took place in the southern ports since it is a reasonable hypothesis that the larger part of English merchant shipping was concentrated in Livorno, while the distribution of exports and the collection of imports was entrusted to the small local fleet – the same category of shipping which the rise of the English 'small ships' from 1664 onwards would do much to undermine.

In the 1670s a sudden expansion in the number of chartered English ships sailing in Italian waters is evident, above all in the south, where the situation of the previous decade was completely transformed. Davies, the consul in Naples from 1672, wrote that while English ships were usually a frequent sight in the port, during the French siege of Messina their numbers had shot up rapidly.[130] Each year approximately 120 merchantmen arrived in Naples: of these, 60 were sailing to pick up cargoes of silk and olive oil to take back to England, while the remaining half took corn and wine on board for other destinations.[131] The leap from 7 to 120 ships was a remarkable one, even more so if we compare it to the 20 ships arriving in Venice and the 100 in Livorno in the same period; it must be remembered, however, that such a high figure was the exceptional and shortlived effect of the siege of Messina.[132]

[127] PRO, SP98/9, Finch to Arlington, Livorno, 16 Jan. 1668.
[128] PRO, SP98/9, Finch to Arlington, Livorno, 6 Feb. 1668 and 9 Apr. 1668.
[129] PRO, SP98/8, Dethick to Williamson, Livorno, 21 Nov. 1667; Finch to Arlington, 26 Dec. 1667.
[130] PRO, SP93/2, 130, dispatch from Consul Davies, Naples, 5 May 1676; SP93/2, 157, dispatch from Consul Davies, Naples, 11 Aug. 1676. The siege of Messina lasted from 1674 to 1678.
[131] PRO, SP93/2, 56, dispatch from Consul Davies, Naples, 24 Sept. 1675 and 29 Oct. 1675.
[132] PRO, CO389/5, 34–35, 'A note of the consulage duty leavyed by his Majestyes Consulls as follows [. . .]' The 'consulage' paid in Livorno had risen from 10 to 15 pieces of eight for each ship, while in Venice it was 30 ducats or approximately £6 per ship.

If the expansion of the 1670s owed much to circumstantial factors, its consequences nevertheless were long-lasting. Writing half a century later the consul in Naples at the time, Edward Allen, reported that the most productive sectors of British industry had never enjoyed such prosperous trading relations with southern Italy. There had been a notable increase in comparison with previous years in the exports of woollen cloth, salt fish and other products. The carrying trade was also thriving, with English ships entirely responsible for the shipment of merchandise out of Naples. They were preferred above the ships of all other nations, and commercial traffic in the Mediterranean was almost entirely entrusted to them.[133]

The close connection between expanding commercial activity and the state of the carrying trade was not merely a question of putting the unoccupied periods between seasonal traffic to good use; it was also related to the advantages which English merchant shipping enjoyed from the outset, thanks to the legislation which controlled imports and exports into England and excluded other carriers. This meant that the cost of freight on intermediate passages was much lower than would have been the case in a freely competitive market.[134]

Here then is a partial explanation for the increasing role played by English ships from the 1670s onwards in trading relations between the 'two Italys'. The same period sees the emergence of an English strategy to take over the Italian market by a process of substitution. With the English ships which loaded olive oil in Puglia and thrown silk in Sicily and Naples for the English textile industry, with the transport of Sicilian corn to Spain, the food supplies taken from the south for the cities of northern Italy, and with the sale of English woollens, which in the 1660s was only possible in the south of the country, we see a revival of the pattern of economic development founded on the industrialised north of Italy and the south of the country which was predominantly agricultural and at the same time a market for the manufactured products of the North's industries. Aymard believes that this pattern had vanished by the beginning of the seventeenth century; its revival certainly takes place within a context which has yet to be properly evaluated. The commercial activity of the English adapted itself in such a way that the dualism of the Italian economy was absorbed into the structure both of its own national economy and of its trading system, which in this very period was expanding worldwide. The first step was to harmonise the London based direction of commercial policy with England's

133 PRO, SP93/5, 137, Allen to Newcastle, Naples, 24 Dec. 1728.
134 Harper, *The English navigation laws*, pp. 278–9.

centre for commercial operations in the Mediterranean, Livorno. This helped to bring into line the confusion engendered by the variety of economic policies which characterised the industrial cities of northern Italy, a fragmentation which threatened to undermine the strategy of the emergent rulers as it had served to protect the vitality of the ruled.

CHAPTER 3

ROUTES AND PORTS

THE ROUTES BETWEEN ENGLAND AND ITALY

In the sixteenth century the pattern of trade between northern Europe and the Mediterranean adhered to what was probably a centuries-old distinction between sea routes and land routes. The distinction was based on the nature of the goods to be transported: luxury commodities, occupying little space but of high unit value, were sent by land, while goods of bulk and weight and comparatively low value were sent with Venetian and Ragusan ships through the Straits of Gibraltar and past the dangerous Bay of Biscay to arrive on the banks of the Scheldt or in the English ports.[1]

From the 1530s onwards, however, there was a clear preference for the continental land route. This was caused in part by the instability in the Mediterranean, which was ravaged by wars and piracy, and in part by an increase in the trade in textiles between the two areas, a key element in their commercial relations, and a growing demand in the English market for Mediterranean luxury commodities.[2] For such goods transportation was a minimal part of the overall cost. Sending goods overland was undoubtedly slower and more expensive, but the greater security and regularity made it a highly attractive option.

The two main transcontinental routes which connected England to Italy started in Antwerp, a centre for international trade until 1564, and in Hamburg, which replaced the Flemish port as the principal northern European entrepôt from 1584 to the 1630s, when the sea routes began to be more regularly used (see Figure 3). In the twenty years which

---

[1] *La Méditerranée*, vol. I, p. 266; W. Brulez, 'Les routes commerciales d'Angleterre en Italie au XVIe siècle' in *Studi in onore di Amintore Fanfani* (Milan: 1962), vol. IV, p. 130.

[2] J. H. Parry, 'Transport and trade routes' in Rich and Wilson (eds.), *The Cambridge Economic History of Europe*, vol. IV, pp. 185–6; Clay, *Economic expansion and social change*, vol. II, p. 123.

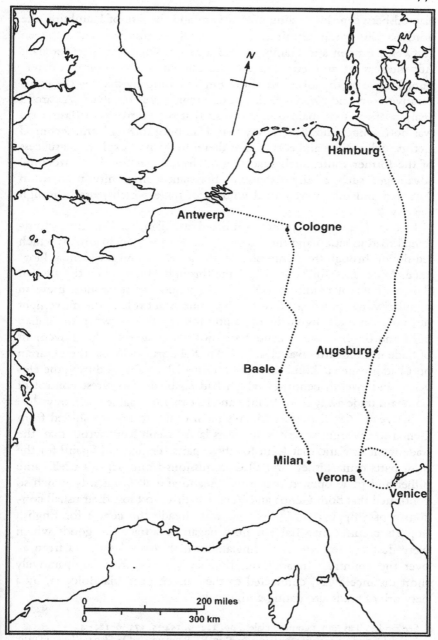

Figure 3   The continental land routes
Source: W. Brulez, 'Les routes commerciales d'Angleterre en italie au XVIIe siècle', *Studi in onore di Amintore Fanfani*, vol. IV (Milan: 1962), p. 177.

elapsed between the decline of Antwerp and the rise of Hamburg, the northern European terminus of the overland route varied between Antwerp, Emden and Hamburg, more or less wherever the Merchant Adventurers set up their headquarters. The choice of route was determined more by the locations of the English company than by the comparative costs and times which the different routes involved. A careful analysis of the two main routes reveals that the Antwerp to Basle road was both longer and more costly than Hamburg to Augsburg: technical factors such as time and cost cannot therefore help to explain the success of the former route; such success must have been based on structural advantages such as the extensive merchant community resident in Antwerp and the international volume of trade which passed through the city.[3]

In Italy the western route terminated at Milan, an important continental road junction and the starting point for the principal roads which led down through the peninsula. All the goods bound for Genoa, Florence, Ancona, or further south, came through Milan, along the ancient Roman lines of communication. Even when the sea routes grew in popularity, Milan managed to retain an important role in the movement of European trade, by virtue of its position as a link between the Italian ports and the markets of central and northern Europe. The movement of trade in Lombardy was closely tied to the port of Genoa; the Ligurian port had pursued a skilful strategy of territorial expansion during the eleventh and twelfth centuries which had enabled it to wrest control of Lombard trade away from Venice and its easily navigable waterways.[4]

Between 1625 and 1628 Milan's main outlet to the sea shifted from Genoa to Livorno, where some years later Joseph Kent wrote that 'the trade from England that went for those parts [France and Spain] for the most parts came hither, and all Commissions from Genova itself came hither and trade opened hence for Milano and all Lombardy which so continued that both Genoa and Venice hath almost lost their usuall concourse of Shipping . . .'[5] Livorno was already the centre for English imports coming into Italy; it now began to attract the goods which were destined for export to England, which arrived by road from all over the country.[6] In addition, Lombardy was only a comparatively short distance away, connected to the Tuscan port, via Bologna, by a network of roads alternating with canals.

[3] See Brulez, 'Les routes commerciales', pp. 124–9, 154–5, 175–6, 181–4.
[4] J. Day, 'Strade e vie di comunicazione' in R. Romano (ed.), Storia d'Italia (Turin: 1973), vol. v, p. 110.
[5] PRO, SP98/4, 198v. (part II), Kent to Bennet, Livorno, 27 Apr. 1663. See pp. 116–17.
[6] Davis, 'England and the Mediterranean', pp. 134–5.

The importance of Lombardy stemmed not only from its fortunate position and the fertility of its soil; its high population density and the productivity of its manufacturing industries were also contributing factors. From 1565 onwards, when the continual attacks of English and Dutch privateers made the Atlantic seaboard route impracticable, Spain used Lombardy, a Spanish viceroyalty, as its Italian base for the Spanish troops and money destined for Flanders.[7] Between 1613 and 1659, warfare raged in the territory of Lombardy itself, bringing disruption to the region's industry, but at the same time providing an important stimulus to the local industries supplying armaments and other military provisions. Finally, Milan was a great city, and, as such, it retained its status throughout the seventeenth century as a centre of conspicuous demand for food and luxury merchandise, as a lively commercial base, and as an essential clearing house for the transit of goods between northern Italy and France and Switzerland.[8]

The Antwerp–Basle road did not serve the area round Venice. Venice had its own communication network with Europe north of the Alps which linked up with the Hamburg–Augsburg route. This route grew in importance in the last quarter of the sixteenth century: a principal cause was the establishment of the Merchant Adventurers' headquarters in Hamburg in 1584. One could travel as far as Venice on this road, although it was frequent practice to leave the road at the important junction of Verona: this deviated from the direct route, but at the same time was connected to Venice by a system of easily navigated waterways, thus reducing the costs of transportation by a considerable margin, especially for those goods destined for the markets further south.[9]

The freedom of movement enjoyed by troops, merchandise, money and letters along the land routes was dependent not only on changing weather conditions and the varying terrain but also on the control wielded both by the local barons, who took the opportunity to levy tolls at various key points along the road, and by the great powers who were on occasion in open conflict over the occupation of some restricted but crucially located site along the route. The wars over Monferrato and Valtellina, in which half the countries in Europe were involved throughout the first half of the seventeenth century, were nothing more than a struggle for control of the communications between Genoa and Milan, or, on a larger scale, between Italy and

[7] PRO, SP98/4, 286 (part II), Kent to Bennet, Livorno, 29 Dec. 1663. See D. Sella, *L'economia lombarda durante la dominazione spagnola* (Bologna: 1982), and Parker, *The army of Flanders*, chapters 1 and 2.

[8] Sella, *L'economia lombarda*, pp. 153–5.

[9] Brulez, 'Les routes commerciales', p. 165.

transalpine Europe. The 'Spanish road' to Flanders used by Philip II in 1565–6 led through Genoa and Lombardy across Piedmont, Savoy, the Franche-Comté and Lorraine, all territories either directly under the dominion of Spain or allied to it. During the Habsburg period the Spanish kings were always careful to forge alliances with the rulers of the countries which lay between their own territories.

Unlike the overland routes, the sea route between England and Italy followed an unvarying course, resembling that taken by the Genoese and Venetian galleys and the modern merchant ships. It led from the port of London, or one of the provincial or so-called 'outports', such as Yarmouth, Plymouth or Bristol, down the English Channel; once past the Bay of Biscay, it followed the Portuguese coast until reaching the Straits of Gibraltar. The comparative absence of alternatives to this itinerary can be seen if we look at the routes followed by the English convoys in the second half of the seventeenth century (figure 2). The lack of variation is also true of the routes within the Mediterranean; with some small variations in the ports of call, ships sailed the same route to Italy, where setting out from Genoa or Livorno, they followed the so-called 'Christian route', down the Tyrrhenian coast, through the Straits of Messina and on to the Levant.

The only other possibility was the so-called 'Islamic route' which, starting from Bizerta or Algiers, crossed the Sicilian channel to the coast of Sicily or to Naples; from here it continued on towards Valona or Albania. This was the route taken by the Turkish fleet; English and Dutch ships took to sailing it at the turn of the sixteenth century: once through the Straits of Gibraltar, they sailed along the North African coast, and then branched off in the direction of Greece, Crete and Syria. The route conveniently avoided the threat of Spanish control at a time when both England and Holland were at war with Spain, but it was both longer and more dangerous than the usual itinerary, and ships were more exposed to the risk of piracy.[10]

Ships normally preferred to take the 'Christian route' because it was shorter and because, sailing from east to west, it provided greater shelter from the winds and currents which made the crossing of the central Mediterranean so hazardous. However, the safety provided by the passage through the Straits of Messina was, from this point of view, only relative. During the siege of the Sicilian port, the currents in the Straits had played an important part in the engagements of the Spanish and French fleets. On the morning of 27 October 1675, for example, the

[10] Braudel, *La Méditerranée*, vol. 1, pp. 122–3; see also P. Earle, *Corsairs of Malta and Barbary* (London: 1970).

scirocco wind was blowing and the current flowing from Sicily favoured the French, pushing their fleet towards Reggio. However, once they were midway across the channel, they were caught off the Calabrian coast by the current which pushed them downstream a quarter of a mile to the south of the Spanish fleet which was waiting to pursue them with the aid of the 'Faro' current and the prevailing wind.[11] Little more than a year before, a French ship, with 20 cannon and 150 crew on board, had been pushed by the same currents towards the coast of Calabria, where it was captured by Spanish galleys; the year before that a similar fate had befallen two English warships.[12]

The winds, above all the scirocco, also made this short stretch of sea treacherous for ships. In February 1675, the Spanish fleet, having fled at the appearance of the French, took up their positions again and pre-pared to confront them. They lined up all their ships and galleys along the stretch of coast which extends from the beach of Scilla as far as Reggio; however, a sudden storm brought on by the scirocco almost dispersed them again. A contemporary chronicler from Messina, Giovan Battista Romano, in his account of the episode, remarks that the scirocco had caused problems for more than one fleet in the waters off the 'Faro'.[13]

'The hazardous channel of the "Faro"', as one contemporary observer described it, had been responsible for many shipwrecks.[14] In May 1614, the Santa Caterina, one of nine Spanish galleys, at the entrance to the channel was driven by the currents against the Calabrian coast where it ran aground; the boatswain and his mate were accused of negligence and hanged on the orders of the commander of the galleys, the Marquis of Santa Cruz. Even English ships, accustomed to wintry conditions and stormy seas, succumbed to the dangers of sailing the Straits. On the night of the 9 January 1677, the Albany, under its captain James Dodesley, ran aground near the 'Faro' owing to atrocious weather and the inexperience of the pilot.[15]

The need for a local pilot when entering and leaving the waters round Messina was a constant concern of the English ships which sailed

[11] E. Laloy, La révolte de Messine: l'expédition de Sicile et la politique française en Italie (1674–1678) (Paris: 1930), vol. ii, p. 268.
[12] PRO, SP93/3, 36, letter from the consul in Naples, George Davies to Joseph Williamson, Secretary of State, Naples, 30 July 1675; SP93/2, 162, dispatch from Davies, Naples, 1 Sept. 1676. On Joseph Williamson, see chapter 1, note 49.
[13] Laloy, La révolte de Messine, vol. i, p. 581.   [14] Ibid., p. 484.
[15] PRO, SP93/2, 186, letter from Samuel Stanier, English consul in Messina, to Williamson, Messina, 15 Jan. 1677; SP93/2, 187v., Stanier to Williamson, Messina, 19 Jan. 1677; SP93/2, 190, Stanier to Williamson, Messina, 23 Jan. 1677; SP93/2, 192, dispatch from Davies, Naples, 2 Feb. 1677.

in the Mediterranean.[16] In the account-books for the three voyages undertaken by the *Bantam* between 1667 and 1670, there is always a heading for the 'pilotage' needed on entering and leaving the 'Faro'.[17] In June 1676, De Ruyter, the commander of the Dutch fleet, which had arrived in the Mediterranean to help the Spanish recapture Messina from the French, had local Sicilian coastal pilots brought on board each ship in order to guide them safely past the dangerous shoals and points along the coast.[18]

Along the sea route from England to the Mediterranean, there were only three stretches where it was possible to exercise a degree of control: the English Channel, the Straits of Gibraltar, and, within the Mediterranean, the Straits of Messina.

All ships sailing west from the North Sea had to pass through the English Channel. The key question of control of these waters emerged in the 1590s, when Genoa and Tuscany bought huge supplies of grain from northern Europe in response to an unexpected demand in Italy; the Dutch and Hanseatic ships which were chartered to carry the supplies had to obtain permits from the English. In June 1591, the Grand Duke Ferdinand wrote to Elizabeth I, asking her 'to grant passports to all the ships and other vessels which the above-named, from Flanders as from Lisbon, are sending to my port of Livorno, especially as they are acting on my behalf to bring corn for my people'.[19] A few days later, a new pass was requested for Decio Doria, Antonio Velluti and Orfeo Amato in their own name and in the name of Nicolò and Francesco Capponi, two gentlemen of Florence, for approximately forty ships from 'Hamburg, Zeeland, and Holland to come to Livorno and to Genoa'.[20] In July, the Grand Duke wrote again to the Queen:

> Besides the supplies of corn collected during the past year and now stored in Hamburg, I should like to have further corn and rye for the coming year: in addition therefore to the passports I have already requested from your loving Majesty, I beseech you with all my heart gra-

[16] 'The voyage of master Roger Bedenham with the great bark "Aucher" to Candia and Chios. Written by himself' in R. David (ed.), *Hakluyt's voyages* (London: 1981), p. 125.

[17] BL, Eg. 2524, 'Book of account of the ship "Bantam", trading to Spain and the Mediterranean, and afterwards sold in the Navy, Capt. Richard Haddock, Commander; 1667–1672'.

[18] Laloy, *La révolte de Messine*, vol. II, pp. 487–8.

[19] PRO, SP98/1, 52, Grand Duke to Elizabeth, Florence, 14 June 1591: 'di concedere Passaporti, a tutti le Navi et robbe che tutti li sopradetti, così di Fiandra, come di Lisbona, s'invijno a Livorno mio Porto, et massime che faranno condurre Grani, come miei agenti, per servitio de miei popoli'.

[20] PRO, SP98/1, 60, Grand Duke to Elizabeth, Florence, 6 July 1591: 'Amburgo, Zelanda e Olanda per venire a Livorno, et a Genova'.

ciously to grant passports and full safe-conduct to all the ships carrying corn from Holland on behalf of Francesco Cambi of Antwerp, or from Hamburg on behalf of Alessandro Rocca, or others to my port of Livorno . . .[21]

Again, two weeks later, we find the Grand Duke requesting further permits for the grain sent by the Florentine Neri Giraldi from Danzig to Livorno on ten English and Flemish vessels.[22] A month later Elizabeth granted more passes in the names of Decio Doria, Antonio Velluti, Orfeo Amato, Francesco and Nicola Capponi, Francesco Cambi of Antwerp and Alessandro Rocca of Hamburg, all of whom were responsible for sending corn to the Grand Duke.[23]

Thus, although England had no major involvement in the transport of grain, its role was still vital because it controlled a crucial part of the sea route between northern Europe and the Mediterranean. Similarly, during the Second Dutch War, the English kept close watch over shipping in the Channel, forcing Dutch ships headed for the south to take the much longer and more dangerous route round Scotland. This strategy together with the attacks of North African pirates succeeded in driving the Dutch completely, if only temporarily, out of the Mediterranean. In 1667, Finch reported that no Dutch ship had passed through the Straits of Gibraltar for two years. Of the five ships which had set sail for the south from Holland in that time, one, carrying an extremely valuable cargo, had been wrecked on the Scottish coast, while the other four had been captured by pirates and taken to the port of Algiers. Finch added that such disasters for England's rivals were more effective than any military success in winning renown for the ships sailing under the Royal Standard and in creating confidence among Italian merchants, with the result that they entrusted their merchandise wholly to English ships.[24]

Spain controlled Gibraltar, together with the stretch of sea known as the Mediterranean Channel, the area of water which lies between the Straits, the coasts of southern Spain and North Africa, and extends to the east as far as Cape Matifou, near Algiers, and Cape de la Nao, south

---

[21] Ibid.: 'Oltre che restano ancora in Amburgho de miei grani provisti fin l'anno passato, io desidero ancora di far venire per l'anno prossimo delli altri grani et Segole, et pero oltre alli altri Passaporti che io ho chiesto all'amorevolezza di Vostra Maestà, la prego ancora, efficacissimamente di cuore che mi voglia far gratia di concedere libero, et amplo Salvacondotto à tutte le Navi, che da Francesco Cambi da Anversa, ò di Olanda, ò da Alessandro Rocca di Amburgo ò da altri per loro saranno cariche di grani, ò segole, ò d'altro, per noleggiarsi et condursi à Livorno mio Porto. . .'
[22] PRO, SP98/1, 62, Grand Duke to Elizabeth, Florence, 24 July 1591.
[23] PRO, SP98/1, 65–6, 'Queen Elizabeth's passport for the Grand Duke's ships'.
[24] PRO, SP98/8, Finch to Arlington, Livorno, 11 Apr. 1667.

of Valencia. The Spanish patrol of the waters, however, was far from effective: the ships from northern Europe carrying corn purchased by the Tuscan Grand Duke continued their journeys normally despite the procrastination of Philip II in granting them their passports.[25] Even during the first half of the seventeenth century, the ships belonging to the rebel Dutch continued to sail and trade undisturbed in the Mediterranean. Devising some effective means of controlling the Straits was a problem which constantly preoccupied both Spain's rulers and its mariners.[26] The installation of cannon on Gibraltar which would be capable of bombarding the ships passing through the Straits was suggested.[27] There was a plan to fortify the small island of Perejil, off Ceuta. Some consideration was even given to the scheme devised by Anthony Sherley, an English adventurer employed in the service of Spain, which envisaged the Spanish occupying the towns of Mogador (Essaouira) and Agadir, and so taking control of Morocco. It proved impossible, however, to control the shipping in the Straits.[28]

In his account of the 1617 peace treaty agreed by Spain, the Empire, Venice and Savoy, Corbett remarks on Spain's inability to establish adequate control over the great shipping routes which lay within its sphere of influence and on the readiness of both the Dutch and the English to appropriate them to their own advantage.[29] Such a view is borne out by the episode which took place in the late autumn of 1620, at a time of heightened tension between England and Spain, when the English fleet, commanded by Sir Richard Hawkins, entered the Mediterranean undisturbed, while the Spanish galleys, which had long been awaiting its arrival, had only recently been called back to port and were anchored in Cadiz, from where they would only be able to set sail again in the following spring.[30]

The only type of control which the Spanish succeeded in imposing was the embargo or closure of its ports to the ships which belonged to hostile countries. This proved an effective device in both the periods when Spain was at war with the United Provinces, 1590–1609 and

---

[25] ASG, Archivio segreto, Spain, busta 2419, letter from Ambassador Cattaneo, 12 Sept. 1591, quoted in Grendi, 'I nordici,' 26.

[26] Braudel, *La Méditerranée*, vol. I, p. 110.

[27] ASV, Alvise Correr to the Doge, Madrid, 28 Apr. 1621, quoted by Braudel, *La Méditerranée*, vol. I, p. 110. Correr thought the project impossible given the distance between the two shores of the Straits.

[28] Braudel, *La Méditerranée*, vol. I, p. 110.

[29] Corbett, *England in the Mediterranean*, vol. I, p. 51.

[30] Ibid. Sir Richard Hawkins (1562?–1622) was an experienced seaman who took part in various expeditions and, as commander of the *Swallow*, fought in the Battle of the Armada.

1621–47. The Dutch who wanted to continue trading with Spain and Portugal and southern Italy could only do so under another country's flag or through foreign merchants. In the winter of 1621–2, the embargo was briefly lifted by the Viceroy in Naples in order to allow Dutch ships to load corn in Sicily and relieve the famine which was afflicting the southern mainland. During the 1630s, Dutch ships were occasionally allowed permits for the transportation of corn or munitions. On the whole, however, trade between Spain and Holland was at a standstill throughout this period, and the effects on Dutch commercial interests in the Mediterranean were serious.[31]

The closure of Spanish ports to the ships of enemy countries could not prevent those ships from entering the Mediterranean; it did, however, cause serious difficulties for the ships from northern European countries, who thus found it necessary to maintain peaceful relations with Spain. The ports of the Iberian peninsula were gateways to colonial as well as local markets; they were rich sources for the silver pieces of eight which were essential for trade in the Levant and in the Far East.

Spain also controlled a crucial stretch of the Mediterranean: the Straits of Messina, the most important part of the 'Christian route', with the Spanish viceroyalties of Sicily and southern Italy on either side. It was normally used by ships from Genoa and Livorno on their way to and from Puglia or beyond, to the 'currant islands' or the Levant. Unlike the Straits of Gibraltar, the narrowness of the sea at Messina meant that cannon could control the passage of ships. In January 1675, don Melchor de la Cueva, in explaining to the Marquis of Villafranca the usefulness of taking possession of the 'Faro' tower, declared his conviction that four cannon placed on the 'Faro' and at Scilla would make the passage of the Straits difficult, not to say hazardous, for the French fleet.[32] In January of the following year, the passage of the *Katherine*, an English ship sailing from Naples to Gallipoli, through the Straits, revealed how effective the Spanish artillery defending the entrance to them could be: it was bombarded as it came in sight of the 'Faro', and the captain, Daniel Tracie, fearing further damage, agreed to berth. Once on land he was held prisoner for three days, while the Spanish claimed the right to search his ship.[33]

---

[31] J. I. Israel, *The Dutch Republic and the Hispanic world, 1606–1661* (Oxford: 1982), pp. 142–3, 285–7; see the same author's 'The phases of the Dutch *staatvaart*' and *Dutch primacy*.

[32] Laloy, *La révolte de Messine*, vol. 1, p. 523. The Straits of Gibraltar are 13 kilometres wide, whereas those of Messina measure only 3 kilometres across at their narrowest point.

[33] PRO, SP93/2, 185, dispatch from the consul George Davies, Naples, 5 Jan. 1677.

If naval squadrons were added to the firing power of the cannon, then the Straits became virtually impassable. In a letter written on 12 January 1675, Valbelle, the French admiral besieged by the Spanish in Messina, wrote that the northern shore of the 'Faro' entrance was normally guarded by Spanish galleys if the wind permitted. When the wind was in the south-east, the Spanish fleet took shelter in Milazzo; when the wind was light, they used oars and sails to defend themselves against the French. Because of their presence, merchant ships ran great risks when they passed through this stretch of water.[34]

The strategic importance of the Straits of Messina as an alternative to the Sicilian channel was well known. In the seventeenth century the Straits were seen to occupy a key position, since Naples and to some degree the rest of mainland Italy received supplies from the ships which sailed from Puglia through this stretch of water. As the French consul wrote: 'Naples is dependent on Puglia alone for its food provision . . . not only Naples, but the whole of Italy is entirely dependent on Puglia for its corn, oil, vegetables, and other such items needful for survival . . .'[35]

In 1672, at a time of widespread famine in the island, the Senate in Messina sought permission from the Viceroy in Naples to obtain supplies from Puglia, on payment in silver. Permission was granted, but withdrawn almost immediately, when it was discovered that the famine affected not only the whole of Sicily but parts of the mainland as well, thus making it essential to ensure that supplies continued to reach the city of Naples. Reduced to desperation, the inhabitants of Messina put three armed ships to sea with the purpose of capturing all the merchant ships carrying corn on their way to Naples and elsewhere. They were so successful that, after only two months, Naples, Campania and the whole of Calabria found themselves in the same condition as Sicily.[36] In order to put an end to the crisis, the Neapolitan authorities chartered two Dutch men-of-war at considerable expense to escort as far as Naples the numerous merchant ships which were waiting to set out from Puglia with cargoes of corn already loaded but which did not dare to for fear of being captured by the inhabitants of Messina.[37]

Some three years later, writing on the eve of the arrival of French

---

[34] Laloy, La révolte de Messine, vol. i, p. 585.

[35] ANF, AE/BI/867, Naples, 1672–1714, 'Mémoire concernant la Marine de Naple et de Sicille. Mémoire de Monseig. le Marquis de Seignelay', undated document, probably written in 1675: 'Naples ne subsiste que par la puille . . . non seulement Naples, mais toute l'Italie depend entierement de la puille par le besoin des grains, huilles, legumes, et autres choses necessaires a la vie . . .'

[36] Ibid.

[37] PRO, SP93/1, 221, dispatch from the consul George Davies, Naples, 16 Feb. 1672.

assistance for the rebels in Messina, the French consul stressed how vital the Straits of Messina were for all the shipping in the Kingdom of Naples, and how easily they could be blocked at the 'Faro' by a handful of forces. The Neapolitans would be forced to bring their supplies of corn overland; the city would be reduced to such a state of want that it would need to turn to Livorno and Genoa for more supplies, as indeed proved to be the case in 1672.[38] The French admiral Valbelle agreed with this strategy; shortly after his arrival in Sicily, he wrote:

> We possess nothing in Italy, but with Messina the King could enrich himself as much as he cares to; at the worst, we would be feared, even if we were not loved. The city's 'Faro', already notorious for the frequent shipwrecks which occur there, would, if the King takes possession of it, be even more renowned for the pain and torment it inflicts on the Council of Spain: all the corn from the Two Calabrias must pass through on its way to the Kingdom of Naples. In wartime we could bring the great city of Naples to its knees because of famine and humiliate the Spanish in the process.[39]

Until the crisis of Messina, the English, with their defensible ships and their convoys, and under the protection vouchsafed them in the Treaty of Madrid, were free to sail the 'Christian route' through the Straits. Even during the Spanish siege of the French forces holding Messina in support of the rebels, both sides allowed English ships to pass through. Indeed, for a certain period, the English enjoyed a privileged position as the only country which had remained neutral in the conflict, and their ships were largely responsible for the transportation of agricultural produce to Naples and northern Italy, to the disadvantage above all of the Dutch.[40] However, when the Spanish blockade of Messina caused problems of supply, the French took to intercepting the English merchant ships on their way from Puglia and forcing them to sell their cargoes at current prices.[41] A lively contraband trade sprang up, which,

[38] ANF, AE/BI/867.

[39] Laloy, La révolte de Messine, vol. I, p. 454: 'Nous ne possédons rien en Italie, et avec Messine le Roi pourrait s'agrandir quand il lui plairait; au pis-aller, on nous craindrait si on ne nous y voulait pas aimer. Son Fare, fameux par tant de naufrages, le serait bien plus à l'avenir par la peine et le tourment qu'il donnerait au Conseil d'Espagne, si le Roi en était le maître, puisque c'est le passage des blés des deux Calabres pour les porter dans le royaume de Naples; en temps de guerre, nous ferions crier famine à cette grande ville et les Espagnols ne seraient pas peu embarrassés.'

[40] PRO, SP93/2, 50, Davies to Williamson, Naples, 3 Sept. 1675. See also Israel, 'The phases of the Dutch staatvaart'.

[41] PRO, SP93/2, 242, Stanier to Williamson, Messina, 30 Dec. 1677; SP93/2, 243, letter from the consul Davies to the Secretary of State, Naples, 4 Jan. 1678; SP93/2, 245, report by the Marquis d'Oppede, chief of justice, police and finance in the French military forces in Sicily, Messina, 16 Jan. 1678.

while it served to enrich the English merchants living in southern Italy, angered Spain, infringed the agreements in the Treaty of Madrid, and, most importantly, damaged the commercial reputation of the English with serious repercussions on the use of English ships for internal Mediterranean trade. Charles II was obliged to intervene with a decree forbidding his subjects to give any form of assistance to the rebels in Messina.[42] The difficulties encountered in the Straits of Messina together with a gradual easing in the relations with the countries of North Africa led to English ships sailing the 'Islamic' as opposed to the 'Christian' route. Stanier, the English consul in Messina, wrote to the Secretary of State that 'since his majesties proclamation, noe English Ships have as formerly hazarded to trafficke here to the dissatisfaction as well of the French as these people, who will not bee capable of the true reason . . .'[43] By the end of 1676, no English ships were using the Straits of Messina; once the peace treaty had been signed with the Algerians, all vessels sailing under the English flag chose to use the Sicilian channel.[44]

THE SEA ROUTE

It was above all the English desire to obtain Levantine and Italian goods directly from the source of supply which led to the revival of contacts by sea between England and Italy, and the rest of the Mediterranean. From the outset, alum, olive oil, currants, citrus fruits and other such goods filled the holds of the northern ships returning from Italy, as formerly they had been the principal cargoes of Venetian and Ragusan ships. During the last thirty years of the sixteenth century, the trade routes overland and by sea coexisted in a kind of equilibrium. From the beginning of the seventeenth century, however, there was a steady growth in the frequency of trading contacts by sea between northern Europe and the Mediterranean, stimulated by the new transoceanic routes, which were much more extensive than those within Europe and the Mediterranean and offered merchants no choice between land and sea. The goods which merchants had until then preferred to send by land were increasingly entrusted to the sea routes, while overland transportation began to take second place. Italian woven silk or silk yarn was an exception: it continued to be transported by land throughout the early seventeenth century; after a period when consignments were divided equally between sea and land, it began to appear as a standard

---

[42] PRO, SP93/2, 85, dispatch from the consul Stanier, Messina, 30 Dec. 1675.
[43] Ibid.
[44] PRO, SP93/2, 181, Stanier to Williamson, Messina, 10 Dec. 1676.

item in the cargoes of the English merchant ships setting out from Livorno.[45] In 1635 we can note a certain indecision in the choice of which route to take in the instructions given by Carlo Labistrat from Antwerp to the Florentine firm, Orazio Corsi, Antonio Rondinelli & Co., although it is true that Labistrat wrote his instructions at different times in the year and perhaps took account of seasonal hazards. In August, he wrote that the silk was to be sent 'to London to Messrs. Abram and Jacopo de la Forastiere in a trunk only in an English armed ship, since no other ships are so well defended . . .'[46] On 29 November, he asked Corsi and Rondinelli to send his goods 'to Verona in the charge of Messrs. Annoni; from Verona they can be sent through Germany, since I think this a better and more secure route to England than sending them by sea . . .'[47] As Jordan Goodman has found from his analysis of the account-books of Florentine merchants in the first half of the century, silk continued to be sent to England overland, even when it would have been extremely easy to load ships in Livorno bound for England.[48]

Another indication that the custom of transporting silks to England on the continental land routes persisted after the 1650s can be found in the 1651 Navigation Act in which raw and manufactured silk is included in the short list of goods not covered by the Act. If it was purchased with the proceeds from the sale of English goods in Italy, silk could be brought overland and then loaded on to English ships in the ports of Ostend, Newport, Rotterdam, Middelburgh, Amsterdam or any other port in the vicinity.[49] In the new measures introduced after the restora-

[45] Davis, 'England and the Mediterranean', p. 135; see also A. Millard, 'The import trade of London, 1600–1640', Ph.D. thesis, University of London (1956), vol. I, appendix 10, table 14; vol. III, table C.
[46] ASF, Archivio Guicciardini–Corsi–Salviati, no. 318, f. 774, quoted in Goodman, 'The Florentine silk industry', p. 126: 'in una cassa per nave a Londra alli Sri. Abram e Jacopo de la Forastiere che sia buon armata, in altre nave non desiderio d'havere carico perché non sono di diffesa come la nave Inghilese . . .'
[47] Ibid., no. 318, f. 77r, quoted in Goodman, 'The Florentine silk industry', p. 127: 'A Verona in condotta di Sri Annoni e di Verona potra esse spedita per Allemagna [perché] mi pare sarà la meglio e più sicura che mandarla per mare in Inghilterra . . .'
[48] Ibid., p. 130.
[49] Harper, The English navigation laws, p. 48. The 1651 Navigation Act gave greater importance to imports than to exports. It stipulated that goods imported into England should come directly from the country of origin or from the port where they were normally loaded on to the ship. They had to be transported by English ships or by ships belonging to the country where they were produced or to the port where they were normally loaded. Exceptions were made to these rules, especially for precious metals, where neither the port of embarkation nor the nationality of the ship was subject to restriction. Furthermore, the goods produced in Spanish or Portuguese colonies could be taken on board in the ports of Spain and Portugal. A final concession

tion of Charles II in 1660, silk was again excluded from the list of goods which had to be imported directly by English ships from the port of embarkation; somewhat later, it was added to a list of articles which benefited from preferential rates of customs duty, if they were imported by English ships.[50]

There is a range of evidence that the overland routes continued to play an important role in the silk trade throughout the second half of the seventeenth century. In 1653, General Bobler halted the customary transport of silk and goathair on the overland routes to London for fear of reprisals on its way through Spanish-held territories.[51] In 1660, three English merchants, Simeon Bonnel, Sir Theophilus Biddulph and Samuel Foote, presented a petition asking to pay customs duties at the rates levied for Italian silk imported from the Netherlands.[52] In 1665, the English resident in Livorno had to refuse the Grand Duke's invitation to the English merchants in Livorno to purchase silk, saying that no orders were arriving from England on account of the great plague and that a backlog of silk already purchased for the English market was waiting in Holland.[53] Two years after this, Finch wrote to the Secretary of State reporting the capture by an English naval squadron of a ship, the *San Nicolò*, on its way from Ostend to London. He mentioned that most of the cargo consisted of goods belonging to English merchants in Livorno, who had asked him to see that they were restored to them.[54] Almost at the turn of the century, the London merchant Samuel Lyons asked that preferential rates of duty be applied to a consignment of Italian silk sent to him from Ostend.[55] In 1702, John Houghton published a survey of silk products imported into England in his journal and noted that some of these, such as velvet, taffeta and Florentine silks, reached England along the overland routes via Holland.[56]

on the port of embarkation was made for the goods of the Levant Company, where the port of embarkation was normally either Scanderoon, which served Aleppo, or Smyrna. The concession was granted at the request of the Turkey Merchants, who wished to retain the possibility of unloading and reloading their ships also in Livorno and other Italian ports. While this concession undoubtedly allowed the Levantine trade routes greater flexibility at a time of difficult reorganisation and harsh competition, it also provided an alternative opening for the activity of 'interloping' or infringement of the monopoly. This flaw led the Levant merchants themselves somewhat later to ask for the concession to be rescinded.

50 Ibid., pp. 52–8, 410.
51 CSP Venetian, v. 29, 1653–4, 8 Feb. 1653, pp. 22–3.
52 CSP Treasury Books, 1660–7, 20 Nov. 1660, p. 36.
53 PRO, SP98/6, Finch to Arlington, Florence, 29 Sept. 1665.
54 PRO, SP98/8, Finch to Arlington, 16 May 1667.
55 CSP Treasury Papers, 1557–1696, 23 Sept. 1696, p. 549.
56 J. Houghton, *A collection for improvement of husbandry and trade*, 21 Aug. 1702.

Table 3.1 *Valuations of commodities (£ per ton)*

Imported goods		Exported goods	
Thrown silk	2,688	Wrought silk	3,920
Raw silk	1,904	Woollen cloth	200–1,000
Cochineal	1,792	Tin	73
Linen cloth	200–1,000	Iron goods	55
Coffee	140	Lead	11
Wool (Spanish)	120	Red herrings	11
Linen yarn	98	Pilchards	7
Cotton (Turkish)	65	Wheat	5.5
Madder	40	Malt	3.5
Flax	35	Coal	less than 1
Pepper	33		
Olive oil (Italian)	28		
Sugar	27		
Wine (Portuguese)	25		
Wine (Spanish)	22		
Currants	21		
Tobacco	21		
Hemp	19		
Rice	15		
Raisins	11		
Iron	10		
Timber (European)	about 1		

Source: Davis, *The rise of the English shipping industry*, p. 177. Davis's valuations are taken from those compiled by the Inspector-Generals of the Customs in 1754 (PRO, Customs, 3–54).

One explanation for the continuing use of the overland routes in the silk trade was the low cost of transportation incurred as part of the overall cost. From table 3.1 it can be seen that silk in all its forms, woven, thrown and raw, is conspicuous for its high value, far higher, with the exception of cochineal, than all other imported or exported goods. As far as the costs of transportation are concerned, to take the example of Florentine silks in 1608, these amounted to between 0.5 per cent and 0.75 per cent according to the type of cloth.[57] Sir Robert Chamberlain in Naples received 5¼ rolls of 'peluche' sent from Florence via Rome, and paid 60 ducats for the cloth and two carlines for their transportation as far as the customs, in other words 0.16 per cent of the cost of the goods.[58]

In 1673, the Cinque Savii alla Mercanzia, the official authorities in Venice responsible for commercial policy, specified the various problems which the transportation of silk by sea presented. In their

[57] Goodman, 'The Florentine silk industry', p. 129.
[58] PRO, SP93/1, 37–41.

opinion, Venetian merchants would be reluctant to give up the advantages of a system of weekly consignments sent overland, incurring an increase of only 4 per cent of total costs, to transport their goods by ship instead: such a method was more irregular than the overland routes, and incurred extra insurance costs; in the absence of insurance, however, there was always the fear that the ship would be attacked and plundered. In any case, there were always the possible hazards of storms, of fire at sea, of fraudulence on the part of the captain, and other such troublesome mishaps.[59]

The misgivings of the Venetian commercial authorities as regards the regularity and stability of maritime transport might be taken in one way as an indication of the irreversible marginalisation which was overtaking the Republic in the sphere of international trade, where use of the sea routes was steadily increasing and in which, within the Mediterranean at least, Livorno was growing in importance. Yet they also serve to encapsulate the conflict between the sea routes, economical and fast, but also irregular and dangerous, and the overland routes, costly and slow, but comparatively predictable and safe.

One reason why the sea routes increasingly prevailed in this competition was the regular service the English ships were able to provide, since they continued to sail in the winter. The arrival of the 'fish ships' in the winter months from December to March put an end to the customary cessation of shipping in the Mediterranean. The elimination of seasonal interruptions in the sea routes diminished one advantage enjoyed by the overland routes, which, although they were less affected by seasonal variation in the weather, were still vulnerable to adverse conditions. On the plains, heavy and continued rain could cause rivers to overflow and bridges to collapse, while snow could block the mountain passes for long periods. Braudel writes that in winter 'the mountains were abandoned by the traveller as well as by the shepherd'.[60] In December 1670, Finch had been recalled to England but had to remain in Florence because of the winter weather; only when the Alpine passes reopened was he able to continue his journey.[61]

Another determining factor in the choice of route for valuable commodities was the protection provided against the greater risks involved in the sea routes. This protection was in part provided by the development of an appropriate insurance market and in part by the system of ships capable of self-defence or attack, if necessary, when confronted by enemy ships or pirates. The two aspects were closely connected; insur-

[59] CSP Venetian, 1673–5, 26 Jan. 1673, pp. 7–8.
[60] Braudel, La Méditerranée, vol. I, p. 247.
[61] PRO, SP98/12, 130–1, Finch to Arlington, Florence, 16 Dec. 1670.

ance premiums were linked to the extent to which a ship was armed enough to defend itself and to the military and diplomatic protection provided for the ships involved in maritime trade. The silk trade only served to emphasise the problem of protection on the sea routes. The greatest security was that provided by the English naval frigates: in early 1660, Sir John Banks instructed his factors in Livorno to invest the capital he had sent them in the finest organzine silk from Messina only on condition that the warships under the command of Captain Poole put in at the port on their way home to England; the goods were to be sent by no other ship.[62]

Banks could probably use Poole's warships, which merchants were normally excluded from using for their goods, because of his friendship and close collaboration with the man who had been responsible since the 1650s for the supply of naval provisions, Denis Gawden. He told Lytcott & Gascoigne, his factors in Livorno, that Poole was a good friend and would certainly do his best to satisfy his request.[63] It is interesting to note that the purchase of the consignment of silk was dependent for Banks on the protection provided on the journey to England: he writes explicitly: 'I perceive the Convoy makes stay att there returne from the Levant in your port which is a good inducement for find Orsoy of Messina or some other Commodity, under soe good conduct . . .'[64] In the event that his silk could not be conveyed to England on Poole's ships, he sends instructions that the goods are to be divided among a number of merchant ships, chosen from those which are accompanied by the convoy, a decision probably dictated by his wish to diminish the risk of transporting such a valuable cargo and also to reduce the insurance costs.[65] He reiterates in another letter:

> My desier and order is that you doe returne me $10000 to 12000 invested in said Commodity (fine orsoy of Messina); which I doe assume myselfe you will take care to provide as you mention of the most Excellence sorte Alwais observeing thatt fine is the most Esteemed and my Cash being in readynesse you will take good opportunity to provide . . . upon good termes And does order that the said Adventure be divided unto

---

[62] KCCRO, Aylesford MSS, U234/B3, Banks to 'Lytcott & Gascoigne' of Livorno, London, 2 Jan. 1660. Sir John Banks (1627–99), was a merchant and prominent financier in the City in the second half of the century. He was a friend of Samuel Pepys, a Member of Parliament, and a Fellow of the Royal Society; John Locke worked for him as his doctor and tutor to his son. He was also a governor of the East India Company and the Royal African Company. He amassed a vast fortune which he left to his heirs, the Earls of Aylesford (see Coleman, *Sir John Banks*).

[63] KCCRO, Aylesford MSS, Banks to Lytcott & Gascoigne of Livorno, London, 2 Jan. 1660.

[64] Ibid., 27 Feb. 1660.   [65] Ibid., 23 Mar. 1660.

three or foure ships or more as best you can: and if possible to procure the same to be receaved unto the States ships. I am perswaded Capt. Poole will doe whatt he Can for me and if you can I would they were all in his ship which I leave to your prudent management desireing you to take notice that my desier and order is that in case the said ships will not take in the same yett thatt you returne my said Effect by severall ships in Company of the said Convoy and that the Bales may be conveniently packed . . .[66]

Banks obtained what he wanted and was able to use Poole's ships for his merchandise. The cargo of the *Leopard*, when it arrived in England, included 2 cases of Florence satin and 3 bales of silk yarn from Messina in addition to the 6 bales of organzine silk. The cost of the freight was extremely low, from 0.54 per cent to 1 per cent of the value of the goods: it is probable that transporting his goods on English warships also allowed Banks to save on insurance costs.[67]

Precise instructions were similarly given for the protection of the transportation of silver pieces of eight. The London merchants John Dethick, John Banks and Giles Lytcott gave orders to one Captain Terlany that, if he stopped in Cadiz or Alicante on his way to Livorno and was able to sell some of the 350 sacks of pepper which had been assigned to him, he was to send the money made from the sale in pieces of eight back to London only on an English ship armed with at least 20 cannon. If the ship had only 16 cannon, then only 6,000 pieces of eight could be loaded. If no such ship were forthcoming, then Terlany was to proceed to Livorno and deliver the money to Giles Lytcott & Walwin Gascoigne, the firm which represented the three merchants' interests in Livorno.[68] Banks gave similarly precise instructions to his factor in Lisbon, Thomas Bridgwood, when he told him to load 2 cases of sugar for Livorno under his name only on a ship armed with a minimum of 16 cannon.[69]

Protection was a determining factor not only in decisions to send valuable commodities by sea; the English were still greatly concerned with protection even when the cargo was of fish. Banks, for example, was constantly reminding the captain of his ship and his factors in Livorno of his concern in this matter. When the *Virgin* was getting ready for its first voyage to the Mediterranean, towards the end of 1659, Banks wrote to its captain, Thomas Hendra, instructing him to go to

---

[66] Ibid., 23 June 1660.
[67] Ibid., Banks to Captain Poole, London, 20 Sept. 1660; U234/A1, Journal, f. 68, f. 76; U234/A2, Ledger, f. 71.
[68] KCCRO, Aylesford MSS, U234/B3, John Dethick, John Banks and Giles Lytcott to Captain William Terlany, London, 11 Mar. 1661.
[69] Ibid., Banks to Thomas Bridgwood, London, 4 Feb. 1661.

Portsmouth where other southbound ships would arrange an escort.[70] When it seemed that, owing to a series of unforeseen mishaps, the ship might not arrive in Portsmouth in time to meet up with the others, Banks sent off a stern rebuke to Hendra, saying that the convoy would certainly not wait for him and that he would rather lose the freight than miss the convoy. He urged him to buy as large a quantity of pilchards as possible, but on no account to miss the convoy.[71]

Part of the risk incurred by shipping could be covered by insurance. Insurance was a practice which had first appeared in the commercial world of medieval Italy, devised as a means of diminishing the burden of risk for the country's merchants. From the outset insurance was almost entirely a matter of maritime insurance, since it was this sphere of activity where the margin of risk was greatest. Insurance was practised in Italy from the eleventh century onwards, and gradually spread throughout the Mediterranean and the rest of Europe.[72] From the beginning of the seventeenth century, the practice extended to English ships, which depended on the thriving insurance market in Livorno, where Florentine merchants, together with Jews, Armenians, and later the English themselves, operated. The growth in the practice of insuring the journeys made by sea between England and Italy was decisive for the development of the sea route, since it served to protect the commercial interests involved from the risks arising from bad weather, piracy and international conflict. One clause in the printed insurance policies which were signed in Livorno reads as follows: 'the Insurers underwrite risks for the above-mentioned merchandise which may occur from all sea-going hazards: fire, jettison, confiscation, plunder by friend or foe, as well as any other conceivable chance, danger, fortune, disaster, impediment or accident which may befall, including fraudulence on the part of the shipmaster, or damage sustained by the merchandise in the hold or while held in customs, until it is unloaded safely in the above-mentioned place . . .'[73] It is interesting to note that the whole range of possible risks is enumerated here, including the possibility of fraudu-

[70] Ibid., U234/B2, Banks to Captain Thomas Hendra, London, 18 Oct. 1659.
[71] Ibid., London, 29 Oct. 1659.
[72] F. Melis, *Origini e sviluppo delle assicurazioni in Italia, secoli XIV–XVI*, vol. 1, *Le fonti* (Rome: 1975); M. A. Benedetto, 'Appunti per una ricerca sul contratto di assicurazione marittima' in *Studi in onore di Giuseppe Grosso*, vol. IV/ (Turin: 1971).
[73] ASP, Consoli del Mare: 'correndo sempre rischio gli Assicuratori in suddette Mercanzie d'ogni cosa di Mare, di fuoco, di getto à Mare, di rappresaglia, rubberia di amici, e nemici, e d'ogni caso, pericolo, fortuna, disastro, impedimento, ò caso sinistro, anchora, che non si potesse imaginare, intervenisse, ò fusse intervenuto, etiam di baratteria di padrone, salvo di stiva, e Dogane per infino à che saranno scariche in terra a salvamento nel luogo dichiarato di sopra . . .'

lence on the part of the ship's captain, one of the problems associated
with shipping which had led the Cinque Savii in Venice to prefer transportation by the overland routes. It was undoubtedly an important consideration, since a ship's cargo was wholly entrusted to the captain, who
thus needed to be a man of proven honesty as well as seafaring ability.
On occasion the captain acted as the factor for the merchandise he was
carrying. Banks, for example, wrote to Captain Terlany on the *St
George*, which had been chartered to sail to Livorno with a cargo of 350
sacks of Malabar pepper, with the suggestion that he disregard the bill of
lading, call at Cadiz and try to sell part or all of the cargo there.[74]

In connection with the issue of insurance, the case of Captain
William Ell was a significant one. Ell's ship, the *Lewis*, had taken on
board at Alexandria a cargo of rice which he was to take to Constantinople on behalf of the Sultan, but he sought refuge in Livorno, where
the English consul, fearing Turkish reprisals on the merchants working
in the Levant, imprisoned Ell and sequestered the rice, which was
transferred to another ship *en route* for Constantinople. At Constantinople, the Cameican refused to accept the rice since it had gone bad,
while the English ambassador in the city declined responsibility for
replacing the supply. The case of Ell is interesting because it was
perhaps the only time that, in response to a request from the Levant
Company and from Cromwell himself, the Grand Duke had the safe
conduct of the English captain withdrawn, thus removing the immu-
nity which Livorno had by long tradition always granted to the mariners who sought shelter in its port.[75] It was as important in the
insurance business as in the carrying trade to maintain an image of
commercial reliability. Developments in the insurance business in
Livorno in turn favoured the growth of insurance. In the 1620s we can
find examples of insurance policies underwritten by the shipmaster as
single insurer, but from the 1650s onwards all policies were underwritten by several merchants with the result that costs were reduced
and risks divided.[76]

As maritime insurance increasingly became a matter of third-party
aleatory contracts, it required both capital for investment and the
interest of individual underwriters in advancing the capital. If risk

---

[74] KCCRO, Aylesford MSS, U234/B3, Banks to Captain William Terlany, London,
11 Mar. 1660.

[75] PRO, SP98/8, Finch to Arlington, Livorno, 14 Mar. 1667; SP105/112, 293,
London, 10 Sept. 1657; CSP Venetian, 1657–9, 28 Apr. 1658, p. 190; CSP Domestic, 1657–8, 10 Sept. 1657, p. 95 and 29 Nov. 1657, p. 197.

[76] PRO, SP98/3, 42, charter party, Livorno, 2 Dec. 1622; ASP, Consoli del Mare.

underlay the contract, then it was not to be excessive, and the 'firm' in question, the country behind the enterprise, had to inspire credibility and confidence.[77] Yet it remained the case that the commercial sphere was not yet divided up into specialised sectors or interests: the merchant insurers of Livorno were the same merchants – Florentines, Jews, Armenians and Englishmen – who were faced with the choice of the safest and most convenient route for their own merchandise. When the Second Dutch War broke out, the Jewish and Armenian merchants who refused to charter Dutch and English ships very probably also refused to insure them.[78] A similar situation arose in the 1670s, for example, during the Franco-Spanish conflict, when all French merchant shipping was halted because no-one was prepared to insure it.[79] It was therefore of crucial importance in maritime trade, for one's own sake and even more for the sake of third parties, to inspire confidence and trust both in potential clients and potential insurers; this explains the stress laid by the English resident in Tuscany on England's reputation, which was founded as much on its own intrinsic merit as on the failings of its competitors.[80]

Once it was firmly established, and despite its attendant inconveniences, the sea route was seen to possess notable advantages: it allowed goods to be brought directly from their countries of origin at a considerably lower cost; the constant change of carrier needed on the overland routes was eliminated, together with the dependence on foreign middlemen; as a result, the costs of transaction were reduced and commercial costs in general and those relating to transportation in particular were re-absorbed and capitalised.[81] In the sixteenth and seventeenth centuries the sea routes, unlike those overland, were still comparatively untried and uncrowded, and mastery over them was a prize waiting to be won by those nations which showed a sense of enterprise and competitiveness, coupled with the technical means and economic organisation needed to claim them and control them.

---

[77] Rapp, 'The unmaking of the Mediterranean trade hegemony', 514–15. Rapp writes that 'the State, not the individual firm, was the relevant unit of competition in early modern international trade'.

[78] PRO, SP98/5, Morgan Read to Bennet, Livorno, 28 Feb. 1664. See also CSP Venetian, 1664–6, 10 Jan. 1665, p. 75.

[79] ANF, AE/B1/695, letter from the French consul in Livorno, François Cotolendy, to the Marquis de Seignelay, 22 June 1674.

[80] PRO, SP98/4, 248, Kent to Williamson, Livorno, 3 Sept. 1663; SP98/8, Finch to Arlington, Livorno, 31 Jan. 1667.

[81] See D. C. North and R. P. Thomas, *The rise of the western world: a new economic history* (Cambridge: 1973).

THE PORT OF LONDON AND THE ITALIAN SEA ROUTES

From the very beginning of maritime trade between England and Italy the paramount role played by the Port of London was apparent, even in comparison with those ports which had formerly been significant: Southampton, for example, which had in medieval times been the favoured port of Venetian and Genoese galleys, or Bristol, from where ships had first set sail to reach Newfoundland or the eastern coasts of the Mediterranean.[82]

The dominance of London over the 'outports' developed in tandem with the increasing importance of Antwerp as a trading entrepôt for north-west Europe. With the Thames estuary directly opposite the River Scheldt, London was favoured by its position in relation to Antwerp. The merchants who had business to do in Antwerp found London so convenient a base that they moved their operations there. From the beginning of the sixteenth century, both the ports of Bristol and Exeter started to decline in importance, although this was also partly caused by the periodical outbreaks of war with France and the worsening political relations with Spain from the 1530s onwards.[83]

As we have seen, the continental land routes linking northern Europe to the Mediterranean and the east ended at Antwerp; along these roads, sweet wines, dried fruit, silk, pepper and spices were brought by Flemish and Italian merchants to supply the markets of the north. Antwerp was also the focus for the huge Mediterranean demand for English woollens, and the continental headquarters of the Merchant Adventurers company, which pursued a prosperous and growing trade in English woollens and encouraged a gradual shift in the market away from the exports of English raw wool in favour of semi-manufactured textiles, that is to say, textiles which had been woven but not yet dyed. The finishing stages of work on these textiles took place in Flanders. The special relationship between London and Antwerp in the distribution of English wool reinforced a development which was already under way in England, whereby the textile production of provincial centres destined for foreign markets tended to converge on the capital. The merchants of East Anglia, Gloucestershire, Wiltshire and Somerset all found it particularly convenient to organise the shipment of their consignments from London.[84]

The Port of London was not only favourably located in relation to

---

[82] In the fifteenth century, ships from Bristol had fished the waters round Iceland; difficulties in trade with Iceland led them in the 1580s to explore the fishing grounds off Newfoundland (see Clay, *Economic expansion and social change*, vol. II, p. 131).

[83] Ibid., p. 111.   [84] Ibid., p. 199.

Antwerp; its communications with the rest of the country made it an ideal centre of collection and distribution. An extensive network of roads led to London, while the Thames itself was an important means of communication. Finally, since London was fortunately placed midway on the sea route between north-east and south-west England, the ships which set sail from its port had easy access to both the southern and the eastern coasts.

London's importance, however, was not solely a question of geographical advantage. Since the city was a focus for the country's import and export trade, many merchants transferred their businesses there from the provincial ports, bringing in their wake capital funds to invest in commerce and industry. Part of the profits from trade were used to finance loans to the aristocracy, while the wealthiest merchants lent to the Exchequer. The government borrowed huge sums from the London merchants, who received farms, patents and monopolies in return.[85]

London was also transformed into the country's largest market for merchandise, thanks to a swift increase in population which outstripped the rest of England (see table 3.2). Given the high cost of transportation, all the forms of economic activity commonly associated with such a growth in population were centred on London and its surroundings.[86] In addition to its sheer size, London was the centre of political power, with its accompanying bureaucracy, and of the law, with the development of the Inns of Court, quite apart from the presence of the royal court itself, a centre of attraction for the provincial nobility. The demand for luxury goods from Mediterranean countries was typical of these classes, and it was their growing demand which led to a shift in economic growth, in the later sixteenth century, from the export market linked with Antwerp to the imported goods brought in from the Mediterranean.[87]

The greater importance of London in comparison to the 'outports' remained constant and unchallenged for almost the whole of the seventeenth century: in 1677, customs revenues in the capital amounted to £597,704, more than eleven times the revenues in Bristol, the second largest English port (£50,946). The revenues of the smaller ports lagged

[85] A. L. Beier and R. Finlay, 'The significance of the metropolis' in A. L. Beier and R. Finlay (eds.), *London 1500–1700: the making of the metropolis* (London: 1986), pp. 15–16.

[86] R. Finlay and B. Shearer, 'Population growth and suburban expansion' in Beier and Finlay (eds.), *London 1500–1700*, pp. 38–9; E. A. Wrigley, *Demografia e storia* (Milan: 1969), pp. 21–5.

[87] Beier and Finlay, 'The significance of the metropolis', p. 13; B. Dietz, 'Overseas trade and metropolitan growth' in Beier and Finlay (eds.), *London 1500–1700*, p. 121.

Table 3.2 *The population of London in comparative perspective, 1550–1800 (000)*

Year	Population of England	Increase (%)	Population of London	Increase (%)	Population of England (%)	Population of cities with more than 5,000 inhabitants	Increase (%)	Population of England (%)
1550	3,010 (2,890)	—	120	—	4.0	—	—	—
1600	4,110 (3,910)	37 (35)	200	67	4.9	125	—	3.0
1650	5,230 (4,855)	27 (24)	375	88	7.2	—	—	—
1700	5,060 (4,570)	−3 (−6)	490	24	9.7	275	—	5.4
1750	5,780 (5,105)	14 (12)	675	38	11.7	540	96	9.3
1800	8,660 (7,710)	50 (51)	950	41	11.0	1,430	165	16.5

Source: R. Finlay and B. Shearer, 'Population growth and suburban expansion', in Beier and Finlay (eds.), *London 1500–1700: the making of the metropolis* (London: 1986), p. 39.

The figures in parenthesis indicate the population of England excluding London.

far behind these: for example, Plymouth with £12,157, Yarmouth with
£9,444 and Falmouth with only £2,876.[88]

London did not merely survive the decline of Antwerp, but drew
new strength from the widened trading networks. The link between
London and the Flemish port had enabled the English capital to attain
its predominance, but the very convenience and proximity of Antwerp
had served to restrict the growth of the English fleet. If we examine
London's position in the context of the progressive expansion of the
national fleet from the end of the sixteenth century onwards, the proportion of London ships in the fleet is consistently higher than those
from the rest of the country, at least until the closing years of the seventeenth century, when the first, limited challenges to the capital's pre-
eminence came from ports on the country's western coast, Bristol and,
later, Liverpool (see table 3.3).[89] A substantial proportion of the country's imports, approximately 80 per cent of the total, arrived in London:
this figure remained unchanged for almost the whole of the century.[90]
An analysis of the homeward routes of merchant ships on their way
back from Italy serves to reinforce this impression of convergence on
the capital: these ships tended to return to London, despite the fact that
they had set out from provincial ports with cargoes of fish and normally
returned with olive oil for use in the textile industries of northern and
western England, areas much closer to the ports of departure than the
capital.

In February 1666, several 'fish ships' in a convoy under the command
of Sir Jeremy Smith arrived in the port of Livorno on their way to
Puglia and Zante.[91] The merchant Thomas Dethick reported that there
were nine ships, four with cargoes of herrings and the rest pilchards, and
all bound for Puglia where they were to collect olive oil.[92] By the
beginning of March, the number of merchant ships had increased: the
consul wrote that 'we have now in all twelve small English shipes in
Port, most with fish all in English Imployment, and by what can learne
goe all for Gallipoli & Zante'.[93]

Having unloaded their cargo in Livorno, or, on occasion, part of it in
Genoa, Civitavecchia, Naples or Messina, and having taken on olive oil

[88] BL, Add. MSS 36785, f. 101, 'Customs – The revenue of His Majesty's Customs in
      the severall ports of England for one year from Michaelmas 1676 to Michaelmas
      1677'. Only those ports which had trading relations with Italy have been taken into
      consideration here.
[89] Clay, *Economic expansion and social change*, vol. 1, p. 202.
[90] Ibid., vol. II, pp. 123, 131; 182; Dietz, 'Overseas trade', p. 131.
[91] PRO, SP98/6, Chellingworth to Arlington, Livorno, 8 Feb. 1666.
[92] PRO, SP98/6, Dethick to Williamson, Livorno, 22 Feb. 1666.
[93] PRO, SP98/6, Chellingworth to Arlington, Livorno, 8 Mar. 1666.

Table 3.3 *The English merchant fleet (percentages in parentheses)*

Year	England	London	Bristol	Yarmouth	Provincial ports
A. Tonnage					
1582	67,000	12,300 (18.35)	2,300 (3.43)	6,800 (10.14)	—
1629	115,000	35,300 (30.69)	6,000 (5.21)	5,800 (5.04)	—
1686	340,000	150,000 (44.11)	—	—	190,000 (55.88)
1702	323,000	140,000 (43.34)	17,300 (5.35)	9,900 (3.06)	183,000 (56.65)
B. Number of English merchant-ships (above 100 tons)					
1582	177	62 (35.02)			
1628	350	132 (37.71)			

Sources: Davis, *The rise of the English shipping industry*, pp. 7, 10, 15, 27, 35; Clay, *Economic expansion*, vol. I, p. 202.
Harper, *The English navigation laws*, p. 282. Harper writes that 'by Charles I's reign, London possessed one-third of the Kingdom's ships, and after 1660 did no more than maintain the same relative position'.

or currants from Zante, such ships would set out on the return journey by first calling again in Livorno to make up the cargo with luxury goods; they would then proceed to London, occasionally stopping briefly on the way in Spanish or Portuguese ports.[94] In March 1664, Kent reported that four English ships, carrying cargoes of olive oil from Puglia and bound for London, had been taken to Algiers.[95] He added that '[there are] now in Port 16 English Shipps ready to Sayle towards London most of them laden from severall parts of Italy'.[96]

An examination of the list of seventeen English ships which left the port of Livorno on 6 March 1663 shows that five of these were carrying freight to Spanish ports, while the rest, of which eight were carrying olive oil and one alum, were returning to London. It is to be supposed that the first group of ships, having unloaded their freight in Spain and then collected their return cargo, would also make their way back to London. This was certainly the case with one of the five ships on the list, the *Virgin* belonging to Sir John Banks, which was carrying corn to Cadiz but later continued its journey to London where it unloaded its normal cargo of Levantine merchandise.[97]

[94] PRO, SP98/5, 'A distinct list of severall English merchants shipes gathered togeather from severall places in this mounth of May to strengthen each the other and in company did sayle from this port of Livorno the 24th May 1664 newe stile.'
[95] PRO, SP98/5, Kent to Williamson, Livorno, 1 Mar. 1664.
[96] PRO, SP98/5, Kent to Williamson, Livorno, 15 Mar. 1664.
[97] PRO, SP98/5, 'In Livorno the 6 March 1663 – English marchants ships departeing this day in company for England Spaine and Portugalle.'

On 24 May 1664, the list of ships leaving Livorno shows twelve vessels, two bound for Amsterdam with olive oil from Puglia and the rest for England. Of these, seven had cargoes of olive oil taken on board at Bari and Gallipoli, while the others were carrying currants from Zante, Greek wine most probably from Naples and lemons from San Remo. Only one ship, an 'oil ship', is listed as returning to Bristol; all the others have London as their home destination.[98] Among these 'fish' and 'oil ships', there was the *Orange Tree*, a small merchant ship from Yarmouth under the command of Thomas Avory, with eight cannon and seventeen crew; it made an annual trip from Yarmouth to Livorno with a cargo of herrings and returned to London via Gallipoli where it collected olive oil.[99]

In January 1676, John Smith & Co. in Naples paid 2,247 ducats to Onofrio Brancato for 149 'salme' and 9 'stare' of 'clear yellow oil' (both these were Neapolitan measurements of capacity), which had been taken on board the English ship *Delfino*, captained by Thomas Gurgeny, in Gallipoli by Alessandro Federighi, acting on behalf of Guglielmo Samuelli. The oil was to be 'delivered to London to the aforesaid Sig. Brancato or his delegate; the which Sig. Brancato has endorsed the bill of lading of the said 1498 "stare" of olive oil to Messrs. Roberto Foot, Gio. Smith and Company or their delegate . . .'[100]

The tendency of English merchant ships returning from Italy with raw material destined for the native textile industry to converge on London was especially pronounced during the last quarter of the century. This period saw the first in a series of protests from the clothiers against the so-called 'Blackwell factors', the London-based merchants who controlled almost the entire English export trade in textiles.[101] The protests were not fuelled by social resentment, nor were they directed against the London merchants' commercial monopoly; opposition was aroused by the extension of the monopoly from control over the selling and buying of textiles to control over the trade in raw materials for the textile industry. The commercial interests of the Blackwell factors included wool, especially Spanish wool, olive oil, alum, dyestuffs, etc.,

[98] PRO, SP98/5, 'A distinct list . . .'
[99] Ibid. See also PRO, SP98/6, Dethick to Williamson, Livorno, 6 Feb. 1666; Chellingworth to Arlington, Livorno, 26 Apr. 1666.
[100] ASBN, AGP, g. matr. 456, f. 1,484, duc. 2,247, 24 Jan. 1676: 'per consignare a Londra a detto sig. Brancato ò ordine; il quale sig. Brancato ne ha girato le polize di carico di dette stara 1498 ogli a loro sig.ri Roberto Foot, Gio. Smith è Compagni ò loro ordine . . .'
[101] See D. W. Jones, 'The "hallage" receipts of the London cloth-markets, 1562–c.1720', *The Economic History Review*, ser. 2, 25/4 (1972), 567–87. See also chapter 5, note 61.

and they were accused of forcing provincial buyers to buy these products from them. Moreover, by limiting or extending credit to the clothiers, they in effect controlled textile production in each part of the country, where they had set up dependents who passed themselves off as clothiers.[102] In George Clark's words, from his *A treatise of wool*, written in 1684:

> the making of woollen cloth is the greatest manufacture of this kingdom . . . wherein many thousands of poor people are employed and set to work, and thereby relieved and maintained; and that since the time that the art of clothing was first known amongst us it has continued free, until the beginning of the late rebellion there sprung up a sort of people who under the name of factors of Blackwell Hall have gotten into their power the management and disposal of most of the cloth that is sold there; and besides are grown to be the greatest merchants of oil and dyeing stuffs, but chiefly of Spanish wool; all goods belonging to the clothing trade, of whom the clothier is forced to buy, the factor having his stock both of cloth and money in his own hands . . .[103]

The convergence of the return routes on London was therefore part of the overall commercial and financial strategy pursued by this small group of City merchants. The network of money and credit often proved to be the determining factor in the success of trade routes which otherwise possessed no advantages. When the Genoese bankers moved the great trade fairs held in Lyons and Chambéry to Besançon at the beginning of the sixteenth century, the movement of trade shifted away accordingly from the direct route through Mont Cenis to the Alpine passes of the Great Saint Bernard and the Simplon.[104] Similarly Persian silk continued throughout the seventeenth century to travel the caravan routes rather than the sea routes, as both the English and Dutch East India Companies wanted, because of the central role played in the silk trade by Armenian and Jewish merchants.[105]

Yet the choice of London as the port of arrival for ships coming from Italy was also due to the city's domination of the export trade in woollen cloth; by the middle of the seventeenth century, 90 per cent of the total value of exports of woollen cloth was controlled by London.[106] Despite this, textiles did not suffice to fill the ships, and

---

[102] G. D. Ramsay, *The Wiltshire woollen industry in the sixteenth and seventeenth centuries* (Oxford: 1943), p. 136.

[103] G. Clark, 'A treatise of wool' (1685), in *17th century economic documents*, pp. 304–5.

[104] Day, 'Strade e vie di comunicazione', p. 117.

[105] PRO, SP98/8, Finch to Arlington, Livorno, 24 Jan. 1667; see V. Baladoni, 'Armenian trade with the English East India Company: an aperçu', *The Journal of European Economic History* 15/1 (1986), 153–62.

[106] Dietz, 'Overseas trade', p. 130. From the end of the sixteenth century, cloth from

there was not enough pepper, which from the 1620s onwards was re-exported from England to the Mediterranean, to make up the cargoes of the merchant ships bound for Italy, from where they were certain of returning with a full cargo. Whereas English ships left Italian ports with their holds filled with wine, oil and fruit, the shipowners had great diffi-culties in assembling even partial cargoes for the outward journeys.[107] One solution to this problem, commonly practised at least until the end of the 1660s, was for the ships leaving London for the Mediterranean to add small quantities of tin or lead, together with fish which was either brought from Yarmouth or taken directly on board at the Channel ports on the way out. Sir John Banks, for example, wrote to Thomas Hendra, the captain in command of his ship, which was carrying a cargo of 200 sacks of pepper and 150 pigs of lead, with instructions to stop at Plymouth on the way and take on board as large a cargo of pilchards, to be supplied by Banks's agent William Addis, as he could fit in.[108] It was more difficult to load the cargo of fish in Yarmouth itself, since the port lay to the north of London and therefore entailed a deviation from the southern route in order to reach it. In 1660, Banks, having decided to send a cargo of herrings to Livorno on his ship the *Virgin*, wrote to his agent in Yarmouth asking him to prepare between 200 and 400 barrels of fish for the Italian market and send them to the 'Downs', where Hendra and the ship would collect them.[109]

THE ENGLISH PROVINCIAL PORTS

As we have seen, London was the destination of most English ships on their return journey from Italy; it also remained the principal port of embarkation for the outward journeys to the Mediterranean, but, in contrast to the return, a number of English provincial ports, from Yar-mouth on the east coast to Bristol on the west, feature significantly. This was true from the very beginning of maritime contacts between England and Italy; the entry bills for the port of Livorno reveal that between 1573 and 1593 there were ninety-five sailings between the Tuscan port and London. In thirty-three cases, the ports of embarkation of the English merchant ships remain unspecified; of the rest, forty-five

Norwich and Norfolk was not sent to Blackwell Hall, although it was exported through London (see Jones, 'The "hallage" receipts', 576).

[107] H. Taylor, 'Trade, neutrality and the "English road", 1630–1648', *The Economic History Review*, ser. 2, 25 (1972), 238; Davis, *The rise of the English shipping industry*, p. 186.

[108] KCCRO, Aylesford MSS, U234/B2, John Banks to Captain Thomas Hendra, London, 29 Oct. 1659.

[109] Ibid., Banks to Thomas Gooch, London, 16 Oct. 1660.

are registered as sailing from London, seven from Harwich, three from Southampton, three from Bristol, two from Yarmouth, two from a place named in the document as Inester, and one from Plymouth.[110] The majority of ships sailing from the outports were 'fish ships' on annual trips to Italy and in particular to Livorno. Most of these came from Yarmouth, and arrived in the Italian ports, in small groups, in pairs, or sometimes singly, between December and March. Their crews were a familiar if occasionally rowdy sight in Livorno.[111]

It is impossible to give a precise figure for the number of ships arriving in Italy from provincial ports in England. On the basis of the type of cargo carried on the ships, however, it is possible to make an approximate distinction between those from Yarmouth and those from Plymouth and Bristol. Herrings were usually brought from the east coast, pilchards from southern ports, while Irish salmon or Newfoundland cod was loaded on vessels in ports in the west or south-west of the country.

In 1667, thirteen of the fifteen ships anchored in Livorno came from Yarmouth. One was the 100 ton *Naples*, with 12 crew and 6 cannon, and carrying a cargo of 800 barrels of herrings and 200 pigs of lead sent by the London merchant John Gould. On 28 January, the *Unity* arrived in the port, with a cargo of herrings and lead, followed on the next day by the *Dove*, which had set out from the East Anglian port via the 'Downs' and Land's End eighteen days before with a cargo of lead and butter. On 5 February, after a journey of thirty-two days, the *Diamant* arrived, with a cargo of lead and 420 barrels of herrings. The following day seven more English ships arrived: the *Yarmouth Merchant*, *Mayflower*, *James*, *Little Eagle*, *Pickarell*, *Mulberry* and *Friendship*, all carrying herrings, tin and calf-skins. Finally, on 27 March, the *Marchant Servant* arrived via Cadiz.[112] In November 1670, seven merchant ships and ketches carrying herrings set sail from Yarmouth for La Rochelle, Bordeaux, Naples, Marseilles, and what is generically termed 'the Straits', in other words, the Mediterranean.[113]

It is probable that the 'fish ships' were partly financed by merchants in the City, as was the case of the *Naples*, and as can also be inferred

[110] Braudel and Romano, *Navires et marchandises*, p. 51.

[111] PRO, SP98/8, Finch to Arlington, Livorno, 2 May 1667.

[112] PRO, SP98/8, Dethick to Williamson, Livorno, 17 Jan. 1667; 31 Jan. 1667; 7 Feb. 1667; 28 Mar. 1667; list of arrivals of 18 Dec. 1667, printed document. On these so-called 'marine lists', see J. J. McCusker, *European bills of entry and marine lists: early commercial publications and the origins of the business press* (Cambridge, Mass.: 1985), and J. J. McCusker and C. Gravestein, *The beginnings of commercial and financial journalism* (Amsterdam: 1990).

[113] CSP Domestic, 1670, 11 Nov. 1670, p. 524.

from Sir John Banks's business dealings; however, it is clear that Yarmouth merchants were directly involved in the export of fish to Italy,
even if their role in the business seems less independent and less well
defined than that played by their Bristol counterparts. Their direct
involvement in decisions taken in London is shown by one piece of evidence: the request made by the English consul in Venice, George
Hayles, in 1672, that his commission or 'consulage' should no longer be
calculated on the basis of the number of ships arriving in Venice, but on
the value of the merchandise they were carrying. The twelve London-
based merchants who specialised in trade with Venice were favourably
disposed to Hayles's petition, but sent a copy to their Yarmouth colleagues with a similar interest in Venice, in order to hear their opinion
before taking a final decision.[114]

Such a view is supported by Ralph Davis, who argues that herrings
were normally transported to Italy on English ships belonging to both
London and Yarmouth shipowners, while the cargoes were bought by
London merchants under the control of an individual merchant or a
small syndicate, the normal way of dealing with goods of low value.[115]
Michell also maintains that the merchants of Yarmouth were better
placed than their Dieppe rivals in being able to dictate terms to their
London colleagues whenever a dispute between the two arose, since
they could count on the support of the government.[116]

Evidence for trading relations between the Italian ports and Plymouth
can be found at the beginning of the seventeenth century, when the 200
ton *Matthew*, belonging to Gualtieri Mattei (i.e. Walter Matthews?), was
included in the list of English vessels captured and sequestered by the
Grand Duke,[117] yet, as for Yarmouth, information on Plymouth is
limited and intermittent. In February 1666, the *Amitie*, captained by
Robert Alderman, carrying a cargo of pilchards, and accompanied by a
convoy under the command of Sir Jeremy Smith, arrived from Plymouth in Livorno, where it was placed in quarantine by the local health

---

[114] PRO, CO/5, 32–34. Hayles's petition was approved by the following 'Citty of
London traders for Venice': J. Robinson, Thomas Bludworth, John Moore, Jeremie
Bonnell, Simeon Bonnell, Ralph Lee, Robert Geffery, John Chapman, George Ra-
venscroft, Christopher Gore, John Cooke, John Pollexfen. The confirmation of the
'Traders for Venice' in Great Yarmouth was signed on 9 Sept. 1672 by George
England, Thomas Cooper, William Burton, John Cooper, James Symonds, Peter
Caulier, Robert Ferrier, Abraham Castell Senior, Thomas Lucas, Thomas Raven.
[115] Davis, *The rise of the English shipping industry*, p. 245.
[116] A. R. Michell, 'The European fisheries in early modern history' in Rich and
Wilson, *The Cambridge economic history of Europe*, vol. v, p. 174.
[117] PRO, SP98/2, 122, 'The names of such English ships as the Duke of Florence hath
present for his service with a note of others that he hath dispoyled this Realme of.'

authorities; a few days later the *Delight*, captain Henry Galsworthy, and the *Welfare*, captain Samuell Peatell, arrived, both with cargoes of pilchards.[118]

Of the twenty-eight 'fish ships' which arrived in the port of Livorno in the first two months of 1667, at least three were certainly from Plymouth: the *Amity, Unity* and *Delight*.[119] On the 27 March, the *Smyrna Factor*, the *Owen & David* and the *Alice & Francis* arrived.[120] In the case of these three ships, it may be doubted whether Plymouth was their real port of embarkation, since ships coming from other English ports could nevertheless still be registered under Plymouth, if they had stopped there on the outward journey in order to join the protecting convoy which would accompany them on their way to the Mediterranean. On the 11 January 1672, the *Toson d'Oro* arrived in Livorno: it had set out from 'London, 75 days previously, from Plymouth 2 months ago, from Malaga 41 days ago, and from the island of "Eris" 5 days before. From Plymouth it left under the protection of a warship . . .'[121] Another example is the *William & Mary*, with a cargo of fish for Naples, which waited in Plymouth in September 1681 for the convoy of warships which were to accompany it, no doubt together with other merchant ships, to its destination.[122] Sir John Banks urged the captain of his ship the *Virgin* to go to Plymouth in order to join the convoy before setting out on its journey to Livorno and Scanderoon.[123]

Plymouth was both the port where the merchant ships *en route* for the Mediterranean met up with their protecting convoys, and where the convoys left them on their return journey, as we can see from the instructions issued to the captain of the warship *Foresight* to accompany all the vessels gathered under his protection in the Mediterranean ports as far as Plymouth.[124]

Ships sailing from other English provincial ports were occasionally seen in Italy: the *Unity*, for example, which made an annual trip from Falmouth to Livorno with a cargo of pilchards.[125] Another Falmouth

[118] PRO, SP98/6, Dethick to Williamson, Livorno, 6 Feb. 1666; Chellingworth to Arlington, Livorno, 15 Feb. 1666.

[119] PRO, SP98/8, Dethick to Williamson, Livorno, 24 Jan. 1667.

[120] PRO, SP98/8, Dethick to Williamson, Livorno, 28 Mar. 1667.

[121] PRO, SP101/80, list of arrivals in the port of Livorno, 11 Jan. 1672, printed document: 'di Londra, manca 75 giorni, di Plemut 2 mesi, di Malaga 41 giorni e dell'isole di Eris 5 giorni. Di Plemut partì di conserva d'una Nave di Guerra . . .'

[122] S. Hornstein, 'The deployment of the English navy in peacetime, 1674–1688', Ph.D. thesis, University of Utrecht (1985), p. 50.

[123] KCCRO, Aylesford MSS, U234/B2, Banks to Captain Thomas Hendra, London, 29 Oct. 1659; 3 Nov. 1659; 16 Nov. 1659.

[124] Hornstein, 'The deployment of the English navy', pp. 51–3, 58.

[125] PRO, SP98/8, Dethick to Williamson, Livorno, 24 Jan. 1667; 4 Apr. 1667; PRO,

ship, the *Brothers*, was sent directly to Naples by its owner, the London
merchant Samuel Foote; its cargo of fish belonged to the London firm
of Jonathan Dawes, John Hill Junior & Co., whose factor in Naples was
one Timoteo Hatton.[126] In December 1670, the *George* and the *Scipio*,
both from Falmouth, arrived in Livorno with 400 and 1200 'hogsheads'
of pilchards respectively.[127] In May 1666, the *Dexterity* from Chester
arrived in Livorno, with a cargo of lead, both refined and unrefined. It
made the same trip again the following year, when it was captured by
Algerian pirates on the homeward journey, after loading a cargo of olive
oil in Puglia.[128]

Contacts between Exeter and the Italian ports were established only
towards the end of the century. In 1680 the shipment of 2,292 lbs of
woollens and in 1686 of 1,280 lbs are registered; similarly, the first evidence for incoming cargoes of oil and currants is found only in 1684.
Direct contacts between the Devon port and Italy remained restricted.[129]

Bristol is an exception among the English outports: in the 1490s John
Cabot had been resident in the city, entrusted by Henry VII with the
task of discovering new lands, and the merchants of Bristol had to
supply him with the capital he needed for his voyages to the west,
receiving in exchange the monopoly of any trade which resulted from
his explorations. It was from Bristol too, where he had perhaps been
born, that John Cabot's son, Sebastian, set out to discover the north-
west passage to the Far East.

It was therefore Bristol seafarers who discovered the fishing grounds
off Newfoundland and who were the first in England to establish direct
links with the Mediterranean, at the end of the fifteenth century.[130]
The city was still famed for its commercial initiative and vitality even at

SP101/80, list of arrivals in the port of Livorno, 11 Jan. 1672, printed document.
There was also a Yarmouth ship called the *Unity*: it is not unusual to find several
ships with the same name; it is occasionally possible to distinguish them by their
port of origin or by the name of their captain.

[126] PRO, SP98/6, Dethick to Williamson, Livorno, 1 Mar. 1666; Finch to Arlington,
Livorno, 1 Mar. 1666; SP98/7, 'Arryved in this port severall mercht ships . . .',
Livorno, 9 July 1666. See also chapter 5, p. 157ff. ASN, Fondo notarile, notaio
Hieronimo De Roma, scheda 1214/4, 100–1. See also pp. 60, 164.
[127] PRO, SP98/12, 128, Dethick to Williamson, Livorno, 15 Dec. 1670; SP98/12, 133,
Dethick to Williamson, Livorno, 22 Dec. 1670. A 'hogshead' was the equivalent of
a large barrel containing 52.5 gallons or 238.5 litres.
[128] PRO, SP98/6, Chellingworth to Arlington, Livorno, 17 May 1666; SP98/8,
Dethick to Williamson, Livorno, 28 Feb. 1667.
[129] W. G. Hoskins, *Industry, trade and people in Exeter 1688–1800* (Manchester: 1935),
p. 44; W. B. Stephens, *Seventeenth-century Exeter: a study of industrial and commercial
development 1625–1688* (Exeter: 1958), pp. 105, 116.
[130] Wood, *A history of the Levant Company*, pp. 1–2; Clay, *Economic expansion and social
change*, vol. II, p. 131.

the end of the nineteenth century: 'all men that are dealers, even in shop trades, launch themselves into adventures by sea chiefly to West India Plantation and Spain'.[131]

With its favourable location, Bristol maintained links with the Mediterranean world, albeit on a reduced scale, throughout the course of the seventeenth century, even when London had established its dominant role. Although its commercial activity was based principally on its dealings with the American colonies, Ireland, France and Spain, trading contacts remained in force with the Mediterranean, notably with Livorno and Venice, where they formed a substantial part of the city's business.[132]

Although it is possible to find Bristol ships, such as the *Peregryne*, which were used for the transportation of Italian alum, the city's Mediterranean trade in the sixteenth and seventeenth centuries consisted largely of imports of consumer goods such as currants from Zante. It thus encroached on the monopoly of the Levant Company.[133] Throughout the first half of the century, Bristol defended its right to 'Free trade unto the Levant partes For Corrans'.[134] In 1618 the local aldermen urged the Merchant Adventurers of the city to refuse the compromise agreement which the Turkey Company had offered them, whereby imports of currants were subject to restriction.[135] The presence of Bristol ships within the area of the 'currant islands' was, on the other hand, accepted and respected by the Levant Company, probably in acknowledgement of Bristol's right of temporal precedence: when, in August 1636, the Levant Company decided to send an English consul to Zante and jointly appointed two men to the post, Thomas Symonds and Henry Hyde, the merchants of the port were duly notified by letter.[136]

The usual cargo taken by Bristol ships to the Mediterranean was fish. The ships worked a triangular route, either stopping on the Irish coast, where they loaded herrings or salmon, or sailing to Newfoundland, where they either fished themselves or, increasingly in the second half

[131] R. North, *Lives of the Norths* (London: 1890), vol. I, p. 156.

[132] P. McGrath (ed.), *Merchants and merchandise in seventeenth-century Bristol*, Bristol Record Society, vol. XIX (Bristol: 1955), p. xxi.

[133] Ibid., pp. 170–1, document n. 267, 'Dispute concerning a Charter Party'. D. H. Sachs, 'Bristol's "little businesses" 1625–1641', *Past and Present* 110 (1986), 88, 90.

[134] P. McGrath (ed.), *Records relating to the Society of Merchant Venturers of the city of Bristol in the seventeenth century*, Bristol Record Society, vol. XVII (Bristol: 1952), p. 213, document no. 433 dated 6 Nov. 1617.

[135] Ibid., pp. 213–17. The dispute between the Bristol merchants and the Levant Company ended in 1632, when the city was allowed to collect 200 tons a year for three years, paying a tax of £4 for every hundredweight. It appears that this agreement in fact dated back to 1612, although its provisions had never been applied.

[136] CSP Venetian, 1636–9, 2 Aug. 1636, p. 402.

of the seventeenth century, bought in cod from the local fishermen to sell in the Spanish or Italian markets.

The triangular route persisted throughout the century. We find a Bristol merchant named Moore swearing under oath that he had been employed as a factor or commercial agent on the local ship *Endeavour*, carrying about 200 tons of cargo, captained by John Totterdell, on its last voyage from Bristol to Ireland and from there to Marseilles, Livorno and back.[137] Similarly the *James*, another Bristol ship, sailed regularly to Italian ports throughout the 1660s; in 1668, for instance, it arrived in Livorno with what was doubtless a cargo of Irish products – hides, tallow, salmon, etc.[138] The merchant ships which arrived in Livorno from Ireland in 1665, for which Finch sought to obtain permission to land from the local health authorities in the wake of the London plague, must also have been from Bristol.[139] The merchants of the city must have found it more advantageous to buy fish in order to sell it on rather than finance fishing activities directly; the fish was bought largely from local communities on the Irish coast which were unaffected by the market economy and where prices were therefore low.[140]

The other three-sided route worked by the ships of the ports in the south-west is much better known. The ships would sail either empty 'in ballast' or with a cargo of salt to Newfoundland, and having fished for cod, would continue on to Spain or Italy. The Newfoundland fishing grounds were probably discovered by Bristol fishermen at the end of the fifteenth century; they were then abandoned to Spanish and Portuguese fishing fleets, which from the 1570s onwards were the object of continual attacks from English ships, which finally succeeded in ousting them. It was well known that sailors from the west of England were enthusiastic privateers.[141] The importance of this trade for the English economy as a whole was stressed by the merchants of Bristol in a petition they presented to Charles II in 1667, in which they asked for greater protection against Dutch and French attacks on the England–Newfoundland–Mediterranean route and in the ports of North America.[142]

---

[137] *Merchants and merchandise*, p. 253, document no. 349, dated 13 Apr. 1660.

[138] PRO, SP98/8, Dethick to Williamson, Livorno, 7 Feb. 1667.

[139] PRO, SP98/6, Finch to the Grand Duke, Florence, 4 Oct. 1665.

[140] Michell, 'The European fisheries', pp. 140–1.

[141] Ibid., p. 157; Clay, *Economic expansion and social change*, vol. II, pp. 132–3; *Merchants and merchandise*, p. xxiv.

[142] The petitioners claim that the trade has been 'of great advantage to your Majesty in divers respects as can be well made out in point of customes from the product of the said trade amounting to att least forty thousand pounds per annum by the importacon of Oyles, wyne fruite and other comodities brought in as returnes from

The documentary evidence we possess on the arrivals of ships from Bristol in Italian ports is meagre. In the twelve months from September 1600, four merchant ships set sail from Bristol for Livorno; in the following year there were five.[143] In 1640 the *Bristoll merchant*, together with the *Northumberland*, was sequestered by the French fleet off Nisida near Naples. It managed to escape and sail on to Bari, where it was to collect a cargo of olive oil, but eight sailors and two merchants who were on board were imprisoned by the Spanish and the ship's cargo, with a value of 20,000 crowns, was sequestered and the ship itself forced to set off empty on the return journey.[144] In May 1664, the *James* was the only vessel not bound for London among the English merchant ships ready to set out from Livorno; it was returning to Bristol with a cargo of olive oil from Gallipoli.[145] In March 1666, the *Gift* arrived in Livorno with 200 hogsheads of pilchards; after a month, it left for Gallipoli with three other ships, returning to Livorno in July with olive oil.[146] In December 1667, the *Mayflower*, under its captain, Guglielmo Treggio, arrived from Bristol via Cadiz with a cargo for delivery to one Christopher Williams consisting of 90 barrels of pilchards, 120 pigs of lead, 10 bales of calf-skins and 15 barrels of galena or lead ore.[147] In March 1668, two Bristol ships, the *Bristoll Merchant* and the *Elisabeth*, sailing from Barbados with sugar, lead, etc., anchored in Livorno. At Cadiz they had been joined first by the *Owen & David* on its way from London, and then at Alicante by the *Saphire*, *Mary Rose* and *Meermaide* on their way to Algiers.[148] In May of the same year, the arrival was registered in Livorno of the *Mercante di Plemua*, with its captain Arturo Plumia, which had sailed from Bristol via Cadiz with a cargo of 60 bales of calf-skins, 500 small pigs of lead, 60 barrels of galena, 30 casks of

Spayne Portugall and Italy for the Fish caught in those Seas, It breedinge yearely many hundred seamen, And being also of great advantage to your Maiesties Subjects in the west of England . . .' (PRO, SP29/224, 55, 'To the kings most excellent Maiestie and to the right honourable the lords and others of his maiesties most honourable privie councell. The humble peticion of the compagnie trading to the Newfoundland from your Maiesties City of Bristoll', Whitehall, 6 Dec. 1667). The text of this document can be found in *Merchants and merchandise*, pp. 257–8, document no. 356, and in *Acts of Privy Council, Colonial series*, vol. II (1613–80), pp. 448–9.

143 *Merchants and merchandise*, Appendix D, p. 279.

144 PRO, SP93/1, 123, newsletter, Naples, 2 Oct. 1640; SP93/1, 128, petition of the English merchants resident in Naples, undated document, in catalogue as '1670?', but, to judge from its contents, more probably the end of 1640.

145 PRO, SP98/5, 'A distinct list . . .', Livorno, 24 May 1664 (see note 94).

146 PRO, SP98/6, Dethick to Williamson, Livorno, 8 Mar. 1666; Chellingworth to Arlington, Livorno, 26 Apr. 1666.

147 PRO, SP98/8, list of arrivals in Livorno, 18 Dec. 1667, printed document.

148 PRO, SP98/9, Dethick to Williamson, Livorno, 12 Mar. 1668.

white sugar, 20 barrels of unrefined sugar, 15 bales and chests of woollens and stockings, a cask of wax and 20 bales of wool from Alicante for
delivery to Christopher Williams. At the same time as the *Mercante di
Plemua*, the *Isabella*, captained by Richard Philips, arrived in Livorno,
carrying 80 pigs of lead, 250 dozen calf-skins, 35 barrels of sugar, 40 says
(a kind of serge) and 80 baskets of soda.[149] In November 1670, a small
merchant ship from Bristol, together with another vessel from the West
of England, bound for Italy, was captured by Algerian pirates.[150] Piracy
was not the only danger, however; in January 1677, in Naples, a mutiny
occurred on the Bristol ship *Howners Adventure* and the captain, Bartho-
lomew Broome, was beaten almost to death. The mutineers were all
imprisoned with the exception of the boatswain and the gunner who
had led the revolt but eluded the authorities by taking sanctuary in a
Neapolitan church.[151]

Such evidence would suggest that in the competition with London
Bristol was capable of stronger resistance than other English provincial
ports. In addition to the *James*, it is possible to find other merchant ships
returning to the city; for example, the two ships accompanied to Marseilles by the warship *Dartford*, under the command of captain Darris.[152]
In reality Bristol held out strongly against the encroaching mercantile
monopoly of the City of London and the gradual concentration of consumer industries around the English capital, some of which – the soap
industry, for example – were in direct competition with long-established manufacturing industries in the west of England.

Opposition to the mediation of Blackwell Hall meant resisting its
monopoly of the cloth trade in general and the monopoly of the Levant
Company in particular, but above all it meant opposition to the control
exercised by this group of London merchants over the provincial textile
industry.[153] The struggle was waged up to and beyond the 1670s, with
London emerging victorious, but not without Bristol giving evidence
of continuing vitality, as when the city shifted its commercial interests
from Newfoundland, increasingly under the control of American merchants, to the West Indies, just at the time when these were of growing
importance for English trade. Its continuing role in English trade with
Italy is shown too by a 1674 report on Livorno which states, among

[149] PRO, SP98/9, 182, list of arrivals in the port of Livorno, 7 May 1668, included
with a letter from Dethick to Williamson (PRO, SP98/9, 180, Livorno, 7 May
1668), printed document.
[150] PRO, SP98/12, Clutterbuck to Williamson, Livorno, 23 Nov. 1670.
[151] PRO, SP93/2, 191, dispatch from the consul Davies, Naples, 26 Jan. 1677.
[152] PRO, SP98/12, Dethick to Williamson, Livorno, 22 Sept. 1670.
[153] See p. 168.

other facts, that many English ships arrive in the Tuscan port, carrying 'goods from Ireland and Bristol, such as leather, staves, salmon and sugar'.[154]

LIVORNO AND THE ITALIAN PORTS

From the very beginning of the revival of commercial contacts by sea between northern Europe and Italy in the 1570s, the port of Livorno, founded thirty years before by the Grand Duke Cosimo I de' Medici, was an indispensable stopping-off point in the route taken by English ships sailing to the Mediterranean. The dominance of the Tuscan port over others in Italy, however, emerged only later, between 1625 and 1628, when, as a result of the conflicts between Spain and France, England chose to concentrate most of its Mediterranean commercial interests there.[155] As Livorno became the focus for the Mediterranean routes, so the port began to free itself from its dependence on Pisa, which had until then functioned as the principal commercial centre of the region with Livorno as a mere landing place. Those merchants who were still resident in Pisa moved their working quarters to the new port; between 1633 and 1642, the new town's population grew by 27 per cent, with a notable increase in the mercantile community, especially in the number of Jewish merchants (see table 3.4).[156]

During the same period, as has been described, the role of Genoa as the seaport serving the city of Milan and its Lombard hinterland was taken over by Livorno. This was a development for which the Genoese were unprepared; as Joseph Kent put it in a report written in 1663, only a few years before, the Tuscan port had been a simple landing-stage 'onely inhabited by a few fishermen rounded with Boggs and a very badd ayre'.[157]

The rapid development of Livorno in the 1620s and 1630s was also recorded by Thomas Mun, who had lived there at the beginning of the century. He wrote that 'within these thirty years the trade of Leghorn is much encreased, that of a poor little town (as my self knew it) it is now

---

[154] Document quoted in G. Battelli, 'Il porto di Livorno alla fine del secolo XVII', *Bollettino storico livornese*, 1/1 (1937), 80–2. Battelli's reference for the document is 'Archivio di Stato di Firenze, Carte strozziane 106, s.1': 'mercanzie d'Irlanda e Bristol, cioè cuoia, doghe, salmone e zuccheri'.

[155] PRO, SP98/4, 198 (part II), Kent to Bennet, Livorno, 27 Apr. 1663.

[156] E. Fasano Guerini, 'La popolazione', in *Livorno: progetto e storia di una città tra il 1500 e il 1600* (Pisa: 1980), catalogue of the exhibition held in Livorno in 1980 in the 'Bottini dell'olio' and the 'Fortezza vecchia', pp. 199–216.

[157] PRO, SP98/4, 198v. (part II), Kent to Bennet, Livorno, 27 Apr. 1663; see pp. 78–9.

Table 3.4 *Population of Livorno*

Years	Total population of Livorno	Jewish population of Livorno	Merchants resident in Livorno in 1642[a]	Tax paid (in 'scudi')
1601	3,118	124	80 Jews	4,622
1609	5,046		33 Frenchmen	1,054
1616	7,509		12 Florentines	1,460
1622	9,103	711	10 Englishmen	1,400
1632	8,392		8 Flemings	1,100
1633	8,642	700	28 other nationalities	1,552
1642	11,954	1,115		
1643	11,597			
1645	10,079	1,250		

Note: [a] These figures have been calculated by Fasano Guarini from a tax document relating to merchants resident in Livorno in 1642. There was a total of 219 *negozianti* and the tax they paid amounted to 11,188 scudi.
Source: Fasano Guarini, 'La popolazione', in *Livorno: progetto e storia di una città tra il 1500 e il 1600*, pp. 199–215. Fasano Guarini writes: 'At the end of the century the population of Livorno appears to number approximately 12,000, despite reaching 17,000 during the 1670s.'

become a fair and strong City, being one of the most famous places of trade in all Christendom'.[158]

Livorno's position was a factor which worked strongly in its favour; it was nearer than Venice and Ancona to the routes taken by the northern European ships on their way to the Levant, and, unlike Genoa, because it was situated midway on the Italian Tyrrhenian coast, it allowed convenient access both to the overland routes leading out of Italy towards northern Europe and to the ports of southern Italy which were important sources of supply.

Yet Livorno's development owed more to the enlightened and liberal policy pursued by its rulers than it did to its geographical advantages. It was declared a free port, where, unlike Genoa or Venice, freedom of movement for merchandise and low customs duties prevailed. The economic benefits were such that it proved cheaper to unload goods destined for the Veneto in Livorno than it was to send them to Venice. In 1628, it was calculated that if a bale to be delivered in Vicenza was sent via Livorno, it cost 1 piece of eight for freight and discharge, and 8 for overland transport to its destination, whereas, if the same item was sent to Venice, the total cost of the operation rose to between 30 and 40 pieces of eight.[159]

[158] Mun, *England's treasure by foreign trade* in McCulloch, *Early tracts on commerce*, p. 139.
[159] Wood, *A history of the Levant Company*, p. 65. Livorno was officially proclaimed a free port in 1675, but had been one *de facto* since its foundation. On Livorno, see P.

When the Genoese proposed a new route from Amsterdam to Genoa to Dutch merchants, crossing the Grisons, as opposed to the old route which went from Amsterdam to Livorno via Nuremberg, the Brenner Pass and Florence, the merchants replied that no duties had to be paid on the old route, with the exception of the customs duty levied at Florence, which in the case of textiles was so reduced as to be negligible.[160] The total costs of transportation were a more important factor in the choice of which route to take than mere geographical considerations. The reduction of customs duties became an indispensable tool in the management of the transit trade, by its very nature fluctuating and subject to wider economic trends, which increasingly characterised the trade in Italian ports in the wake of the decline in the country's export industries.[161] The distinction in Tuscany between the port at Livorno and the manufacturing centre in Florence was doubtless to the state's advantage, since the combination of industrial and shipping activity in one place might well have proved an impediment to the free circulation of goods. Both Genoa and Venice were slow to establish this distinction, and this delay had fatal consequences for their shipping activity; both cities found themselves inexorably excluded from the worldwide networks under the control of merchants and shipowners from northern Europe.

International trade as it affected Italian ports in the second half of the seventeenth century increasingly involved the transit trade; this in turn exacerbated the problems already inherent in the political divisions of the country and in the rivalry between its various states. The absence of unity, which may have been one of the contributing factors to Italian economic growth in earlier centuries, was now, in the changing context of international trade, a further handicap in the competition with the emergent northern European powers.

The 1660s saw the ports of northern Italy locked in a struggle to attract the transit trade of Dutch and English ships. Both Genoa and Villafranca were declared free ports and competed to emulate Livorno by offering foreign merchants privileges and exemptions.[162] The English saw clearly the benefits which could accrue to them from the rivalry

Scrosoppi, 'Il porto di Livorno e gli inizi dell'attività inglese nel Mediterraneo', *Bollettino storico livornese* 1/4 (1937), 339–77; 'Attività commerciale nel porto di Livorno nella prima metà del secolo XVII', *Bollettino storico livornese* 3/4 (1939), 41–65; J.-P. Filippini, 'Il porto di Livorno e il regno di Francia dall'editto di porto franco alla fine della dominazione medicea', in *Atti del convegno 'Livorno e il Mediterraneo nell'età medicea'*, pp. 179–201.

[160] Day, 'Strade e vie di comunicazione', pp. 112–13.
[161] Ibid., pp. 107, 113.
[162] PRO, SP98/8, Finch to Arlington, Livorno, 21 Mar. 1667.

ROUTES AND PORTS 117

between the various ports, and between Livorno and Genoa in particular, while, at the same time, they exploited the concessions made by
Spain in southern Italy, or those offered by the Duke of Savoy in order
to tempt them to transfer their business to Villafranca, with the result
that their commercial organisation was strengthened while Italy's was
further weakened.[163]

The English well understood the role played by the port of Livorno
as a transit port in the context of English commercial interests in the
Mediterranean. In a 1668 report to the Secretary of State, Finch wrote:

> As to the Erecting a Factory at Villafranca with Submission to your Lord-
> ship I conceave thus. That it is so farr from Spoyling the English Interest, as
> it much advanceth it: for your Lordship must Looke upon Legorn as a Scale
> of trade or magazin for other parts, Our English Merchandise that is landed
> there, being not consumd' in the place: nor in the Great Dukes Territoryes,
> but bought up by other Merchants to be transferrd' to other places, and if
> such Merchants want at Legorn, the English Principalls themselves send
> them to convenient places. So that if there was no Such place as Legorn
> the Consumption of Our Commodityes would be much the same, to
> which adding this Consideration; that Our Woollen Manufactures are
> banish'd here and in most parts of Italy, they making Use onely of so
> much of Ours as they cannot be without: Whosoever Wee leave they
> loose by us, and Wee nothing by them, save the Convenience of a free
> Port: which as it is a convenience, so consequently the more free Ports
> Wee have the greater is the Convenience in itselfe: but the greater Still;
> in that they being two; We shall be Us'd better in them both but the greatest
> convenience by Erecting this free Port will be; the getting as I hope, a free
> Vent for our Woollen Manufactures in the Dominions of the Duke of
> Savoy, and a free passage through them to adjacent parts: which Example
> being once made, other Princes must follow this President, or be in
> danger of loosing Our Trade which is most beneficiall to them.[164]

About a year before this report was written, Finch had informed
London that Italian rulers were easily able to control all aspects of their
local economies, because their states were small and they were experienced in government. Furthermore, since their power was absolute,
they could change laws as they saw fit, blocking imports and exports
from year to year and imposing new taxes as need arose. It was therefore
in England's interests to negotiate a series of trading agreements with
the various Italian states. Finch advised that English trade in Livorno
should be organised on a permanent basis and better conditions obtained

---

[163] PRO, SP98/6, Finch to Arlington, Livorno, 1 Feb. 1666; SP98/8, Finch to Arlington, Livorno, 24 Jan. 1667; Livorno, 11 Apr. 1667; Florence, 13 June 1667;
Florence, 5 July 1667; SP98/9, Finch to Arlington, Livorno, 12 Mar. 1668.
[164] PRO, SP98/9, Finch to Arlington [Florence], 21/31 May 1668.

from the Grand Duke, especially as regards England's Dutch rivals. It would prove most practical to start negotiations with the Genoese, with whom an advantageous agreement could probably be reached, since the city was a free port and was also in competition with Livorno. It was also in the interests of the Genoese to maintain good relations with England for two reasons: the revival of the Levant trade in the port had been supported and protected by the English, and Genoa's trading links with Spain, in particular the convoys which carried Spanish pieces of eight to the city, could at any moment be broken off by the English fleet stationed in the Mediterranean. Finch also suggested that if the English were to approach Savoy

> who is now endeavouring by allwayes to render Villafranca a place of Trade, anything will be offerd' to invite the English thither . . . But . . . What is agreed with Genova a place of Trade will have more Influence on the Great Duke who next after them is to be Articled with and unlesse his Highnesse grants what Genova admitts the Port of Legorn will be infallibly ruind' by the recession of the English to his œmulous Neighbours of Genova.[165]

Finally, Venice would be the most difficult of the Italian states to negotiate with; nevertheless, given the dependence of the city's currant trade on England and its war against the Turks, the Venetians would be likely to accede to any reasonable request.[166]

The attractions of Livorno, however, did not consist simply of a more advantageous regime of customs tariffs; it was also the most modern and fully equipped port in the Mediterranean. From 1544 onwards, when the last ship left Porto Pisano and Livorno became the new port of Tuscany, the Grand Dukes had pursued a farsighted policy of making the port work efficiently. All necessary facilities were provided: a new customs-house was built in 1546, at the same time as the arsenal. Two new jetties were begun in 1569; it took just five months in 1590 to build the new fortress, and the deep-water dock for the great sailing ships was dug equally rapidly the following year.[167]

The Canale dei navicelli connecting the port to the Arno at Pisa was begun in 1560, giving easier access to the river than the river estuary, which had hitherto been used for the goods which were to be sent inland. The construction of the canal had also required the rechannelling of water from the marshland surrounding Livorno, thus improving the quality of the air. The concern to connect the port to the inland and beyond is shown clearly in the *motu proprio* of 14 April 1606, which

[165] PRO, SP98/8, Finch to Arlington, Livorno, 25 July 1667.   [166] Ibid.
[167] Braudel and Romano, *Navires et marchandises*, pp. 20–1.

established the administrative entity of the Capitanato Nuovo and so extended Livorno's territory, giving the port increased regional importance.[168]

A new town, with a large rectangular drill-ground and a grid-like street plan, was built around the port, and an appropriately heterogeneous and open-minded population was sought to fill it, 'an "American" people . . . with opportunities for the humblest members to make their fortunes'.[169] The Medici were tireless in seeking to attract people, ships and capital to Livorno. The Jewish community was particularly welcome: in February 1548, Cosimo had invited them to come 'out of Spaine and Portugall, that he knew were oppressed by the Inquisition & were rich and tradeing merchants, he granted larger Priviledges which they confesse they enjoy noewhere else . . .'[170] In 1663, the influx of Jews from Spain and Marranos from Portugal showed no signs of stopping; entire families arrived on every ship from the Iberian peninsula. The Jewish community in Livorno was contented and thriving; its merchants were regarded as the wealthiest and most active participants in the town's trade.[171] Their presence ensured that Livorno became part of an international network of trade; it led to increased contacts with North Africa and provided a thriving carrying trade with which ships from northern Europe could profitably employ the seasonal periods of non-activity characteristic of Mediterranean navigation and earn themselves valuable currency for trade in the Levant.

The same hospitality was extended to Armenians, who were merchants and shipbuilders. In the 1660s Antonio Bogus was famous in Livorno; he was the owner of six ships, the equivalent of a third of the Livorno fleet, which regularly worked the western and eastern Mediterranean routes, especially to Lisbon and Smyrna, as well as visiting the ports of North Africa such as Tunis.[172] The consul Chellingworth described him to the Secretary of State as follows:

> The Chelibee; Antonio Bogus, a Converted Turke, vastly rich, & a great Person with His Highnesse, the GDuke; hath one ship already in the French service; called the Soria merchant, alledged under Constraint, & indeed she was carried in from Tunis & now hee is sending the Isabella,

[168] R. Mazzauti, 'Il territorio livornese', in Livorno: progetto e storia di una città, p. 81.
[169] Braudel and Romano, Navires et marchandises, pp. 24–5.
[170] PRO, SP98/4, 198 (part II), Kent to Bennet, Livorno, 27 Apr. 1663.
[171] PRO, SP98/4, 215 (part II), Kent to Bennet, Livorno, 18 May 1663.
[172] PRO, SP98/6, Dethick to Williamson, Livorno, 22 Feb. 1666; Chellingworth to Arlington, Livorno, 12 Apr. 1666 and 3 May 1666; letter from the King of England to the Grand Duke, 16 July 1666; Chellingworth to Arlington, Livorno, 16 Aug. 1666; SP98/8, Dethick to Williamson, Livorno, 24 Jan. 1667 and 21 Mar. 1667; SP98/9, list of arrivals in the port of Livorno 14 Jan. 1668, printed document.

that, in warr may well carry 46 Gunns, they are both Dutch built vessells, & this yeare as hee saith, hee bought them here, they have passed under the GDukes Banner, & and are mann'd with severall nations.[173]

It is probable that the presence of Armenian merchants in Livorno contributed to the continuing trade in Persian silk along the overland caravan routes and across the Mediterranean to Livorno.[174]

Many bandits and pirates were attracted to Livorno with the guarantee of an amnesty for their former crimes, excluding that of *lèse majesté*, and the promise of protection; many English privateers in particular sought refuge there after the 1604 peace treaty was concluded between England and Spain, at the personal invitation of the Grand Duke.[175] In April 1610, he sent Lewkner Bosswell (or Bosfield), an English captain in his service, to Palermo with a letter of pardon together with two letters from Sir Robert Dudley addressed to a pirate by the name of Ward, in an attempt to persuade him to enter his service and become a Catholic. Boswell also carried a letter of pardon from the Grand Duke for other English pirates, such as Lawson Denbow, in command of a Dutch ship, and his deputy Glafield, as well as for one Sky. A similar invitation was extended to the English pirates at Mamora, who had become wealthy on the plunder of ships belonging to Spain and other countries, again with the offer of absolution from their crimes and conversion to Catholicism.[176] It was not surprising therefore that Livorno became the leading Mediterranean market for plunder; in 1630 Giovan Battista Salvago in a letter to the Doge wrote that:

Algiers and Tunis are full of merchants of all nationalities — Livornese, Corsican, Genoese, French, Flemish, English, Jewish, Venetian and others. These merchants buy the plundered goods and send them to the free port of Livorno where they are distributed throughout the whole of Italy. Shipments of the goods are also sent to Genoa, Villafranca, and Nice under the Savoy rulers, and from Nice to Marseilles, but most are

---

173 PRO, SP98/6, Chellingworth to Arlington, Livorno, 29 Mar. 1666; Bogus is referred to throughout as 'the Chelibee', i.e. a native of Cilicia, the south-eastern region of Anatolia. See p. 51.
174 PRO, SP98/8, Finch to Arlington, Livorno, 24 Jan. 1667.
175 Braudel, *La Méditerranée*, vol. 1, p. 566.
176 PRO, SP93/1, 28, Robert Kinge to Cecil, Palermo, 16 Apr. 1610; see also Corbett, *England in the Mediterranean*, vol. 1, pp. 10, 20, 57–8. Mamora or Mehdia, a port on the Atlantic coast of Morocco, was a notorious refuge for English pirates. It was situated at the mouth of the river Sebu, north of Sallee, another port which was notorious for its pirates and where many industrious Moriscos had fled when they were driven out of Spain in 1609–11. The port of Mamora was destroyed in a Spanish raid in 1611: some pirates transferred their activities to ports on the North African coast; a handful moved to the coast of southern Ireland (see Davis, 'England and the Mediterranean', pp. 127–8).

sent to Livorno . . . However many ships lose their other markets when
they're seized by pirates, they all eventually find their way to Livorno.
This trade in plunder is the real incitement to piracy; if it didn't exist, the
plunder would go to waste in Barbary and the pirates, with their useless
booty, would lose interest . . .[177]

The years which saw the development of the new port of Livorno
were also the period in which the English economy began to revive
after the stagnation which had afflicted it in the first two decades of the
century. In the 1630s, together with the development of the free port of
Dover, the pattern of English trade routes shows a marked shift away
from the ports of Spain towards those of Italy.[178]

In Finch's view, English merchants had encouraged Livorno's
growth and were alone responsible for the volume of trade in the port,
despite the equally if not more favourable privileges extended to the
Dutch;[179] half the trade in the Tuscan port was English, and without
the English much of the other half would disappear.[180] England's supremacy was for Finch uncontestable:

> English trade in Legorn brought into this Port in Commodityes the
> value of 50 thousand Dollars for every thousand the Dutch brought, and
> that every thousand Dollars of English Commodityes yielded more profit
> to Legorn than ten thousand in Dutch Commodityes . . . there is no
> proportion between the English and the Dutch trade in the Mediterra-
> nean . . . the Dutch . . . bring not the hundreth part of the profitt to the
> Port . . .[181]

In addition to the key role which the English seem to have played in
the development of Livorno, it is important to define Livorno's role in

---

[177] C. Masi, 'Relazioni fra Livorno ed Algeri nei secoli XVII–XIX', *Bollettino storico livornese* 2/2 (1938), 183–4. Masi's article is the transcript of a report drawn up by the
dragoman Giovan Battista Salvago for the Doge of Venice. Salvago had been sent to
'Barbary' by the Venetians in order to obtain the freedom of the Venetian hostages
held as slaves in the Berber States: 'in Algeri et in Tunisi risiedono mercanti Livornesi, Corsi, Genovesi, Francesi, Fiamminghi, Inglesi, Giudei, Veneziani e d'altri
stati. Questi comprono tutte le robbe predate e le mandano alla scala franchissima di
Livorno e di là si diffondono per tutta l'Italia. Se ne fa parimenti qualche spedizione
per Genova, Villafranca e Nizza sotto Savoia, e da Nizza per Marsiglia; ma l'invia-
mento *è per Livorno* . . . Quanti vasselli perdono l'altre piazze nel rapto de corsari,
tutt'alfine danno fondi in Livorno. Il dispaccio delle prede è il vero fomite del corso
altrimenti le robbe depredate morirebbero in Barbaria, et il Corsaro, in bottini
inutili, si raffrederebbe . . .'
[178] Taylor, 'Trade, neutrality and the "English road" ', p. 248.
[179] PRO, SP98/6, Finch to Arlington, Florence, 29 Sept. 1665; Livorno, 22 Feb. 1666.
[180] PRO, SP98/8, memorandum from Sir John Finch to the Grand Duke, 24 Nov.
1667.
[181] PRO, SP98/9, Finch to Arlington, Livorno, 23 Jan. 1668.

the system of England's commercial relations with other countries. Livorno was essential to English navigation in the Mediterranean as a port where ships could take on provisions, and where maintenance and repair work could be carried out, and new equipment supplied if necessary.[182] Throughout the seventeenth century, Livorno was regarded as 'a Magazin and Scale of the English Levant Trade'.[183] From the beginning of the century, Livorno was seen as primarily important in the context of England's Levant trade. At the end of the 1620s, Sir Peter Wyche passed through Livorno on his way to take up his appointment as ambassador in Constantinople and wrote of the town:

> The trade which our English Marchants have in this port is very greate . . . where it is endeavoured to give them all incouragement to persever. Our Marchants which doe reside here, approve well hereof, and understand this place to bee most comodious for theire trade, it being unto them a fitt seate for theire Commerce into the Levant, and they now transport at this present in their shipping . . . about three Soe thousand pounds sterling in Spanish coyne . . .[184]

Apart from its facilities for provisioning, carrying out repairs and reorganising the cargoes, or the possibility of acquiring there the expensive textiles produced in the industrial centres of northern Italy, Livorno in itself had very little to offer: Salvago noted that 'little can be extracted from the town itself',[185] while Thomas Mun observed that 'the moltitude of ships and ware which come hither from England, the Low Countries and other places, have little or no means to make their returns from thence but only in ready money, which they may and do carry away freely at all times'.[186] Lewes Roberts added that a million ducats in cash were exported from Livorno annually.[187] If we examine the three Mediterranean voyages made by Sir John Banks's ship the *Virgin* between 1659 and 1662, we can see that the goods unloaded at

[182] BL, Eg. 2524, 'Book of accounts of the ship "Bantam" . . .' See Oppenheim, *A history of the administration of the Royal Navy*; D. A. Baugh, *British naval administration in the age of Walpole* (Princeton: 1965).

[183] PRO, SP98/8, Finch to Arlington, Livorno, 4 Apr. 1667, 11 Apr. 1667.

[184] PRO, SP98/3, 79, Sir Peter Wyche to Conway, Livorno (on board the *Sampson*), 27 Feb. 1627. Sir Peter Wyche (?-1643), the son of the merchant Richard Wyche, knighted in 1627, was the English ambassador to the Ottoman court from 1627 to 1641. Sir Edward Conway was created baron in 1624 and viscount in 1626. He was Secretary of State for the Northern Department from 1623 to 1628. See *Il commercio inglese nel Mediterraneo dal '500 al '700*, pp. 336, 338.

[185] G. Pagano de Divitiis, 'Il porto di Livorno fra Inghilterra e Oriente', *Nuovi studi livornesi* 1 (1993), pp. 43–87; Masi, 'Relazioni fra Livorno ed Algeri', p. 184: 'del paese poco s'estragge'.

[186] T. Mun, *A discourse of trade*, in McCulloch (ed.), *Early tracts on commerce*, p. 139.

[187] L. Roberts, *The treasure of trafficke*, in McCulloch (ed.), *Early tracts on commerce*, p. 69.

Livorno consisted of lead, fish, pepper and 'Suffolk cloth', whereas when the ship set sail again for Scanderoon and Aleppo, its cargo was entirely comprised of silver pieces of eight, part 'weighty' and part 'good ordinary', to a total value of approximately $16,000.[188] Coleman remarks that Banks's commercial transactions in the Mediterranean during the 1660s involved rather more than a simple exchange of goods, in so far as trade with Livorno and Cadiz principally supplied silver pieces of eight.[189]

Thus Livorno played a crucially important part in England's Levant trade as a centre where English exports or re-exports could be converted into valuable currency. It is probable that this was also true for those ships which traded only within the central Mediterranean, and, after calling at Livorno, continued to their destinations of the Morea and the 'currant islands', which, as we have seen, may have been part of the eastern Mediterranean geographically, but in commercial terms belonged within the Italian system. In a document which can be dated to the end of the seventeenth century, it is stated that one should try to buy currants in Venice before the cash and ships for the cargo were sent to Zante and elsewhere, as with the purchase of olive oil in Livorno and Naples before the merchant ships were sent to collect the supply in Puglia. This system would have led to a reduction and stabilisation of prices and to the payment of the sums owed in Venice in the same coin as the English received for the sale of their fish or other goods. In this way, two drawbacks for English trade could be avoided: the danger of transporting money and the cost of the premium or agio or of bills of exchange.[190]

In the closing years of the seventeenth century the English merchants resident in Venice complained about having to pay for their acquisitions in valuable money and at high cost, because, unlike fish, the price of Corinth raisins was not fixed by the city authorities. Moreover, they were obliged to accept all kinds of coinage in payment for their goods, whereas they were expected to pay for the currants they bought and the customs dues they incurred in silver ducats and gold zecchins only.[191]

A technique occasionally used to avoid carrying cash to Venice was to transfer the equivalent sum by means of bills of exchange from Livorno, which was usually the point where freight charges were collected for all the ships which arrived in Italy. This method was used with the *Thomas & Daniel*, for example, which, in addition to a cargo of lead and tar bound for Venice, was also carrying freight goods for Genoa and Livorno. The money for the freight was collected in

[188] KCCRO, Aylesford MSS, U234/B2–B3, passim.
[189] Coleman, *Sir John Banks*, p. 26.   [190] PRO, CO388/9, 344 ff.
[191] PRO, SP104/198, ? June 1696.

Livorno and transferred to the Venetian agent of the shipowners, Aloisio Morelli, who was also responsible for the sale of the cargo and, if necessary, for advancing the proceeds in pieces of eight to Venice. The ship with the cash then continued to Zante, where the captain was to buy currants.[192]

It is clear that Livorno played a different role for those English ships which kept to the Italian routes and generally sailed as far as the Puglian ports for olive oil, the transaction for which had been effected by the trading network connecting Livorno and Naples. In these cases Livorno acted as a centre for credit on the basis of the guarantee of the English goods about to arrive.

Naples played a marginal role as a port, as an outpost of Livorno, despite its central importance for trade on the mainland of southern Italy. Its port was designed more to impress than provide secure harbour for the ships which anchored there, and it was only occasionally the final destination of English merchant ships, which more usually called at Naples to deliver the residual part of the cargo they had brought from England or the freight they had carried from Livorno.[193] The French consul in Naples, François Boccardo, in a memorandum written in 1686, asserted that in Naples there was little to be taken on board.[194]

The English ships in search of a cargo for the return journey usually left Livorno to collect barrels of olive oil in the Puglian ports, Gallipoli in particular.[195] In the 1660s there were so many 'fish ships' sailing to Gallipoli that it was thought appropriate for the port to have its own resident consul as distinct from Naples, since it was 'a Port which our English Shipping frequent yearly in considerable numbers to lade oyles, and where they want the Support of a Consull to appeare with courage & boldnesse in their interest by his Majesties authority . . .'[196] The importance of Gallipoli stemmed partly from two factors: its convenient position on the southernmost extremity of the heel of the Italian peninsula, and its excellent cisterns for the conservation of olive oil which

---

[192] PRO, HCA/13, 131, 'The personall answers of Nicholas Cholwell made to the peticions and articles of a certaine pretended allegations in fact given against him the 21st of October 1681 . . .', 12 Nov. 1681. The document refers to a voyage which took place in 1677–9.

[193] PRO, SP93/1, 130, 'Sommario della rellazione del Regno di Napoli', undated.

[194] ANF, AE/B1/867, 'Mémoire concernant le Consulat de Naples', probable date: 18 June 1686.

[195] See M. Visceglia, 'Il commercio nei porti pugliesi nel Settecento: ipotesi di ricerca' in P. Villani (ed.), Economia e classi sociali nella Puglia moderna (Naples: 1974), p. 100.

[196] PRO, SP93/1, 149, Kent to Williamson, Naples, 13 May 1664.

gave it a virtual monopoly over the export of high-quality oil.[197] Yet Gallipoli was also included within the advantageous system of transactions for the purchase of Puglian oil, a system controlled by the English merchants resident in Livorno and Naples, and it was this, rather than the port's location on the return route of the merchant ships sailing back from the Levant, which was the basis of its importance. It was certainly no intermediate port of call, but a specific destination for the return cargo.[198]

This phenomenon of ships leaving Livorno for Puglia empty of cargo simply extended what was an already established feature of commerce in southern Italy during the seventeenth century, the so-called 'empty ships' which used to leave the port of Naples in order to collect food supplies in the provincial ports further south.

[197] J. Davis, *Società e imprenditori nel Regno Borbonico, 1815–1860* (Bari: 1979), p. 98; P. Chorley, *Oil, silk, and Enlightenment: economic problems in XVIII-century Naples* (Naples: 1965), p. 30.

[198] See P. Macry, *Mercato e società nel regno di Napoli: commercio di grano e politica economica nel '700* (Naples: 1974), p. 78.

CHAPTER 4

IMPORTED GOODS

ENGLAND AND ITALY: BALANCE OF TRADE AND BALANCE OF PAYMENTS

It is difficult to assess the value of trade between England and Italy in the seventeenth century: useful primary sources are scarce, and generally of relevance only for London, and Italy's lack of political unity makes the country's commercial situation difficult to analyse. What information is available has been gathered here in order to provide an approximate picture of commercial relations between the two countries.

One fundamental feature is that England's trade balance with the rest of the world was in deficit at the beginning of the seventeenth century and remained so in the 1660s, whereas by the end of the century there was a marked inversion of the trend (see table 4.1). In the specific case of trade with Italy, the picture is somewhat different: England's trade balance remains sharply in deficit until the second half of the eighteenth century, when the first signs of surplus appear (see table 4.2).

Table 4.1 *Estimated figures for England's foreign trade (£000)*

	1663–1669	1669–1701
London exports	2,039	2,773
Outport exports	1,200	1,660
Re-exports	900	1,986
Total exports	4,100	6,419
London imports	3,495	4,667
Outport imports	900	1,182
Total imports	4,400	5,849

Source: Davis, 'English foreign trade, 1660–1700', p. 160.

126

Table 4.2 *Value of trade between England and Italy (£000)*

	1669–1701	1771–1773
Exports		
Italy	114	821
Venice	35	84
Total exports	149	905
Imports		
Italy	355	762
Venice	50	84
Total	405	846

Source: Davis, *The rise of the English shipping industry*, p. 256.

A contemporary document containing figures for imports and exports in the Port of London alone for the years 1663 and 1669 is confirmation that trade between England and Italy was firmly to the latter's advantage, with the rate of imports almost doubling that of exports (see table 4.3). Any extrapolations must be made with caution from figures which relate to so brief a period of time, but if we compare the two series of figures by category, several points emerge. The Mediterranean was the leading market for English goods and the increase in exports to the area shows that its significance continued to grow. If we look at individual countries, there was an increase in English exports to Italy and, to a lesser extent, to Portugal. The Levant market remained stable, while there was a slight decline in exports to Spain. Imports from the Mediterranean for these two years show a slight overall decline, especially from Spain and Portugal, but there was a marked increase in the quantity of goods arriving in England from Italy and the Levant.

It appears therefore that Italy was the only Mediterranean country to show an increase in trade with England, both in terms of exports and imports, even though Spain, despite the negative trend, remained the most important overseas market for English goods. The deficit of the English trade balance in relation to Italy throughout the seventeenth century is reflected in all the Italian states.

Towards 1696 English merchants involved in trading with Venice declared that 'each year the English bring fish of all kinds to Venice to the value of 100,000 ducats, and take in return quantities of currants worth double this sum'.[1] In what was probably an exaggerated estimate,

[1] PRO, SP104/198, ? June 1696. The exchange rate between England and Venice was 1:5, so that 100,000 ducats was the equivalent of £20,000 sterling.

Table 4.3 *Foreign trade from the Port of London*

	Exports			Imports		
	Sterling (£ s d)	% of Mediterranean total	% of overall total	Sterling (£ s d)	% of Mediterranean total	% of overall total
1663						
Italy	170,478.19.00	18.76		353,564.08.00	27.13	
Spain	425,280.01.00	46.78		558,437.05.00	42.85	
Turkey	167,661.00.00	18.45		304,363.14.00	23.35	
Portugal	145,061.17.00	15.96		86,691.08.00	6.65	
Mediterranean	908,481.17.00		44.91	1,303,056.15.00ᵃ		32.44
Mediterranean	908,481.17.00		44.91	1,303,056.15.00ᵃ		32.44
Rest of Europe	927,603.02.00		45.85	1,867,763.10.00		46.50
American colonies	105,909.18.00		5.23	484,641.02.00		12.06
North African Potentates	56,766.05.00		2.80	384,671.18.00		9.57
Far East	24,051.02.00		1.18	15,886.13.00		0.39
Overall total	2,022,812.04.00			4,056,019.18.00		
1669						
Italy	210,209.13.00	20.22		391,426.11.00	30.42	
Spain	470,765.08.00	45.28		448,819.09.00	34.88	
Turkey	191,458.00.00	18.41		378,741.07.00	29.44	
Portugal	167,178.04.00	16.08		67,692.00.00	5.26	
Mediterranean	1,039,631.05.00		50.38	1,286,679.07.00		30.66
Mediterranean	1,039,631.05.00		50.38	1,286,679.07.00		30.66
Rest of Europe	819,366.18.00		39.71	1,863,370.19.00		44.40
American colonies	107,791.12.00		5.22	605,574.02.00		14.43
North African Potentates	54,402.14.00		2.63	432,869.02.00		10.31
Far East	40,102.10.00		1.94	7,646.07.00		0.18
Overall total	2,061,274.19.00			4,196,139.17.00		

Note: ᵃ I have modified the figures taken from the document in this one case by transferring the sum for imports of currants from Turkey from the heading 'Turkey' to the heading 'Italy', since the 'currant trade' is for the purposes of this study considered to be part of the Italian trading area, although it belongs in geographical terms to the Levant.
Source: BL, Add. MSS 36785

another document of the same date puts England's trade deficit with Venice at £100,000, sent from London via Amsterdam in pieces of eight.[2]

A detailed document from the Levant Company corrected the merchants' estimates, and reduced the deficit to a figure which varied

[2] PRO, CO388/1, 75, c. 1690.

between £50,000 and £81,500.[3] Little credence can be given to the
figures advanced by Hubland and Gold, in this same period, which
purport to show that England's trade balance with the Venetian
Republic was in credit to the amount of £72,900, a remarkable increase
both in the volume and the value of exports from the Port of London.
The two merchants maintained that they had never sent any silver to
Venice throughout the course of their working lives, nor did they
know of any other merchant who had;[4] their assertion, however, con-
tradicts all the other surviving evidence, both for this period and
earlier.[5]

In Naples, English merchants similarly found that 'the revenue from
the merchandise they sell is not enough to cover the purchase of the
goods they export, which means they are obliged to bring in money by
means of bills of exchange, as they do in Livorno, Genoa and Venice
. . .'[6] Half to three-quarters of the value of the imports was paid in cash,
an estimate confirmed by Neapolitan documents of the period: in one it
was asserted that the English and Dutch 'do not obtain money from the
Kingdom but bring great quantities of it in because the price of the oil,
corn, vegetables, and silks they buy from us far exceeds the price of the
goods they sell'.[7] Such a state of affairs reflects the overall condition of
Naples's trade balance with other countries, which was in its favour
throughout the seventeenth century, given that the value of its exports
was much higher than that of its imports.[8]

If a deficit was registered in the English balance of trade with Naples
and Venice, then it is certain that this was also true of its trade with
Tuscany, which had remained the centre of Italian manufactured

[3] PRO, CO388/1, 78, 'Mr Dodington's Papers – The Turky Companys Opinion concerning the Venice Trades', c. 1690.
[4] PRO, CO388/1, 80, 'Mr. Hublands & Mr. Golds papers in answer to Mr. Badingtons
concerning the Venice trades', c. 1690.
[5] PRO, CO388/9, 344 ff., c. 1700; SP98/9, 242–5, letter from John Finch to Arlington, Florence, 3 July 1668. See Davis, *Aleppo and Devonshire Square*, pp. 196–7;
and Pagano de Divitiis, 'Il porto di Livorno'.
[6] PRO, SP93/3, 6, 'Raggioni – Per le mercanzie che s'immettono dall'Inghilterra in
questo Regno di Napoli', undated document, probably included with a letter from
the consul Davies of 20 Dec. 1689 (PRO, SP93/3, 3, 21): 'perché il ritratto di dette
mercanzie che immettono non basta a pagare il prezzo della robba che estrahono,
sono necessitati far entrare il denaro conforme fanno, facendo le tratte, così in
Livorno com'in Genova e Venezia . . .'
[7] BNN, MSS XI, D, 18, 'Discorsi vari sopra la stampa e publicazione della moneta
nell'anno 1689': 'invece di cavar denari del Regno ve ne portano maggior quantità
perché servendosi delli nostri ogli, grani, legumi e seterie il prezzo di queste supera di
gran lunga quello delle loro merci'.
[8] R. Romano, 'Napoli: dal Viceregno al Regno. Storia economica' in R. Romano
(ed.), *Napoli dal Viceregno al Regno* (Turin: 1976), pp. 26–7.

exports. The London merchants claimed that they bought more silk in Florence than the rest of Europe did, while the English resident in the city noted the huge quantity of Florentine silk imported by the English, amounting to more than half of all local production.[9] In 1666 the Grand Duke was told that Charles II knew that his subjects imported silk from Tuscany to a value far in excess of the goods they exported to the state.[10] Four years later, the English again emphasised the benefits which their custom, far outweighing that of all other countries put together, brought to the port of Livorno and the whole of Tuscany: the Florentine silk industry was largely dependent on the English market.[11] The disproportion of exports to imports was particularly marked from 1663 onwards, when Tuscany blocked the import of woollen cloth from abroad.[12] A deficit in England's balance of trade with Genoa is an equally plausible assumption: the value of England's imports from the city – velvet, citrus fruits, paper, olive oil, etc. – must certainly have exceeded the value of the cloth, fish and minerals it exported to the Genoese.[13] Throughout the course of the seventeenth century, therefore, England sought to balance its trade with Italy; it succeeded in doing so with the carrying trade, currency exchange and invisible transactions.

The importance of the Italian trade routes for English shipping was stressed both by Girolamo Alberti, the Venetian secretary in London, and Lord Falconbridge, a former ambassador in Venice. Falconbridge listed the privileges which Venice offered English merchants and asserted that 'even if all the profits derived from the sale of salt fish were to be invested in currants, provided the merchants lose no capital, though they may make no profits, it is still to the advantage of the nation to encourage the trade, for the sake of the shipping, which is the chief asset of England'.[14] It was indeed the case, as we have seen, that

9 PRO, SP98/9, Finch to Arlington, 12 June 1668; SP98/8, memorandum from Finch to the Grand Duke, 24 Nov. 1667; SP98/12, 83, memorandum from Finch to the Grand Duke, 2 Nov. 1670.

10 PRO, SP98/7, Finch to the Grand Duke, Florence, 19 Nov. 1666.

11 PRO, SP98/12, 83, memorandum from Finch to the Grand Duke, 2 Nov. 1670.

12 PRO, SP98/6, Finch to Arlington, Livorno, 22 Feb. 1666; SP98/8, Finch to Arlington, Florence, ? Aug. 1667; SP98/9, Finch to Arlington, Livorno, 5 Mar. 1668; 8 May 1668.

13 PRO, SP105/113, 136, letter from the Levant Company to George Legat & Co. of Genoa, London, 23 Nov. 1672; SP98/8, Finch to Arlington, 7 Mar. 1667; Dethick to Williamson, Livorno, 16 May 1667; KCCRO, Aylesford MSS, U234/B2, Sir John Banks to Thomas Dethick & Co. of Livorno, London, 27 Nov. 1657; SP98/7, 'An exact accompt given unto his Excellency the Prince of Monacoe of the loss & damidges sustained by the fraighters and owners of the shipp "Equity". . .', 8 Dec. 1667.

14 CSP Venetian, 1673–5, 23 Nov. 1674, p. 313.

the crisis in Italian shipping provided the English with excellent opportunities. Another important factor in favour of English trade was the trading profits which derived both from the transportation of exported and imported goods and from the direct control at home and abroad of commercial transactions. Thomas Mun wrote at the beginning of the century:

> The value of our exportations likewise may be much advanced when we perform it our selves in our own Ships, for then we get not only the price of our wares as they are worth here, but also the Merchants gains, the charges of ensurance and fraight to carry them beyond the seas. As for example, if the Italian Merchants should come hither in their own shipping to fetch our Corn, our red Herrings or the like, in this case the kingdom should have ordinarily but 25s. for a quarter of Wheat, and 20s. for a barrel of red herrings, whereas if we carry these wares our selves into Italy upon the said rates, it is likely that wee shall obtain fifty shillings for the first, and forty shillings for the last, which is a great difference in the utterance or vent of the Kingdoms stock.[15]

If we look again at the report produced by Hubland and Gold concerning English trade at the end of the seventeenth century (table 4.4), and compare its figures with those given by the Levant Company, it can be seen that both sets of figures assess the value of imports at approximately £80,000. As regards exports, the figures are similar for the ships and cargoes originating from provincial ports, but Hubland and Gold overestimate by at least a third the number of ships and the value of goods leaving London. It is interesting that the two merchants have, however, also taken into account the revenue from transport expenses, the earnings derived from local trade and freight within the Mediterranean, and the trading percentages, the so-called 'commercial benefits'. In the calculations given in the document, these items amount to just under a third of the overall value of exports (32.25 per cent), of which 18 per cent comes from re-exports, 7.45 per cent from transport, and 6.77 per cent from commissions on English exports. From the 1570s onwards English merchants had sought to secure this margin of profit in a sector where they were aware of running a trade deficit; the framework within which they conducted trade was by necessity monopolistic.

From the outset English ships were almost entirely responsible for transportation. From the beginning of the eighteenth century onwards the appearance of any ship from a Mediterranean country in the Channel was an infrequent occurrence, while any possibility of Dutch

---

[15] Mun, *England's treasure*, p. 129. 'Quarter' = 28 lbs/12.70 kg.

Table 4.4 *English exports to Venice, c. 1690*

Ships	Goods	Provenance	Value (£)
6	herrings, lead		10,000
3	salmon		2,500
1	lead, hides	Chester	2,000
1	lead, calfskins, woollens	Bristol	1,500
2	pilchards	Plymouth	3,000
8	lead, tin, pepper, 'calicoes', copper, Barbados sugar, ginger, woollens[a]	London	90,000
4	sugar	Lisbon	25,000
2	various	Spain	4,000
27	charter of 27 ships		12,000
	profits from English exports at 10%		10,900
Total			160,900

Note: [a] Average value for each ship = £11,250.
Source: PRO, CO388/1, 80–2.

participation in the English import trade had already been excluded in a 1615 decree which anticipated the Navigation Acts by allowing only English ships to import goods from the Mediterranean and only from certain ports.[16] Moreover, the sale of English products and the purchase of foreign goods was controlled by a network of English merchants who were resident in the various centres of trade abroad, and who added commission fees of between 2 per cent and 6 per cent to revenue. The commercial benefits went far beyond the percentages taken by the agents. The presence of English merchants abroad helped maximise shipping profits in two ways: first, by helping to reduce the time required for loading and discharging the cargo on the outward and return journeys, and second, by organising the chartering of English ships for freight within the Mediterranean. In Venice, where 50 per cent of English trade was in the hands of Italian and Dutch merchants, the English lost not only the 6 per cent commission on imports and exports, but were also disadvantaged in chartering their ships by the direct competition with both Venetian and Dutch merchants.[17]

Direct control of England's trade with foreign countries, both of imports and exports, was essential: Finch was of the opinion that it was necessary to prevent a community of Florentine merchants establishing itself in London, even if they were solely concerned with the trade in Tuscan silk. An opening would thus be created in the tight-knit system

[16] Davis, *The rise of the English shipping industry*, pp. 242, 302–3.
[17] PRO, SP98/5, letter from Sir John Finch, Florence, 13 June 1665; SP98/8, Finch to Arlington, 7 Mar. 1667.

of exchange monopolised by the English, which would in time exclude them from the distribution of silk within England, since Tuscan firms would naturally prefer to send their best material to their fellow-countrymen working in London. At the same time, the Italians would have an opportunity to infiltrate the export trade in English woollens, perhaps with a view to discrediting their quality and introducing Italian textiles in their stead. If such a firm of Florentine merchants were allowed to operate freely in England, Finch continued, it would not only cause serious problems for the English merchants resident in Livorno by reducing their share of the trade-revenue but also remove their role both in the import of Tuscan silk into England and in the export of English woollens into Italy, as the price of the latter would necessarily rise, since it would no longer be exchanged with a local product, making it less competitive against Italian goods.[18]

SILK AND SILK ARTICLES

From the end of the sixteenth century onwards, there was a steady rise in English demand for Italian silks, the consequence of greater and more widespread prosperity together with an enhanced regard for external appearance. The anonymous author of the tract entitled *Britannia Languens* criticises the fashion for foreign silk for its negative effects on the balance of trade:

> The English Formerly wore or used little silk in City or Countrey, only persons of Quality pretended to it; but as our National Gaudery hath increased, it grew more and more into Mode, and is now become the Common Wear, nay the ordinary Material for Bedding, Hanging of Rooms, carpets, Lining of Coaches and other things; and our women, who generally govern in this case, must have Foreign Silks . . . of the humour are the Gallants and such as they can influence; and most others, Our Ordinary Peoplle, especially the Female, will be in Silk, more or less, if they can . . .[19]

The second half of the sixteenth and the first half of the seventeenth centuries saw dress assume the significance of a status symbol in English society; this phenomenon was accompanied by a corresponding and remarkable increase in the demand for foreign silk. Fashions began to change rapidly and unexpectedly and there was a taste for extravagant

[18] PRO, SP98/6, Finch to Arlington, Florence, 8 May 1666; SP98/8, Finch to Arlington, Florence, ? Aug. 1667.

[19] *Britannia Languens, or a discourse of trade: shewing the grounds and reasons of the increase and decay of land-rents, national wealth and strength; with application to the late and present state and condition of England, France, and the United Provinces* (London: 1680), p. 186.

silver and gold embroidery on clothes.[20] The monarchs themselves were not immune: Elizabeth I's customary parsimony was set aside when it came to her clothes, while James I and his son Charles I after him frequently changed their wardrobes. The monarch's tastes set an example for the court, and the fashions thus established circulated more widely as wealth increased among the higher social classes. English men followed fashion as attentively as the women: an unmarried queen courted by suitors and a king with homosexual leanings were both appreciative of well-dressed men and thus encouraged male fashions. Men were frequently the most addicted to silk clothes, embroidery and lace.[21]

After the apparent interruption of this trend with the sobriety of the Commonwealth period, the taste for fashion revived with renewed strength with the return of Charles II from exile in France. The English enthusiasm for foreign fashions is reflected in the new 'comedy of manners': the masterpiece of this genre, written in 1676 by the courtier and playwright George Etherege, is entitled *The man of mode*. The early-eighteenth-century essayist and journalist Richard Steele ridiculed the exaggerations of fashion in the *Tatler*, with an attack on the latest style of skirts, which were worn so wide that it was impossible to get through doorways and required as much material as five ordinary skirts. To illustrate his point that 'there might be more agreeable ornaments found in our own manufacture than any that rise out of the loom of Persia', Isaac Bickerstaffe, the pseudonym used by Steele in his essays, tells the story of a wealthy great-aunt, whose various attempts at marriage are successfully blocked by her family, who, in order not to lose her inheritance, get her to dress in 'a suit of flowered satin' or 'a white sarsenet hood' or 'cherry coloured ribands', with the result that her various suitors are frightened off by the prospect of excessive expenditure.[22]

It is therefore unsurprising that Sir John Banks, foreseeing at least one of the consequences of Charles II's return, should have asked for supplies of silk of all kinds, both in the form of yarn and cloth. When these transactions were nearly concluded, he wrote to his correspondent in

---

[20] L. Stone, *The crisis of the aristocracy 1558–1641* (Oxford: 1967), p. 257. Stone writes: 'Foreign observers like van Meteren were struck by the fashion-consciousness of the English. Tailors anxiously crouched behind the pillars in old St Paul's watching for a new cut of doublet or a novel pair of hose displayed upon the gallants exhibiting themselves in the aisles.'

[21] Ibid., pp. 257–8.

[22] Sir Richard Steele, *The Tatler*, ed. L. Gibbs (London: 1953), 'The case of the petticoat', no. 81, pp. 156ff.; 'Unhappy consequences of women's love of finery', no. 93, pp. 176–9.

Livorno: 'if you have fully invested my effects into silke, I doe hope (if upon reasonable termes bought) will heer turne well to accompt heer being a generall rise in all sorts of that Commodity Especially fine. And in case your Gally from Sicily arrived timely wherby you might furnish yourselves before you had any notice of any rise heer, it may doe very well.'[23]

Several factors made Italy the leading European centre for silk production at the end of the sixteenth century: its industry, in particular its textile industry, was the most advanced in Europe, its raw materials were of the highest quality, and, if necessary, it could easily obtain extra supplies from Spain or the Levant, the other principal producers of raw silk in the Mediterranean.[24] The sixteenth century was a period of success and prosperity for the silk industry in which Italy led the way, not only in the industrial heartland of the north but also in the south, which witnessed an industrial revival which lasted until the middle of the seventeenth century. In Naples, possibly as a result of its vast urban expansion in the second half of the sixteenth century, the production of luxury goods flourished unexpectedly; laces, silks, braids, light cloths, silk cockades in all colours, were fashionable articles in demand all over the continent.

Once the English merchants had eclipsed their Italian counterparts, they continued to obtain supplies of silk and silk articles from both northern and southern Italy. Among the records of transactions concluded by the English merchants in Naples, for example, we find in August 1654 the company 'Lee, Hatton, & Gardiner' making a payment for 'new manufactured silks', black silks, and cloths.[25] In 1669 the firm 'Gould, Broching & Littleton' bought '62 pezzi ritorti', while in 1670 'Gio. Smith, Roberto Foot & Co.' paid a local merchant, Francesco Ventre, 'for several cloths of silk sold to various captains of English ships'.[26]

Significant changes took place in Italian silk manufacture from the 1660s onwards. Venice redirected its production towards the manufacture of articles of higher cost and quality, intended for the German and

[23] KCCRO, Aylesford MSS, U234/B3, Banks to Lytcott & Gascoigne of Livorno, London, 17 May 1660.
[24] Goodman, 'The Florentine silk industry', pp. 79 ff. See also F. Edler de Roover, 'Andrea Banchi, Florentine silk manufacturer and merchant in the fifteenth century', *Studies in Medieval and Renaissance History* 3 (1966), 238.
[25] ASBN, Banco di S. Giacomo, 'giornale copiapolizze' 'matricola 229', partite di ducati 500, del 21.8.1654; di ducati 155 e ducati 500, del 31.8.1654.
[26] ASBN, Banco AGP, 'giornale copiapolizze' 'matricola 429', partita di ducati 6.3.15, del 23.11.1669; 'giornale copiapolizze' 'matricola 442', partita di ducati 121.?.2, 22.11.1670: 'per tanti drappi di Seta venduti à diversi Capitani di navi Inglesi'.

above all Levantine markets where Venetian products still managed to compete strongly against ascendant foreign industries.[27] Venice's special relationship with the Levant is reflected in the way English merchants would buy Venetian damasks only when they needed to send gifts to the Sultan and his officials in order to win Ottoman support.[28]

As imports of silks from Venice began to disappear, there are signs of a lively English interest in Florentine silks, dating back to the 1630s, when the sea routes between northern and southern Europe were beginning to prevail over the traditional land routes and Livorno was emerging as the leading port in the network of Mediterranean trade: in other words, when the volume of trade between England and Italy was growing rapidly. The increase in English imports of Tuscan silk may in part be ascribed to the change of trade route and the frequency of contact with Livorno, but changes within the Florentine silk industry may be more significant. During the first half of the seventeenth century, the Florentine industry gradually abandoned the manufacture of costly and richly designed cloths, characteristic of sixteenth-century production, in favour of plainer and cheaper silks; the trend, in other words, was the opposite of the developments in the Venetian silk-man-ufacturing industry.[29]

The reasons for such radical changes may be found in the report sent to the Venetian Senate by the Republic's Secretary in London, Giro-lamo Alberti, who was of the opinion that luxurious Venetian textiles would not succeed in the English market, and concluded that it was not worth disturbing the prosperous trade with the Levant for one of uncer-tain profit. He regarded the Florentine commercial strategy as mistaken: the city's silks were of inferior quality, and had lost both their reputation and their market, with the result that the city's looms now lay almost completely idle.[30] The English resident Finch had made a similar obser-vation some years before that 'of late the Italians sending silkes of a Worse Fabrique which they could afford at Lower Rates hath occa-sioned the stop of that trade and ceasing all Commissions'.[31] The truth was that while there existed a strong English demand for silk, it was for silk of average quality; the industry in Florence had adapted itself to this demand, lowering the quality of its product and probably managing to absorb the English orders which during the first half of the century had

---

[27] CSP Venetian, 1671–3, 4 Nov. 1672, pp. 309–10.
[28] PRO, SP105/113, 180, letter from the Levant Company to Hales & Hobson in Venice, London, 19 June 1668. See Pagano de Divitiis, 'Il porto di Livorno'.
[29] Goodman, 'The Florentine silk industry', pp. 49–51.
[30] CSP Venetian, 1671–3, 4 Nov. 1672, pp. 309–10.
[31] PRO, SP98/8, Finch to Arlington, Florence, ? Aug. 1667.

Table 4.5 *Florentine silks, March 1663*

	Number of pieces	Percentage
Rasi (= satins) (black, coloured, plain and patterned)	347	34.9
Ermesini (= sarsenets) (black, coloured 'a Fiorentino, Lucchese, Genovese')	308	31.0
Taffeta (black, coloured)	192	19.3
Tabi (= tabby, silk taffeta) (black, coloured)	54	5.4
Cataluffe (black, coloured with patterning)	32	3.2
Damaschi (= damasks) (black, coloured)	23	2.3
Saie (black, coloured)	12	1.2
Dobbletti (black, coloured with patterning)	9	0.9
Filatucci (black, coloured)	4	0.5
Zenzadi (black, coloured)	4	0.5
Grosse Grane (= grosgrain) (black, coloured)	2	0.25
Manti (black, coloured)	2	0.25
Baiette (black)	2	0.25
Zetani (black, coloured with patterning)	2	0.25
Brocatelli (= brocades) (coloured)	1	0.1
Total	994	

Source: Goodman, 'The Florentine silk industry in the seventeenth century', figure 11, p. 52. English equivalents, where these exist, are given in parentheses.

been met by the manufacturing industries in southern Italy. Alberti writes that 'only light silks are sent to England'.[32]

If we analyse the variety of silks produced in Florence, we can note that taffetas, sarsenets, and satins, the cloths most in demand in England, account for 85.2 per cent of local production in 1663, an indication that the city's silk industry was almost entirely geared to meeting the demands of the English market (table 4.5).[33] The decision of Venice to follow a diametrically opposed manufacturing policy, together with its veto on the export of silks to England, can be seen as a protectionist move, designed to avoid the pressures which Florence faced and to combat the likelihood of competition from the new English silk industries, which could supply the market with counterfeit Venetian textiles, as had happened in the woollen trade in the Levant, with damaging economic consequences. By improving the quality of its products, Venice further widened the gap which already existed between English and Italian silk production. The strategy of closure was, moreover, in accor-

[32] CSP Venetian, 1671–3, 18 Nov. 1672, pp. 315–16: 'vengono inviate in Inghilterra solo sete leggere'.

[33] PRO, SP98/8, memorandum from Finch to Grand Duke, 24 Nov. 1667; Goodman, 'The Florentine silk industry', p. 35.

dance with Venetian commercial policy as a whole, which, as we have seen, was designed to limit as far as possible English intervention in the Republic's trade and conserve what remained one of its key industries. Florence, on the other hand, by reducing drastically the production of higher-quality silks, which was more labour-intensive and time-consuming to produce, aimed at lowering the cost of manufacture in order to compete more effectively against its rivals, including perhaps those in the south, which produced silks of average quality. Finding itself excluded from the markets of northern Europe, southern Italy turned to Spain, from where its silks were most probably re-exported to the colonies in the New World.[34]

The silk manufacturing industries of Florence employed unskilled labour for the most part; when English orders dried up in the 1660s on account of the great plague, the city's poor went hungry, an indication of how vital the English market was to the economy of the Tuscan state.[35]

Exact figures for English imports of Florentine silks are lacking; however, it is justifiable to assume that they accounted for over half of the city's total production.[36] Bearing this in mind and working on the basis of the production figures provided by Goodman for the city's silk industry in the period between 1608 and 1739, a plausible estimate would be that in the 1660s and 1670s English merchants imported approximately 6,000 pieces of silk each year from Florence (table 4.6).

If we examine the figures for Italian silk imports into England for the years 1663 and 1669 (tables 4.8 and 4.9), we can observe the beginning of a trend which was to develop throughout the rest of the century. There is a gradual reduction in the import of manufactured articles and a corresponding increase in the import of thrown silk or silk yarn; such an increase was probably related to the rise of the English silk industry, which succeeded in dominating the domestic market in the sixty or so years between the 1660s and the 1710s.[37]

The English had been quick to discover how to spin the raw silk they imported from the Levant and the Far East, and in London a company of 'Silk throwers' was duly established. An Act of Parliament at the end of the century had sought to promote and support the industry by banning the import of thrown silk from abroad with the exception of Italian organzine silk.[38] The Italians had kept the secret of spinning

---

[34] BNN, MSS xi, D, 18.
[35] PRO, SP98/6, Finch to Arlington, Florence, 29 Sept. 1665.
[36] PRO, SP98/8, Finch to Arlington, Florence, 22 Nov. 1667.
[37] P. Earle, *The making of the English middle class: business, society and family life in London, 1660–1730* (London: 1989), pp. 18–21.
[38] PRO, SP104/98, 'An account of the King of Sardinia's prohibiting the exportation

Table 4.6 *Production rates of the Florentine silk industry, 1608–1739*

Year	Number of pieces
1608 April–March	10,306
1618 April–March	9,293
1628 April–March	9,769
1638 April–March	9,995
1647 April–March	10,276
1648 April–March	9,781
1649 April–March	8,689
1650	8,706
1653 January–December	9,583
1654 January–December	10,947
1662	10,416
1665	10,177
1673 January–December	11,478
1738	15,516
1739	15,509

Source: Goodman, 'The Florentine silk industry in the Seventeenth Century', figure 8, p. 35; Goodman has taken his figures until 1673 inclusive from ASF, Miscellanea Medicea, n. 994 (vecchio), and for 1738 and 1739 from ASF, Carte Bartolomei, n. 214, ins. 57.

organzine silk over many generations; to reveal the technique was a crime punishable by death. Since it was indispensable for English weavers, who used it, in combination with silk yarn from the Levant and the Far East, to form the warp, the English had no choice but to import it from Italy already spun. Thomas Lombe wrote in 1722:

> Organzine Silk (here commonly called Italian Thrown Silk) is made out of Raw Silk, by Winding, Spinning and Twisting it. Of this Silk is annually Imported (and for the most part consumed in England) about 12 or 15,000 Bales, and the Quantity every yeare increasing bought in Italy at high Rates with ready Money, or sent by the Italians to be sold here for their own Account, which cost the Nation above £100,000 per annum more than the same quantity might be Imported for in the Raw Silk, Employs no Silk Throwers here, nor any of our poor to Wind Spin or Twist it, but has been hitherto brought from Italy ready worked and fitted for our Weavers use, for want of the Art of doing it here.[39]

At the time Lombe was writing, organzine silk was imported into

of raw silk, with a brief state of the silk trade in England. Humbly offered to the right honourable the Lord Viscount Townshend', undated document, possibly written September 1722. According to Thomas Lombe, the Act of Parliament is '2nd William & Mary, Chap: 9'.

[39] Ibid.

England principally from Piedmont, Bologna or Bergamo, but in the 1660s and 1670s imports were still largely of Sicilian provenance; Sicilian organzine was essential for the Genoese silk industry, as it had been for its Tuscan counterpart until the beginning of the century. In England there was also a demand for other types of silk yarn produced in southern Italy – the so-called *seta in peli in 50* and *in 40*, as well as the cheaper *seta matazella* and *seta cusirini*, large quantities of which were normally exchanged for woollens supplemented by small amounts of cash to make up the price.[40]

Imports of Italian as opposed to Levantine raw silk remained low until the end of the seventeenth century, although the two kinds were not in direct competition; Italian raw silk was of better quality and greater strength, and catered for a different market.[41] The raw silk which was imported into England was used largely in the manufacture of small articles such as stockings, ribbons, braiding and trimming, etc. Venice, as we have seen, was opposed to the export of its own silk cloth into England, but was disposed to supply the English market with the raw silk produced on its mainland territories, especially since the end products did not threaten Venetian manufacture. Alberti suggested switching such exports from the land routes via Bologna to the sea routes, which would bring the Republic greater profits from customs duties and increase the activity in its port.[42]

From 1668 onwards, the English also began to buy raw silk and silk yarn from Piedmont. Finch had been sent samples of Piedmont silk by his correspondent in Turin; he had had them examined by local experts in Tuscany, although he did not reveal where he had obtained them. The experts thought it was from Bologna, the type and quality most in demand on the English market at the time. The price was particularly advantageous, since '. . . silke altogether consists of the Labour of the Poor, and where they are many and live cheap as in that country, they can Worke at Easy rates'.[43]

Silk ribbons, trimmings and hems, used to add a touch of luxury to middle-class dress, were made in England from the 1660s onward and, in the context of the domestic market, probably replaced the previous imports of such items from southern Italy. Occasionally, the articles manufactured by the English, such as silk stockings, won new markets abroad – in 1627, 'silk stockings from Naples' were still being exported from Livorno for England, but forty years later in 1665 we find English silk

---

[40] ASBN, accounts of the English merchants resident in Naples.
[41] See Davis, *Aleppo and Devonshire Square*, chapters 8 and 9, in particular pp. 136–7.
[42] CSP Venetian, 1671–3, 18 Nov. 1672, p. 316.
[43] PRO, SP98/9, Finch to Arlington, 29 May 1668.

stockings arriving in Italy. England was quick to protect its products on the Italian market: it prevented one George Floxe or Flush, a London-based silk weaver, from setting up a small firm in Livorno in partnership with several Frenchmen, including a certain Robustell, to make silk stockings. They had petitioned the Grand Duke to grant them the monopoly of such production and to ban the import of similar products: the English resident commented:

> the very introduction of the fabrick simply without the exclusion of others, would be notably prejudiciall and therefore I have made severall Contrivances to prevent the English weavers' alienating that Trade from England; but if my designs should be ineffectuall, It were more than ne-cessary that he should be commanded home and in such case I would demand him of the G. Duke, and at worst cheat him aboard some English vessell, and send him home.[44]

Unlike the manufacture of small silk articles, which, as we have seen, were being successfully exported by the 1660s, the production of silk cloth was only then just beginning. This sector of the English textile industry was greatly stimulated by the arrival of the Huguenots from France in 1685 after the revocation of the Edict of Nantes and by the imposition of exorbitant customs duties on the importation of French silk, yet it was not until the 1720s that English production of silk cloth was sufficiently great to meet most of the domestic demand.

From the beginning of the eighteenth century, raw silk and silk yarn formed the steadily increasing bulk of Italian exports of silk products to northern Europe, while silk cloth gradually disappeared. Silkworm farming in Italy was also affected by great changes in this period: the principal areas for the cultivation of mulberry trees and silkworm farming moved northwards, from Sicily and Calabria to the Veneto and Piedmont; by the end of the eighteenth century, these two Italian regions accounted for two-thirds of all European production, i.e. approximately 7,000,000 lbs.[45]

CURRANTS AND OLIVE OIL

After 1570 there was a large increase in English imports of Italian agri-cultural products, especially currants and olive oil, both from the

[44] PRO, SP98/6, Finch to Mr Godolphin, Florence, 29 Dec. 1665. Sir William Godol-phin (1634?–1696) was a member of the Royal Society and an ambassador; in 1667 he was sent to negotiate the commercial treaty of Madrid. In 1668 he was knighted. In 1669 and 1671 he returned to Spain, on the first occasion as a special ambassador and on the second as permanent ambassador. He converted to Catholicism during a serious illness; although he was recalled to England in 1678, he chose to remain in Spain.
[45] Aymard, 'La transizione dal feudalismo al capitalismo', pp. 1150–1.

Adriatic regions of the country. The English demand for currants continued to grow until the end of the seventeenth century. It has been calculated that English imports of currants at the end of the sixteenth century amounted to 2,300 tons, the maximum limit set by the Levant Company, a figure which remained in force until 1633 and was calculated on the basis of the English market's capacity to absorb the supply. A crisis affected the market in 1660 or thereabouts, provoked by the extortionate taxes and demands of the Venetians, but a recovery was rapidly under way by 1663.[46] Some historians maintain that the quantity of currants imported between 1600 and 1640 quadrupled.[47] The high demand from northern Europe led the countries and regions which produced and exported currants, Zante above all, to adopt a single-crop system of cultivation; this resulted in overproduction and a swift reduction in prices, which meant that the same amount of money fetched ever larger quantities.

Although the figures relating to the second half of the century (table 4.7) are incomplete and merely indicative, they nevertheless show that during the course of the century imports doubled while their value halved. In the forty years from 1660 to the end of the century, it appears that English imports accounted for 70 per cent of the production of the 'currant islands'.[48]

Strange as it seemed to some, the English used currants exclusively for culinary purposes. At the beginning of the century we can already find some Englishmen criticising their fellow-countrymen for their inability to 'digest breads, pastries, broth and bag-puddings without those currants',[49] while a document dating from the end of the century declared that the 30 per cent of total currant production which remained after the English had taken their supplies was distributed throughout northern Europe by the Dutch and in Italy and southern Germany by the Venetians 'in all Which places this Comodity is Imployed in Apothecaries shopps not in Cooks shopps and Kitchings as here in England . . .'[50]

As we have said, English ships sailing to the Mediterranean followed two different routes from Livorno. The larger merchant ships continued

---

[46] Wood, *A history of the Levant Company*, pp. 24, 70. See also CSP Domestic, 1591–4, ?.(May).1592, p. 227; CSP Venetian, 1661–4, 21 Aug. 1661, p. 32; 2 Sept. 1661, p. 36; 30 Dec. 1661, pp. 88–9; 28 Apr. 1662, pp. 135–6; 8 July 1662, pp. 159–60; 19 Jan. 1663, p. 227; 3 Mar. 1663, p. 233; 8 Nov. 1663, p. 268; PRO, SP105/149, 60–1.

[47] Davis, 'England and the Mediterranean', p. 72.   [48] PRO, CO388/1, 75–82.

[49] W. Lithgow, *Travels and voyages* (1609)(Leith: 1814), p. 56; S. Richardson (ed.), *The negotiations of Sir T. Roe in his embassy to the Ottoman Porte, from the year 1621 to 1628 inclusive, containing . . . his correspondence* (London: 1740), pp. 10–11.

[50] PRO, CO388/1, 75.

Table 4.7 *Imports of currants*

Year	Tonnage	Sterling per ton	Total value ($£$)
end 1500 (1)	2,300		
1663 (2)	1,573 approx.	44	69,232
1669 (2)	1,999 approx.	44	87,963
1690 (3)	3,000	23–4	70,000
1700 (4)	4,000	10–11	41,400

Sources: (1) Wood, *A history of the Levant Company*, p. 24. (2) BL, Add. MSS 36785. These figures have been taken from the section on English imports from Turkey and therefore include currants coming from Zante, as well as small quantities from other islands and the Morea. According to an estimate taken from a document dating from the end of the seventeenth century (PRO, CO388/1, 75v), England imported 250 tons of currants from the Morea or 5 per cent of the 5,000 tons from the 'currant islands'. The figures for these two years refer only to arrivals in the port of London and do not include imports arriving in Bristol (according to the agreement of 1632, these must have amounted to 200 tons annually: see McGrath, 'Records relating to the Society of Merchant Venturers of the City of Bristol' in McGrath (ed.), *Bristol Record Society*, vol. XVII, pp. 215–16). In the original document the quantities of currants are calculated in hundredweights or 'cwt.'; these have been converted to tons in the table. (3) PRO, CO388/1, 78ff., *Mr Dodington's Papers. The Turkey Company's Opinion concerning the Current Trade*. There is another report from the same period (PRO, CO388/1, 75ff.), in which the imports of currants are estimated to be 5,000 tons, as opposed to 7,000 tons from the Ionian islands: at $£25$ per ton, this gives a total value of $£125,000$. I have preferred to use the figures given in the Levant Company document because they largely match the figures given in Hubland and Gold's report from the same time: this puts a value of $£69,000$ on English imports of currants (PRO, CO388/1, 8off.). (4) PRO, CO388/9,7344ff. In this document it is claimed that projected expenditure for the purchase of 4,000 tons of currants was $208,000, the equivalent of $£46,800$ ($1 = 54 d/pence), with a unit cost of $52/ton = $£12/ton; this was reduced to $46/ton = $£10$–$£11$/ton with the unexpected abundance of that year's crop.

on to Zante for currants, while the smaller vessels sailed to the Puglian ports, in particular Gallipoli, to collect the olive oil which the English merchants resident in Naples had bought in readiness for the ships' arrival. The figures we possess for this trade do not allow us to draw definite conclusions, only general indications. From tables 4.8 and 4.9, concerning imports arriving in the port of London in 1663 and 1669, it can be seen that the value of imports of olive oil comes third in position after silk and currants; moreover, 1669 shows a notable increase over the earlier year. There are no figures for imports in Exeter; they probably started to arrive only at the end of the century when the city saw a revival of its export trade to the Mediterranean.[51] Information is simi-

---

[51] See Hoskins, *Industry, trade and people*, pp. 94, 99; and Stephens, *Seventeenth-century Exeter*, pp. 116, 177.

Table 4.8 *Italian imports arriving in the Port of London ,1663*

Goods	Quantities	Unit cost (£ s d)	Total value (£ s d)	Percentage
Manufactured silk	47,072 lbs	2.05.00	105,912.00.00	29.95
Thrown silk	61,596 lbs	00.20.00	61,596.00.00	17.42
Raw silk	23,506 lbs	1.05.00	29,382.10.00	8.31
'Capitall silk'	140 lbs	1.10.00	210.00.00	0.05
	132,314 lbs		197,100.10.00	55.73
Glasses	6,464 dozen	00.06.00	1,939.04.00	
Lenses	289 dozen	12.00.00	3,468.00.00	
Spectacles	1,471 dozen	00.15.00	1,103.00.00	
Glass beads	36 gross	00.12.00	21.12.00	
Glass necklaces	363 gross	1.15.00	635.05.00	
			7,167.01.00	2.02
Venetian gloves			62.08.00	
Brooms			20.00.00	
Paper			266.10.00	
			348.18.00	0.09
Whole coral	2,357 lbs	1.10.00	3,535.10.00	
Pieces of coral	2,360 lbs	00.02.06	295.00.00	
	4,717 lbs		3,840.10.00	1.15
Olive oil	1,422 tons	32.00.00	45,504.00.00	12.87
Currants	31,469 cwt	2.04.00	69,231,16.00	19.58
Total			323,192.14.00	

Industrial products = 32% approx.

Source: BL, Add. MSS 36785. In the original, currants are listed among imports from Turkey.

larly sparse for Bristol, where annual imports of oil, much lower than those in London, must have amounted, in the 1660s, to approximately 500 tons each year, in line with an overall downward trend caused by the decline in the west of England's textile industries and the concentration of the soap-manufacturing industry in London.[52]

As far as the beginning of the import trade in Italian olive oil is concerned, Davis is of the opinion that this got under way only towards the 1630s, a half-century later than the 'currants' trade and then grew steadily for the rest of the century, coming to replace Spanish and Portuguese supplies almost entirely.[53] It is true that in the years leading up to 1630, as we have seen, Italy replaced Spain as the centre of English commercial interests and the port of Livorno emerged as the main entrepôt

[52] *Merchants and merchandise*, Appendixes G, H, I, pp. 284, 286, 288.
[53] Davis, 'England and the Mediterranean', p. 136.

Table 4.9 *Italian imports arriving in the Port of London, 1669*

Goods	Quantities	Unit cost (£ s d)	Total value (£ s d)	Percentage
Manufactured silk	39,457 lbs	2.05.00	88,778.05.00	22.68
Thrown silk	87,216 lbs	1.00.00	87,216.00.00	22.28
Raw silk	14,563 lbs	1.05.00	18,203.15.00	4.65
	141,236 lbs		194,198.00.00	49.61
Glasses	5,980 dozen	00.06.00	1,794.00.00	
Spectacles	587 dozen	00.15.00	440.05.00	
Glass necklaces	801 gross	1.15.00	1,401.15.00	
			3,636.00.00	0.92
Brooms			15.00.00	
Paper			87.10.00	
			102.10.00	0.02
Whole coral	5,821 lbs	1.10.00	8,731.10.00	
Pieces of coral	3,768 lbs	00.02.06	471.00.00	
	9,589 lbs	00.02.06	9,202.10.00	2.25
Olive oil	2,278 tons	32.00.00	72,896.00.00	18.62
Currants	39,983 cwt	2.04.00	87,962.12.00	22.47
Total			367,997.12.00	
Industrial products = 23.63% approx.				

Source: BL, Add. MSS 36785.

for northern European ships plying the Mediterranean routes.[54] However, English imports of olive oil go back far beyond the 1630s, the only difference being that formerly English ships would sail to Venice for Puglian olive oil, as they did for currants, and not directly to the regions which produced these commodities. While Puglia, unlike Zante or Cephalonia, belonged not to Venice but to the Spanish viceroyalty of Naples, it was in the nature of things part of the commercial sphere of the Venetian Republic. Venice had always regarded the eastern coast of southern Italy, with its access to the Adriatic routes, as of vital strategic importance; on two occasions, in 1495 and again in 1528, the Republic had occupied the Puglian ports with military force.[55] The region was a highly important source of foodstuffs and raw materials, such as the olive oil which was used in the Venetian textile industry and in the manufacture of soap.[56] In the closing decades of the sixteenth century, after peace had been concluded with Turkey, Venice played an

[54] Taylor, 'Trade, neutrality, and the "English road"', 248–9.
[55] G. Pagano de Divitiis, *Il napoletano Palazzo di Venezia* (Naples: 1980), pp. 32–3; N. Nicolini, 'Il consolato generale veneto nel Regno di Napoli', *Archivio storico per le province napoletane*, n.s. 13 (Naples: 1927), 59–119.
[56] Rapp, *Industry and economic decline*, p. 275.

active role in the revival of Mediterranean trade; the increase in the imports of olive oil, rising from 10,000,000 lbs a year in the period 1580–5 to 15,000,000 lbs in the period 1592–8, was part of this revival. The supply of olive oil was almost exclusively from Puglia; half was destined for re-export, while the rest was for domestic consumption: 33 per cent for soap manufacture, 11 per cent for food, and 6 per cent for the textile industry.[57]

A proportion of the re-exported product must have found its way into the holds of English merchant ships sailing in the Adriatic, since as early as 1583 we find Elizabeth I granting a six-year patent to members of the Venice Company, which gave them the monopoly of imports of currants, wine and oil from Venice. This group of merchants was subsequently incorporated into the Levant Company, who were, however, no longer allowed to levy direct duties on the imports of these goods from Venetians and English merchants who did not belong to the Company.[58] Evidence that the English were trying to circumvent Venice in obtaining supplies of currants and olive oil dates from the beginning of the seventeenth century.[59]

In 1625 the Venetian government introduced a new tax on oil, which was doubled in the following year; it proved a highly damaging move for the city's commercial interests, since the ships which had until then sailed to Venice now preferred to continue on to other ports. There was, in addition, an outbreak of plague in 1629–30, which led to an exceptional dearth of oil in the city, since no Venetian ships were allowed to land in Puglian ports for fear of spreading contagion. The epidemic reduced the city's population and brought about a standstill in the local textile and soap-manufacturing industries, with a consequent reduction in the demand for oil to less than half of what it had been in the preceding period.[60] These years also saw a great proportion of the trade which had hitherto passed through Venice transfer to Livorno. In 1629 the Venetian ambassador in London complained to the Senate that 'the few remaining pockets of English trade in Venice' had moved to Livorno.[61]

Until this period currants had been purchased in Venice, but from 1630 onwards ships began to sail directly to the 'currant islands', in particular to Zante, where local factors or correspondents settled, who came

---

[57] S. Ciriacono, *Olio ed Ebrei nella Repubblica veneta nel Settecento* (Venice: 1975), p. 15; D. Sella, *Commerci e industrie a Venezia nel secolo XVII* (Venice: 1961), pp. 132–4.

[58] Wood, *A history of the Levant Company*, pp. 18–20, 35–6. See above, pp. 6–7.

[59] CSP Venetian, 1607–10, 20 Mar. 1609, pp. 246–7.

[60] Ciriacono, *Olio ed Ebrei*, pp. 17–18.

[61] Wood, *A history of the Levant Company*, p. 66. CSP Venetian, 1629–32, p. 116.

to replace Venetian merchants entirely, and where two consuls acting
on behalf of the Levant Company were appointed in 1636.[62] The same
changes can be found occurring in the oil trade. In 1635, there were
complaints in Venice that the sheer number of English merchant ships
loading oil in Puglia was causing problems of supply.[63] The nature and
effect of these changes can be seen in a Venetian official document
dated August 1636 which declares that:

> Representations have often been made of the hurt done to the customs
> by goods brought by ships from the West coming to lade oil in Apulia,
> *which first came here*. With regard to the measures to be taken in order to
> induce English and Flemish ships to come to this city and to encourage
> trade, be it resolved that for two years the oil brought to this city for the
> West, Flanders and England be free of all *export duty*, and that it pay the
> same import duty as the oil of the Levant, which is only two thirds that
> paid by oil of Apulia. That oil not exported within the term of four
> months and eight days shall pay the entire import duty and shall only be
> exempted from the export duty. That those who export the oil shall
> leave a pledge that it is to be taken to the countries aforesaid.[64]

We find a similar change if we look at Venetian commerce from a
Neapolitan perspective. In the first half of the seventeenth century, an
English document declares that the kingdom of Naples 'has abundant
supplies of corn, oil, wine and silk. There is much maritime trade with
the Venetians, and strong ties exist between them and the people of
Calabria and Puglia.'[65] Yet in 1689, in a memorandum presented to the
Viceroy, the English consul in Naples remarks that 'although Venice
once took large quantities of oil from these regions [i.e. the provinces of
Bari and of Lecce], today little is taken'.[66] By this period the import of
oil from Puglia was in the hands of the English merchants resident in
Livorno working in collaboration with their agents in Naples.

Despite this trend, the Venetians made a further attempt in 1672 to
attract the trade in Puglian oil for northern Europe back to Venice by
offering special tariff exemptions and benefits for the cargoes destined
for England, Flanders, Holland and Hamburg. In the same year Aloisio
Morelli, an 'agent of the English merchants', is recorded as loading a
cargo of olive oil on the English ship *Sommissione*, without having to

[62] Davis, 'England and the Mediterranean', p. 136; see also above, p. 110.
[63] CSP Venetian, 1632–6, 24 Mar. 1635, p. 353.
[64] CSP Venetian, 1636–9, 2 Aug. 1636, p. 36.
[65] PRO, SP93/1, 130, 'Sommario della relazione del Regno di Napoli': 'grande abbon-
danza di grano, olio, vini e sete. Commercia molto per mare con i Veneziani, a cui
le popolazioni della Puglia e della Calabria sono molto affezionate'.
[66] PRO, SP93/3, 6, 'Raggioni . . .', cited in note 6: 'benché Venetia estraheva quantità
di detti ogli da esse provincie hoggi è poca l'estrattione che ne fanno'.

pay the full rate of customs duty.[67] These facilities did encourage a partial return of such trade to Venice – small Venetian coasters started to work the Adriatic and in the late 1690s, when English imports of olive oil from Venice were valued at £1,000, we find the city's merchants beginning to undertake consignments directly.[68]

A large part of the trade in olive oil remained tied, however, to Livorno; as it had already done for the consignments of corn which arrived in the town, the Tuscan port sought to construct the storage facilities which would make it a great entrepôt for Mediterranean oil. In 1698 building was started on the so-called 'Bottini dell'Olio' a construction which housed about 200 slate-lined cisterns, capable of storing up to 15,231 barrels of oil, situated near to the dockyard to which it was connected by a network of canals.[69] The German traveller Martini had visited the building during his stay in Livorno in 1725–7 and wrote about it in his account of the town: 'The traveller who wishes to gain an idea of what is involved in wholesale trade or of the efforts made by the Grand Duke to transform Livorno into a suitable centre for such trade by building storage facilities for merchandise, should visit the town's vast warehouse for storing oil.'[70]

About a third of the oil imported by the Venetians was used in the manufacture of soap. During the fifteenth century Venice had superseded Spain as Europe's leading producer of the so-called 'Castiglione' soap, which, being hard, white and perfumed, was sold as a luxury commodity in the countries of northern Europe, including England, where the locally manufactured soap was made with animal fats and was soft, dark and malodorous as a result. The Venetians used olive oil from Puglia instead of tallow, and in place of potash imported a particular type of ash, rich in soda, from Syria, which made the soap solid and easy to perfume with various fragrances.[71] Venetian soap manufacture remained for a long time one of the Republic's leading export industries, until the seventeenth century, when emigrant Venetian artisans

---

[67] CSP Venetian, 1671–3, 14 May 1672, p. 209.

[68] Ciriacono, *Olio ed Ebrei*, p. 21.

[69] G. Piancastelli Politi, 'I Bottini dell'Olio' in *Livorno: progetto e storia di una città*, pp. 341–50. The building's façade bears the following inscription: 'Ne quid in hoc Mediterranei emporio subditorum indigentiae, aut mercatorum comoditati deesset Cosmus III Magnus Aetruriae dux, pubblica olei receptacula, princeps providentissimus, magnifice extrui jussit, an. salut. MDCCV.'

[70] Ibid., p. 347; the document is kept in ASL, Biblioteca Manoscritti, f. 106. Georg Christoph Martini, author of *Reise von Rom nach Livorno und durch Toscana*, also made a drawing of the interior during his stay in Livorno (see Piancastelli Politi, 'I Bottini dell'Olio', pp. 347–9).

[71] Lane, *Venice: a maritime republic*, pp. 160–1.

were attracted to the better economic conditions in Genoa and Livorno and took with them the secrets and techniques of their trade, with the result that the two cities were able to compete with Venice.[72] In all probability Bristol may also have been involved in the industrial espionage of Venetian processes; as we have seen, Bristol was the first English port to establish trading contacts with the Mediterranean area and between the sixteenth and seventeenth centuries the city had seen a growth in the import of luxury goods from Spain and the rest of the Mediterranean world.[73] The history of the soap-manufacturing industry in the city was doubtless influenced by these contacts. The first appearance of such activity in Bristol dates back to the 1200s and a certain Richard of Devizes; 'Bristol soap' ('grey soap' and 'black soap') is also mentioned in an early official document.[74] No further information is available until 1618, when the city authorities tried to enforce the exclusive use of olive oil in the manufacture of soap, on pain of a penalty ranging from a £10 fine to imprisonment. The nineteenth-century local Bristol historian John Latimer describes the requirement as 'an outrageous attempt to promote the interests of merchants trading to Southern Europe': it was withdrawn after a month, only to be reintroduced five weeks later. Latimer thought the order was still scandalous, since this second enforcement raised the penalty to £40 and was based on the false assumption that olive oil was the only fat used by honest workmen in the manufacture of soap. The regulation clearly proved difficult to enforce, for in 1624 a new decree was issued, which reduced the fine for non-compliance by two-thirds.[75] This series of measures would seem to indicate that a policy was beginning to emerge in Bristol during the early decades of the century to produce soap which could satisfy the demands of the domestic market for luxury goods, in direct competition with Mediterranean imports, and that, in order to achieve this goal, the same raw materials which were used in the Italian industry were required in England.[76]

The Bristol soap industry soon came into conflict with the interests of London financiers, who were beginning to invest their capital in consumer industries such as soap, beer, sugar, glass, etc.[77] Yet it appears

---

[72] Rapp, *Industry and economic decline*, pp. 8–9, 36; Rapp, 'The unmaking of the Mediterranean trade hegemony', 510.

[73] Sachs, 'Bristol's "little businesses" ', 88, 90.

[74] H. E. Matthews (ed.), *The Company of Soapmakers, 1562–1642*, Bristol Record Society, vol. x (Bristol: 1940), p. 4.

[75] J. Latimer, *The annals of Bristol in the seventeenth century* (Bristol: 1900), p. 67.

[76] *The Company of Soapmakers*, pp. 236–7.

[77] Latimer, *The annals of Bristol*, pp. 121 ff. See C. Wilson, *England's apprenticeship 1603–1763* (London: 1965), pp. 9, 83.

from remarks made by the contemporary observer John Houghton that a similar shift to using Italian raw materials in the manufacture of soap can also be found in London. In the 1630s whale-oil, much cheaper than olive oil, was still being used to make soap which could certainly not compete with the imported Italian product, yet the decade also sees a series of arguments between the 'Soap-Patenteas' of Westminster and the 'Soap-Boilers' of London which led to a ban on the use of fish-oil in the manufacture of soap.[78]

By the second half of the century, it was fully acknowledged and accepted in Italy that 'no other oil apart from olive oil' could be used either in the manufacture of soap or in the textile industries.[79] For the latter, olive oil was second in importance only to wool itself as a raw material; whereas Genoa and Florence could rely on local production, Venice was obliged to import it either from the eastern Mediterranean or, more usually, from Puglia. Lombard and German merchants, as we have seen, would then be supplied from the oil which Venice chose to re-export.

Oil was used in the treatment of wool before it was spun; it was essential in the combing of worsteds and in the carding of woollens.[80] As Houghton explains, writing at the very beginning of the eighteenth century, oil was used to treat the raw wool so that 'the Hairs shall not entangle or curle one with another, but may be drawn out at length to shew its staple, and also to be more ready for spinning'.[81] The quantity of oil used depended on the quality of the cloth which was to be produced and on the raw wool which went to make it. In the Veneto, for example, four parts of wool required on average one part of oil, to which one part of soap had to be added for every sixteen parts of wool.[82] The importance of oil in the textile industry is indicated by the way each increase in the duty on oil was directly reflected in the final cost of the manufactured cloth: the constant rise in the prices of Venetian woollens from the 1620s onwards is usually ascribed to the increases in duty on oil, which became for the wool-workers one of the principal items of expenditure in the whole manufacturing process.[83]

---

[78] Houghton, A Collection, 26 Apr. 1700.

[79] D. Grimaldi, Memoria sulla economia olearia antica e moderna e sull'antico frantojo di olio trovato negli scavamenti di Stabia (Naples: 1783), p. 34: 'altra qualità da olio; fuorché quella che si ricava dalle ulive'.

[80] R. de Roover, 'A Florentine firm of cloth manufacturers : management and organisation of sixteenth-century business' in J. Kirshner (ed.), Business, banking and economic thought in late medieval and early modern Europe: selected studies of Raymond de Roover (Chicago: London: 1974), p. 94. See also the introduction to K. G. Ponting (ed.), Baines's account of the woollen manufacture of England (New York: 1970), p. 38.

[81] Houghton, A Collection, 26 Apr. 1700. [82] Ciriacono, Olio ed Ebrei, p. 151.

[83] Ibid., p. 20; Rapp, Industry and decline, p. 180.

The English tried to replace olive oil with cheaper kinds, such as rapeseed oil, but, although it was useful for lighting, it proved disastrous in the wool industry. The factor in Livorno for the English company, Fairfax & Barnsley, wrote to his London partner that 'There is no marvel why the worm breeds in cloths for, since the planting of rapeseed in England, the clothiers have got a trick to mix that oil with olive oil and the first will never scour out, which, lying long packed, breeds a worm.'[84]

Puglian oil was not as refined as the oil from Lucca, Genoa or Provence, but it was better than Calabrian oil, which was used almost exclusively in the soap-manufacturing industries of Marseilles; as the best available ordinary oil made in Italy, the Venetians chose to acquire it as the most appropriate product for use in their textile and soap industries. Puglia was also the only region which consistently produced a surplus of oil, thus guaranteeing supplies to the countries which needed to import it.[85]

The English focused their commercial interests increasingly on Puglia from the 1630s onwards, to Spain's disadvantage. From the figures in table 4.10, which relate only to imports of olive oil into London during the 1660s, it can be seen that while the quantity of imports of Spanish oil remained significant, they were overtaken by the Italian product, despite the identical unit cost of oil in both countries and the greater proximity of Spain. Other factors, apart from the quality of Italian oil, lay behind the English preference for the Puglian product.[86] The quality of Puglian oil was familiar, since it had been used for so long and so successfully by the Venetians. By taking most of the oil produced in Puglia for its own industries, England was competing directly with Venice for supplies of raw materials. With oil in short supply, Venice was forced to turn to the poorer quality oil from the Morea and the Greek islands.[87] Apart from currants, Puglian oil was the only return cargo which Italy could supply in abundance: 'oil . . . fills the ships' holds, and makes it easier to transport other goods', as a Venetian document from the mid eighteenth century puts it.[88] The circuit of which Livorno and Naples

---

[84] PRO, SP46/84, 188, letter from John Fairfax to George Warner, Livorno, 10 May 1642.

[85] G. Palmieri, *Pensieri economici relativi al Regno di Napoli* (Naples: 1789), pp. 35, 40.

[86] See G. Palmieri, *Osservazioni su vari articoli riguardanti la pubblica economia* (Naples: 1790), pp. 83, 116.

[87] PRO, SP93/3, 6, 'Raggioni. . .'

[88] ASV, Cinque Savii alla Mercanzia, Consoli, 163, letter from G. Michiel and G. F. Hamman to the 'Deputati del Commercio', 20 Sept. 1749, quoted in R. Romano, 'Il Regno di Napoli e la vita commerciale nell'Adriatico' in R. Romano (ed.), *Napoli: dal Viceregno al Regno*, p. 137: 'L'Oglio dà il pieno ai Bastimenti; et facilita il traffico delle altre generi'.

Table 4.10 *Imports of olive oil arriving in the Port of London*

Country	1663			1669		
	Tonnage	Sterling per ton	Total value (£)	Tonnage	Sterling per ton	Total value (£)
Italy	1,422	32	45,504	2,278	32	72,896
Spain	718	32	22,976	2,558	32	81,856
Portugal	897	32	28,704	245	32	7,840
	Average 1663–1669					
Italy	1,850	32	59,200			
Spain	1,638	32	52,416			
Portugal	571	32	18,272			

Source: BL, Add. MSS 36785

formed part continued to operate. Purchases were agreed in Livorno, with the oil, together with *seta cuserina* from southern Italy, normally being exchanged for English woollens, a transaction which functioned both as an advantageous method of payment and as a way of promoting exports.[89]

The division between the north and the south of Italy thus continued to exist under a somewhat different guise: the south of the country remained a source of raw materials and at the same time provided a market for the goods imported from foreign countries, while, with the presence of the English, northern Italy saw its former role as the country's centre of industrial production marginalised to that of mediation.

[89] ASBN, Accounts of English merchants in Neapolitan public banks, *passim*; PRO, CO388/9, 388.

CHAPTER 5

EXPORTED GOODS

LEAD AND TIN

La Rondine, the first English ship to arrive in Livorno on 25 June 1573, was not carrying goods which were new to Italy. The goods which comprised its cargo – bells, whole or in fragments, tin, lead, wool, kerseys, and a few woollens – were familiar items to the Italian markets, previously exported to Italy overland or in the holds of Venetian and Ragusan ships.[1] What occurred in the 1570s was simply a change in the means of transport. Before the war with Turkey in 1571–3, Venetian merchants traded with northern Europe: each year five or six ships would set out from Venice for Cephalonia, Zante and Candia, where they would buy currants and wine to take to England, from where in turn they would fetch kerseys, woollens, tin and other commodities. In the 1580s, on the other hand, English ships traded directly with the islands under Venetian rule, and, with the active participation of the islanders, bought currants and new wines in exchange for cloth, tin and silver.[2]

The tin mines of Devon and Cornwall had enabled England to enjoy a centuries-old monopoly in the supply of the metal to the continent. Even in the mid fifteenth century, when all Mediterranean trade was under the control of Italy, exports of tin and raw wool and imports of wine remained firmly in the hands of English merchants.[3]

Exports of English lead were still negligible in the 1530s, but conquered the European markets from the 1580s onwards.[4] The dissolution

---

[1] Braudel and Romano, *Navires et marchandises*, p. 50.
[2] Braudel, *La Méditerranée*, vol. I, p. 562.
[3] Clay, *Economic expansion and social change*, vol. II, pp. 104, 106.
[4] I. Blanchard, 'English lead and the international bullion crisis of the 1550s' in D. C. Coleman and A. H. John (eds.), *Trade, government and economy in pre-industrial England: essays presented to F. J. Fisher* (London: 1976), p. 21.

of the English monasteries, initiated under Henry VIII in 1536, resulted in vast quantities of lead from the destroyed buildings flooding the European markets and led to a sudden reduction in prices in England. In an attempt, therefore, to lower the costs of production, new techniques for the extraction and fusion of the metal were introduced, first in the Mendip mines and then throughout the country. In 1564 the national market for lead was once again thriving; the expansion in trade in the years from 1564 to 1579 brought with it a rapid increase in the exports of lead, at first from Bristol and later from London. By 1580 the sources of the supply of European lead had undergone a fundamental shift from the centre to the periphery, in other words, from central Europe, which had dominated the market for lead from medieval times onwards, to England.[5]

In the two centuries between 1500 and 1700 there was a notable increase in the production of lead and tin. The annual production of tin stood at 600 tons in 1500; this rose to 800 over the period 1525 to 1550, and had reached 1,870 tons a hundred years later. Lead production showed an even steeper increase over the same span of time, from 625 tons in 1500 to 28,000 tons in 1705–6.[6]

These two branches of the English mining industry depended heavily on foreign demand and on the markets of southern Europe and the Mediterranean region in particular.[7] According to Braudel, the Dutch were drawn to the Mediterranean by its need for corn, whereas the English returned to the area because of the high demand for lead and especially tin.[8] There was a strong need for both metals in the countries of the western and eastern Mediterranean. Two English vessels were forced to land in Marseilles in 1590 simply because the city urgently needed the cargoes of lead and tin which they were carrying. Bernardino de Mendoza, the Spanish agent in England, was of the opinion that the Sultan showed such hospitality to the English because he was interested in their exports of tin, which had started to reach Turkey a few years before. At the time Mendoza was writing, five merchant ships were anchored in the Port of London waiting to set sail for the Levant with a cargo of tin worth 20,000 crowns. The European need for armaments and munitions lay behind this widespread demand.[9] Tin was an important component in the manufacture of bronze cannon, which were then beginning to replace the old cannon made of iron, and lead was needed for bullets. In 1565, no fewer than 200 quintals of lead were

---

[5] Ibid., pp. 33–6.   [6] Clay, *Economic expansion and social change*, vol. II, p. 58.
[7] Ibid., pp. 106–8.   [8] Braudel, *La Méditerranée*, vol. I, pp. 560–6.
[9] Ibid., vol. I, pp. 560–6, 622–8.

bought for the ammunition on the ship *La Goletta*.[10] In August 1663 an English merchant sold 2,000 pigs of lead to the Papal State, which was preparing for armed conflict with France; they were sent, at immense cost, along the River Arno from Livorno to Florence, and then loaded on to mules to be carried to Bologna.[11]

Apart from its military uses, lead was also required in the production of pewter and in building work, where it was used in the manufacture of tiles, piping and glass for window-panes, as well as for decorative fittings and in coloured paint. The quantities of lead needed to make tiles or water-pipes were disproportionately large: more than 50 kilogrammes of refined lead were needed for 1.5 metres of piping; a ton of lead covered less than 6 square metres of roof. Tin also had other functions: it was used in the production of objects made of bronze and good quality pewter, in the casting of bells as well as of printing type.[12]

England's strong position in the supply of these metals to the continent was due in part to the increase in production which followed on the introduction of technical innovations and in part to a reduction or containment of costs relative to those of European production, a state of affairs which was maintained throughout the seventeenth century.[13] English supplies of lead and tin were especially advantageous because of the low cost of the outgoing transit goods, which, owing to the lack of competition, amounted to less than half the cost of incoming goods.[14] Lead and tin also helped to fill the half-empty holds of the ships bound for the Mediterranean for valuable cargoes. Unlike other standard English exports, a cargo of lead or tin helped to ballast the ships in the water.[15] Detailed figures on the quantities of lead and tin exported to Italy are unavailable; our figures for exports from the Port of London for the years 1663 and 1669 (table 5.1) show that the two metals taken together accounted for 13.12 per cent and 16.66 per cent respectively of total exports in those two years, with more lead exported than tin. Despite the lack of figures, it is certain that the two metals were important exports in England's trade with Italy. In the 1660s, lead always formed part of the cargoes of the ships arriving in the port of Livorno; a report from the English consul in the city speaks of the arrival 'of eyght

[10] Ibid., vol. II, p. 858.
[11] PRO, SP98/4, Kent to Williamson, Livorno, 3 Aug. 1663.
[12] Clay, *Economic expansion and social change*, vol. II, pp. 57–9.
[13] Blanchard, 'English lead', p. 34; PRO, SP98/8, memorandum from Finch to the Grand Duke, 24 Nov. 1667.
[14] PRO, SP98/7, 'An exact accompt . . .', 8 Dec. 1667.
[15] Davis, *The rise of the English shipping industry*, pp. 180, 229.

Table 5.1 *Exports of English woollens and metals to Italy from the Port of London, 1663 and 1669*

Goods	Unit cost in £sd	1663		1669	
		Quantity (pieces)	Value (in £sd)	Quantity (pieces)	Value (in £sd)
Serges & perpetuanas [a]	3.00.00	18,820	56,460	26,160	78,480
Norwich stuffs	2.10.00	4,741	11,852.10.00	9,556	23,890.00.00
Minikin, Bayes	7.00.00	1,871	13,097.00.00	1,586	11,102.00.00
Bayes double	6.00.00	1,198	7,188.00.00	1,650	9,900.00.00
Bayes single	2.15.00	1,262	3,470.10.00	1,120	3,080.00.00
Kerseys	1.10.00	1,740	2,610.00.00	1,004	1,506.00.00
Long cloths	12.00.00	1,500	18,000.00.00	1,393	16,716.00.00
Short cloths	8.00.00	1,010	8,080.00.00	1,203	9,624.00.00
Spanish cloths	14.00.00	250	3,500.00.00	450	5,740.00.00
North dozens (double)	10.00.00	24	240.00.00	107	1,070.00.00
North dozens (single)	5.00.00	10	50.00.00		
Devon dozens	2.10.00	35	87.10.00		
Cloth rashes	3.10.00	170	595.00.00		
Pennistones	4.10.00	45	202.10.00		
		32,676	125,433.00.00	44,229	161,108.00.00
Tin	3.15.00	2,404cwt.	9,015.00.00	2,326cwt.	8,722.10.00
Lead	11.00.00	1,763 'ffodder'	19,393.00.00	1,716 'ffodder'	18,876.00.00
			28,408.00.00		27,598.10.00
Total value			153,841.00.00		188,706.10.00

Note: [a] The names of the different cloths are listed as they appear in the original.
Source: BL, Add. MSS. 36785.

English ships with leade and fish, this week hath brought ten more with same Cargoe al in Safety . . . we yet want other two but doe heare of the miscarriage of none, they Come al to very Good occasion and have brought near 5000 piggs leade'.[16]

In the export of these two metals, London was of secondary importance to the provincial ports, where they were normally taken on board.[17] Tin was mined in Cornwall and was loaded on occasion at Falmouth and Plymouth, together with pilchards; more frequently, ships would leave London carrying pepper, woollens, sugar, lead, etc. and then call at the ports along the southern coast to make up their cargoes

[16] PRO, SP98/8, Chellingworth to Arlington, Livorno, 7 Feb. 1667.
[17] PRO, SP98/4, 291, Kent to Williamson, Livorno, 7 Jan. 1664. See also Clay, *Economic expansion and social change*, vol. II, pp. 107–8.

with consignments of fish and tin.[18] Most English merchant ships carried lead and herrings to Italy, the herrings coming to London from Yarmouth.[19] Lead was mined in many parts of the country; cargoes of it were loaded in London and other ports, Bristol in particular, which supplied Spain with lead for the whole of the sixteenth century and where the export trade in this commodity was flourishing in the 1660s.[20] The merchant ships which set out from Bristol for Newfoundland carried cargoes of lead as ballast on the outward journey across the Atlantic and sold it on when they finally reached the Mediterranean;[21] the practice continued later when their transatlantic voyage took them to Barbados for sugar rather than to Newfoundland.[22]

FISH

Fish was a cargo which, to an even greater extent than lead and tin, left from provincial ports and for which as a result it is difficult to evaluate the quantity and the value of exports. The only source on which it is possible at present to base an estimate of the importance of fish to the English export trade are the figures for the three years from 1699 to 1701 drawn up by Ralph Davis. These show that English exports of food products amounted to 11 per cent of the total export trade; fish accounted for 39 per cent of this amount, making it the principal exported food product, and 4.28 per cent of the overall figure (table 5.2). However, these figures do not include Newfoundland cod, which, according to an estimate for the year 1706, would have had an annual value of £130,000.[23] Yet it is certain that English exports of fish to Italy during the seventeenth century were far more important than these limited figures might suggest, although only an approximate quantification and evaluation of this branch of England's trade with the Mediterranean can be attempted.

By using figures which refer to the same period of time, and assuming that there were no marked variations in the volume and the value of these exports over that period, if we take Finch's calculation that

[18] PRO, SP98/8, Chellingworth to Arlington, Livorno, 28 Mar. 1667; list of arrivals in the port of Livorno, 11 Jan. 1672.
[19] PRO, SP98/8, Dethick to Williamson, Livorno, 17 Jan. 1667; 24 Jan. 1667; list of arrivals in the port of Livorno, 14 Dec. 1667, 16 Dec. 1667, 18 Dec. 1667.
[20] PRO, SP98/8, list of arrivals in the port of Livorno, 18 Dec. 1667; Blanchard, 'English lead', pp. 22, 24.
[21] Davis, The rise of the English shipping industry, p. 205.
[22] PRO, SP98/9, Dethick to Williamson, 12 Mar. 1668.
[23] Clay, Economic expansion and social change, vol. II, p. 152. See also H. E. S. Fisher, The Portugal trade: a study of Anglo-Portuguese commerce, 1700–1770 (London: 1971), p. 17.

Table 5.2 *Domestic exports from England, average of 1699–1701*

	Sterling	Percentage
Woollens	3,045,000	68.7
Other manufactures		
Metal goods	114,000	
Leather	87,000	
Silks	80,000	
Hats	45,000	
Fustians	20,000	
Miscellaneous	192,000	
Total	538,000	12.1
Food stuffs		
Fish	190,000	
Grain	147,000	
Refined sugar	32,000	
Butter	21,000	
Miscellaneous	98,000	
Total	488,000	11.0
Raw materials		
Lead	128,000	
Tin	97,000	
Coal	35,000	
Skins	24,000	
Salt	20,000	
Miscellaneous	58,000	
Total	362,000	8.2
Grand total	4,433,000	100.0

Source: Clay, *Economic expansion*, vol. II, table 14, p. 145. Clay has taken the figures from Davis, 'English foreign trade 1660–1700' and 'English foreign trade 1700–1774'. Figures rounded up to nearest 1,000.

exports of herrings to Italy in 1667 amounted to 11,000 barrels, and match this figure up with the price which we know was current in Venice in 1672, £2 4s, we obtain a total value of £26,400. This figure represents approximately 6 per cent of the total value of exports from London in 1667.[24] It must be remembered that this figure is for herrings only; it does not include the pilchards which came from ports on England's southern coast, Irish salmon, or the Newfoundland cod brought over by the ships from Bristol (table 5.3).

As far as figures for English production are concerned, if we take Michell's calculation that in the 1660s 3,500 lasts constituted an average quantity of cured herrings, each last comprising 12 barrels, we have a

[24] PRO, SP98/8, Finch to Arlington, Livorno, 18 Apr. 1667; CO389/5, 34 ff., 1672.

Table 5.3 Exports of English fish to Venice

Year	Ships	'Fish ships'	Total exports (£)	Value of fish (£)	Percentage
1672	20	(11)	58,200	14,700	25
1690[a]	12–14	7–8 (58%)	60,000–70,000	(16,000 approx.)[b]	(25)
1690[c]	27	11 (41%)	160,900	15,500	9.63
1690[d]		5–6	24,000	12,000	50

Types of English fish exported to Venice in 1672 (£1 = 5 ducats)

Quantity (barrels)	Quality	Unit cost (ducats)	Total cost (ducats)	Total cost (£)	Percentage
3,000	herrings	12	36,000	7,200	49
1,667[e]	pilchards	15[f]	25,000	5,000	34
500	salmon	25	12,500	2,500	17
5,167			73,500	14,700	100

English exports to Venice in 1672

Commodity	Quantity	Unit cost (ducats)	Total value (ducats)	Total value (£)	Percentage
Fish	5,167 barrels	12–25	73,500	14,700	25
Lead	3,000 pigs	1,400 per 100	42,000	8,400	15
Sugar	1,000 chests	100	100,000	20,000	34
Pepper	600 sacks	60	36,000	7,200	12
Various	100 bales		40,000	8,000	14
			291,000	58,200	100

Notes: [a] There are three different estimates for the year 1690: this figure is taken from f. 78 under the heading 'The Turkey Company's Opinion concerning the currants Trade'.
[b] This figure is calculated as 25 per cent of the total value.
[c] F. 80, 'Mr. Hublands & Mr. Golds Papers in Answer to Mr. Dodingtons concerning the Venice Trade'.
[d] F. 75, untitled.
[e] In the original document, the quantity is '1,000 hogsheads': this is equivalent to 278 tons which equals 1,667 barrels.
[f] The original price was 25 ducats per hogshead.
Source: PRO, CO389/5, 34–5, for figures relating to 1672; PRO, CO/1, 75–82, for figures relating to 1690. Deduced figures in parentheses.

total of 42,000 barrels of herrings, of which the 11,000 barrels exported to Italy in 1667 represent 26.19 per cent. Thus more than a quarter of the total English production of smoked herrings in this period was destined for the Italian market, a clear indication of its importance to the trade.[25] This is confirmed by the fact that at Yarmouth herrings were

[25] Michell, 'The European fisheries', p. 170.

prepared with special care for the Italian market, and were known as 'Leghorn red herrings'. In January 1703, Houghton writes that the herrings were in general 'perfected in the Space of a Month, for the sale at Home, but for those that are design'd for the Streights or Mediterranean six weeks are required'.[26]

When, in October 1660,[27] John Banks was negotiating the purchase of 300 barrels of herrings to be sent to Livorno, he urged his correspondent in Yarmouth to make sure that the fish was conserved and prepared in the appropriate way for Livorno and the other Italian markets, an instruction he reiterated a month later in another letter.[28] When his ship failed to meet up in the 'Downs' with the boat from Yarmouth carrying the barrels of herrings which he had ordered, he wrote to the captain of the *Virgin* with the instructions that if he called at Dover, he was to load 'what herring you can So as you be Sure they be well cured and fitt for Leghorne markett, whereof you must be very carefull or our money is as well in the kennel'.[29]

It seems probable that while the export trade in English fish to Italy was not particularly significant in terms of its value, it was notable for the numbers of English ships which were engaged in it. Out of the twenty English ships which are registered as arriving each year in Venice in the 1670s, the majority were 'fish ships', with only two or three carrying sugar from Lisbon.[30] Towards 1690 a contemporary estimate calculates that out of the twelve to fourteen English ships arriving each year in Venice, four or five were chartered to carry sugar from Portugal, while seven or eight were carrying cargoes of fish to an approximate value of £10,000; the rest had cargoes of lead, tin, pepper, cotton, sugar, ginger, skins and woollen cloth amounting to a value of £60,000–70,000 (table 5.3).[31]

Fish was a useful export, in that, like lead and tin, it filled the holds of the ships and gave them greater stability; it also served to offset the overall lack of national products which could be exported to Italy, a shortage which was a constant feature of English trade with the Mediterranean throughout the seventeenth century. Banks wrote to his factors in Livorno in August 1661 with the news that 'the "Virgin" hath bin ready these 20 days to proceed for ffish but as yett very few Pilchards

[26] Houghton, *A Collection*, 15 Jan. 1703.
[27] KCCRO, Aylesford MSS, U234/B3, Banks to Thomas Gooch, London, 21 Sept. 1668.
[28] Ibid., 16 Oct. 1668.
[29] Ibid., Banks to Captain Thomas Hendra, London, 26 Oct. 1660.
[30] PRO, CO389/5, 35, petition of George Hayles, English consul in Venice, 1672.
[31] PRO, CO388/1, 78, 'Mr Dodington's papers – The Turky Companys opinion concerning the currant trade', c. 1690.

taken as we despaire of her lading therefore doe intend her to you and she will soone be Dispatched with few goods'.[32] Throughout the century fish remained a key commodity in England's export trade. In an article on how to increase English exports, John Houghton illustrated the different types of fish and the methods used in their conservation, and then suggested that the consumption of foreign commodities needed to rise in order to export a larger quantity of domestic products – English merchants would seek out new markets and would sell more fish, amongst other English products, in exchange for the goods which they imported.

Michell observes that the discovery of the market of Livorno was more significant for the expansion of the English fishing industry than Cecil's introduction of 'fish days'. Once it had established contact with Spain and Italy, the English fishing industry adopted the competitive strategy of 'economic warfare' which had been used in the textile industry, driving out traditional suppliers by offering similar products at lower prices, and on occasion resorting to physical aggression in the process. The south-western English ports won back control of the Newfoundland cod trade, which had first been discovered and then abandoned by English ships from Bristol, with a strategy of continual piratical attacks on the Spanish and Portuguese fishermen who had taken it over in the absence of the English. The red herrings prepared in Yarmouth were not completely unfamiliar to the Italian market, but replaced products formerly supplied by the French fishing industry; in Yarmouth itself the technique of smoking herrings was thought to have originated in Calais.[33] The pilchards from Plymouth were able to compete directly with Mediterranean pilchards, which they resembled in appearance and for which the same technique of salting was employed.[34]

Fishing was regarded in England as a highly profitable economic activity and as such was the object of much government attention from Elizabethan times onwards. The industry began to be seen in the second half of the sixteenth century as a kind of training school for sailors and its fleet as a reserve of ships which could be used in case of international conflict. From the 1570s onwards, a policy was followed which tended to exclude all foreign intervention and to encourage the use of English ships for the export of fish.[35]

Unlike Venice and Genoa, which distributed their supplies of fish to

[32] KCCRO, Aylesford MSS, Banks to Lytcott & Gascoigne, London, 22 Aug. 1661.
[33] Michell, 'The European fisheries', pp. 154, 157, 178.
[34] Houghton, A Collection, 5 Feb. 1702; 29 Jan. 1702.
[35] Harper, The English navigation laws, pp. 29–31. The 1651 Navigation Act restricted

the local market in the city and the surrounding areas, Livorno kept only a small proportion of the fish which came into the port for local consumption. It distributed the fish either overland to Lombardy or by sea to central and southern Italy. English merchants regarded both Milan and Naples, which functioned as centres of distribution for their own surrounding regions, as highly important markets; Houghton asserts that the interruption in exports to these two cities brought about by the war had created serious problems for the domestic fishing industry.[36]

In view of the time-consuming complexity of the distribution routes throughout Italian territory and the perishable nature of the product, it was the prime responsibility of the English merchants resident in Livorno to ensure that the fish was distributed swiftly. They therefore availed themselves of the services of correspondents who acted as wholesalers in the various Italian centres for the trade and who in their turn ceded the consignments 'on commission' to local merchants.[37] As has been described,[38] the majority of the 'fish ships' tended to arrive in Livorno, a phenomenon which damaged English trade by leading to a sudden saturation of the market and a consequent collapse in prices. In 1667, for example, nineteen 'herring ships' are registered as arriving in Italy: of these, three had gone straight to Genoa, one to Venice, one to Naples, one to Civitavecchia, while the remaining thirteen had all gone to Livorno, oversupplying the local market and drastically reducing profits.[39] A more balanced distribution of fish among the various Italian ports was therefore thought desirable and a company was established not in order to create a monopoly but with the sole purpose of regulating the fish trade and its price structure in the Italian market. As Finch wrote, 'fish is a merchandise (especially Herrings and Pilchards) that endures in this Country but for three moneths; and there being a necessity of a quick vent, if there be not in the severall places a fitt distribution there's a necessity of losse'.[40]

In order to create a more efficient distribution of fish in Italy, therefore, it was first necessary to reorganise the routes taken by the 'fish ships': the first moves in this direction were taken in the 1660s, and included the appointments of English consuls in Naples, Civitavecchia,

the export of fish to English ships; the 1660 Act maintained the liberalisation which had begun under the Commonwealth.

[36]   Houghton, *A Collection*, 14 May 1703.
[37]   ASBN, Banco di S. Giacomo, 'giornale copiapolizze' 'matricola 393', partita di ducati 126.1.16 del 2.9.1676.
[38]   See above, p. 62.
[39]   PRO, SP98/8, Finch to Arlington, Livorno, 18 Apr. 1667.
[40]   PRO, SP98/8, Finch to Arlington, Florence, 13 June 1667.

Messina, Trapani and Gallipoli. At the same time an increasing number of merchant ships sailed directly to the ports south of Livorno. Among these there was, for example, the *Civitavecchia*, which was carrying 993 barrels of herrings to Timoteo Hatton in Naples,[41] and the *Hannibal*, which left part of its cargo of pilchards, woollens, lead, pepper, etc. in Livorno before continuing on to Naples, Messina and Scanderoon.[42] Banks likewise displayed his customary shrewdness when, in December 1660, on the eve of sending a ship with a consignment of 1,000 barrels of smoked herrings in his name and that of his partners Gyles Lytcott and Thomas Hill, he advised his correspondents in Livorno to divert the ship's destination to Civitavecchia if they thought this an advantageous move. He had given the same advice regarding a consignment of 420 barrels of salmon four months earlier.[43]

One problem in organising the distribution of fish was the strict health regulations, which required each ship to present a 'patente' or bill of health on arrival declaring that it came from a port which was free of infection, what type of cargo it was carrying, the number of people on board and so forth. Only by presenting this 'patente' for inspection were the crew allowed to disembark and start unloading the cargo. If the number of persons on board registered on the 'patente' did not correspond with the number counted on arrival, permission to berth was withheld. Similarly, some categories of merchandise were subject to quarantine, for the duration of which they were transferred to the local lazzaretto; woollen cloth was included among these, and always had to be stored away for a period in order to be 'purged', but all types of conserved fish, for which the term 'salumi' was curiously used, were exempt from such a requirement.[44]

In the autumn of 1665, in the immediate aftermath of the great plague of London, the English export trade in fish had to confront the likelihood that its ships would not be given the *pratica* or permission to

---

[41] ASBN, Banco di S. Giacomo, 'giornale copiapolizze' 'matricola 315', partita di ducati 846.2.5 del 6.4.1667; 'giornale copiapolizze' 'matricola 314', partita di ducati 215.?.16 del 15.4.1667.

[42] PRO, SP101/77, Livorno, 11 Jan. 1668; SP101/76, Livorno, 6 Nov. 1668; SP101/98, Livorno, 28 Dec. 1674; SP98/8, Dethick to Williamson, Livorno, 19 Dec. 1667; list of arrivals in the port of Livorno, 16 Dec. 1667; Chellingworth to Arlington, Livorno, 19 Dec. 1667; 2 Jan. 1668.

[43] KCCRO, Aylesford MSS, U234/B3, John Banks, Gyles Lytcott and Thomas Hill to Lytcott & Gascoigne of Livorno, London, 3 Dec. 1660; Banks to Lytcott & Gascoigne of Livorno, London, 24 Aug. 1660.

[44] See C. Ciano, 'La sanità marittima nell'età medicea', *Bollettino storico pisano*, *Collana storica*, vol. xv (Pisa: 1976). The use of the term 'salumi' to cover all types of conserved fish, including smoked fish, derived from the fact that the most familiar method of conservation was salting, as with Newfoundland cod or with meat.

unload their cargoes when they arrived in Livorno in the following spring. This would have slowed down the whole distribution process considerably and threatened the entire annual export of fish. The health authorities in Livorno were slow to reach a decision. A memorandum was presented to the Grand Duke in which it was made clear that any possible closure of the Tuscan port to the 'fish ships' would be highly damaging both to the subjects of the Grand Duke and to the town of Livorno itself. It was pointed out that the Spanish King had promised the English ambassador that 'permission to disembark is now freely given to all ships from Scotland and Ireland and shall likewise be extended to all ships from England carrying consignments of "salumi" or other goods which are not normally subject to quarantine'.[45] Genoa would willingly accept the English ships if they were turned away from Livorno. Moreover, the voyage from England was a long one and took place during the winter; consignments of preserved fish had never hitherto been subject to quarantine.[46]

With these arguments in his favour and despite the negative decision of the Viceroy of Naples, Cardinal d'Aragona, who had ignored the directives of his own master, the Spanish King, and closed the southern ports to English ships, including Gallipoli with its supplies of olive oil, the English resident in Livorno obtained permission to unload all the fish which had just arrived in the port on the 'fish ships' under the escort of Sir Jeremy Smith. The Grand Duke's concession gladdened and astonished the English merchants in Livorno, who had not expected him to give way.[47] Permission to land was even extended to the ship *The Brothers*, which was carrying a cargo of 500 barrels of pilchards and had been refused entry into the port of Naples because the number of men on board did not match the figure given on the 'patente'.[48]

In the following year an argument arose between the English and the health authorities in Livorno when it was discovered that the English ships had tried to circumvent the ban on the import of animal skins by concealing them among the fish. The authorities had ordered that all imported barrels of herrings were opened and placed in quarantine, which would inevitably have spoilt the merchandise, since the fish

---

[45] PRO, SP98/6, memorandum from Finch to the Grand Duke, Florence, 4 Oct. 1665: 'che tutti li vascelli che vengono di Scotia ò d'Irlanda hanno di haver prattica libera ed il simile per tutti li vascelli che vengono d'Inghilterra carichi di salumi, o altre mercanzie negl'altri tempi non sottoposte a Lazaretto'.
[46] Ibid.   [47] PRO, SP98/6, Finch to Arlington, Pisa, 8 Feb. 1666.
[48] PRO, SP98/6, Dethick to Williamson, Livorno, 1 Mar. 1666; ASN, Fondo Notai, notaio Hieronimo de Roma scheda n. 1214/4, 100v.–101, 'Protestatio pro Thimoteo Hacton', 11 Feb. 1666. See above, pp. 60, 109.

could not be supplied from Yarmouth quickly enough to allow for such a long delay in distribution within Italy.[49]

As we have seen, herrings were the main type of fish exported from England to Italy. For the most part they came from Yarmouth, where the annual catch took place in September and October; small quantities of herring were also found in the ports along the southern coast. Pilchards were found, as Houghton wrote, 'In the Sea, near the extream Parts of Cornwal, about the towns of Pensance and St Iv's, and also along the South Shoar, even to Devonshire';[50] unlike herrings, they were not smoked but salted and pressed, nor did their export to Europe have to take account of competition from Dutch exporters. Limited quantities of salmon were also exported; like the herrings from Yarmouth, the salmon was brought down from Scotland to London and loaded on to the merchant ships bound for the Mediterranean. As we have seen, Irish salmon was fetched from local ports in Ireland by Bristol merchant ships and carried directly from there to southern Europe.[51] Finally, it should not be forgotten that although Newfoundland cod was caught in remote waters, it was nevertheless an integral part of the English fish trade in the Mediterranean region.

Inevitably there has been speculation as to why Italy, which should have been capable of supplying itself, needed to import such vast quantities of fish. The explanations which have been advanced range from the growing depletion of fish stocks in Mediterranean waters to a sudden increase in the population of southern Europe. What is clear is that Italy remained heavily dependent on supplies of English fish throughout the seventeenth century.[52] In February 1653 the Venetian resident in Naples wrote that the Anglo-Dutch war had created problems for the city's supply of fish: its population 'suffers from time to time in the matter of feasts and fast days as happened recently with the capture of an English ship which was on its way to these waters with a cargo of Lenten comestibles'.[53]

With the disappearance of the Catholic obligation to fast in England, it is probable that a surplus of fish was created which found an outlet for distribution in the continental markets, especially in southern Europe where such religious rules not only persisted but were growing stronger in contrast to the Protestant nations of northern Europe. It has been said that the English returned to the Mediterranean in order to satisfy the

[49] PRO, SP98/8, Finch to Arlington, 28 Feb. 1667; 7 Mar. 1667.
[50] Houghton, A Collection, 29 Jan. 1702.
[51] Michell, 'The European fisheries', p. 166.
[52] CSP Venetian, 1653–4, 18 Feb. 1653, p. 27.
[53] PRO, SP101/83, Notice from Venice, 18 Mar. 1673.

European demand for munitions on the one hand and the hunger on fast-days on the other.[54] In this connection it has been observed that in the coral-fishing colonies established by Marseilles on the coast of North Africa the third main item of expenditure after oil and wine was salt fish, reflecting both the strict observance of the religious rules which required the consumption of Lenten fare on many occasions throughout the year, and the scarcity, high cost and greater perishability of meat.[55]

Italy, with its innumerable churches, convents, monasteries, religious colleges and seminaries, together with the vast Papal court and an almost entirely Catholic population, was undoubtedly an attractive market for the English fishing industry. It is a pleasing historical irony that the red herrings of Yarmouth, one of the most fervently Puritan of English towns, found their way on to the dining tables of the Pope and the College of Cardinals in Rome, although it should not conceal the underlying and more serious observation that the cost of preparing and transporting herrings made them too expensive a dish for the poorest sections of the population.[56] Such an observation contrasts with Finch's words to the Grand Duke, when he stressed that the Italians were able to buy from the English essential products at a lower price, such as lead, tin and 'that little salt fish, they cannot do without unlesse theyr poor suffer'.[57] Yet the problem should perhaps be seen not so much in terms of the class divisions of seventeenth-century Italian society as in terms of the distinction between the country's urban and rural populations.

WOOLLEN CLOTH

Unlike the products of the mining and fishing industries, which originated for the most part from provincial ports and made up the bulk of English exports in terms of volume, woollen textiles were exported largely from the port of London and comprised the most valuable commodity in the English export trade. Cloth by itself might not serve to fill the holds of the merchant ships, but it made up their cargo and was the most important item they carried in terms of the country's balance of trade with the continent. As the figures in tables 5.4 and 5.5 show, textiles were the most significant English export throughout the seventeenth century, and their total value rose steadily. On the proportion of

---

[54] Braudel, *La Méditerranée*, vol. I, p. 566.
[55] P. Masson, *La Compagnie du Corail: étude historique sur le commerce de Marseille au XVIe siècle et les origines de la colonisation française en Algérie, Tunisie* (Paris, Marseilles: 1908), p. 93.
[56] Michell, 'The European fisheries', pp. 172, 177.
[57] PRO, SP98/9, memorandum from Finch to the Grand Duke, 24 Nov. 1667.

Table 5.4 *Commodity structure of English exports in the seventeenth century*
(£000)

	London			England
	1640	Average		Average 1699–1701
		1663–69	1699–1701	
Woollens:				
'old draperies'	582 ⎫ 1,097	1,512	2,013	⎰ 1,284
'new draperies'	515 ⎭			3,045 ⎱ 1,761
Other manufactures	⎱ 31	222	420	538
Foodstuffs	⎰ 60	62	138	488
Raw materials		243ᵃ	202	362
Total	1,188	2,039	2,773	4,443

Note: ᵃ Exports of lead in 1663 were particularly high.
Sources: Clay, *Economic expansion*, vol. II, pp. 143–4. Clay bases his figures on those provided by Fisher, 'London's export trade in the early seventeenth century'; Gould, 'Cloth exports, 1600–1640'; Davis, 'English foreign trade 1660–1700'.

Table 5.5 *Commodity structure of English exports in the seventeenth century*
(percentage)

	London			England
	1640	Average		Average 1699–1701
		1663–69	1699–1701	
Woollens:				
'old draperies'	48.9 ⎫ 92.3	74.2	72.6	⎰ 29.0
'new draperies'	43.3 ⎭			68.7 ⎱ 39.7
Other manufactures	⎱ 2.6	10.9	15.1	12.1
Foodstuffs	⎰ 5.1	3.0	5.0	11.1
Raw materials		11.9ᵃ	7.3	8.2
Total	100	100	100	100

Note: ᵃ Exports of lead in 1663 were particularly high.
Sources: Clay *Economic Expansion*, vol. II, pp. 143–4. Clay bases his figures on those provided by Fisher, 'London's export trade in the early seventeenth century'; Gould, 'Cloth exports, 1600–1640'; Davis, 'English foreign trade 1660–1700'.

the English export trade represented by textile products, it should be observed that the leading position occupied by woollen cloth remains constant but at the same time shows signs of gradual but inexorable decline. The role played by London in this branch of English trade also shows variations over the course of the century. Up to 1750, London increased its share of the export trade in textiles from 60 per cent to 90 per cent, a near monopoly; by the end of the century, however, this had been reduced to 72.6 per cent, owing to the re-emergence of provincial ports such as Exeter and Bristol.[58]

Turning now to the intended markets for English woollen cloth (table 1.2), we can see that during the first half of the century the traditional markets of northern continental Europe were replaced by those of southern Europe: by the 1640s demand for English woollens in the two markets was almost equal, but twenty years later, in the 1660s, acquisition in southern Europe exceeded that in the north (table 1.2). The concentration in London of the Mediterranean export trade in woollens continued until the end of the century, while exports of textiles and of other goods from the rest of the country returned to the traditional northern European outlets as a result of the revival in trade between ports on the English southern coast and the Atlantic coast ports on the continent.[59] Italian ports were not entirely unaffected by this revival in the export trade from the English 'outports' at the end of the seventeenth century,[60] but it remained restricted in scope. The export of English textiles to Italy stayed largely in London under the control of the Blackwell Hall and Leaden Hall merchants.[61]

The re-opening of commercial contacts with the Mediterranean region at the end of the sixteenth century and the peace treaty signed with Spain in 1604 gave the export trade in English textiles, which in the markets of northern Europe was beginning to stagnate, an opportunity to diversify and expand. In pre-industrial England, the textile industry still operated essentially as a craft, and there was no possibility of lowering the market price of the product by reducing labour costs; the only way for the industry to expand was to seek out new products and new markets rather than attempt to increase demand in its traditional ones. A first step in this direction had been made with the substitution of manufactured articles for raw wool, demand for which was tied to a limited number of markets in Flanders and northern Italy. Yet by the end of the sixteenth century the English textile industry was once again confronted with the problem of market saturation.[62]

---

[58] A. L. Beier and R. Finlay, 'Introduction: the significance of the metropolis' in *London 1500–1700*, p. 15; Dietz, 'Overseas trade', pp. 119, 130; Clay, *Economic expansion and social change*, vol. II, p. 151; Ramsay, *The Wiltshire woollen industry*, p. 119. See also Hoskins, *Industry, trade and people*, and Stephens, *Seventeenth-century Exeter*.

[59] Hoskins, *Industry, trade and people*, p. 70; Stephens, *Seventeenth-century Exeter*, p. 103.

[60] Stephens, *Seventeenth-century Exeter*, p. 116.

[61] See Jones, 'The "hallage" receipts', 567–8; woollen cloth was exported via the London market of Blackwell Hall. After the city of Norwich had resisted sending its textiles to Blackwell Hall, in 1631 it was decided to sell the 'old draperies' at Blackwell Hall and the 'new draperies' at Leaden Hall (ibid., 575–6). See p. 113.

[62] Fisher, 'London's export trade', 156–7.

The appearance of kerseys, woollen cloths which were both lighter and inferior in quality to the broadcloths which were exported semi-finished by the Merchant Adventurers to the markets of northern Europe, and in particular Antwerp, signalled an important advance in the English textile industry's attempt to diversify and expand.[63] Kerseys were sold mostly in Antwerp to Italian merchants who re-exported them to the Levant. Yet neither broadcloths nor kerseys were suitable for the new markets of Spain and Italy; it was English contact with these new regions which stimulated the production of new textiles, the so-called 'new draperies', which were more appropriate for the climate of the Mediterranean and the taste of its peoples.[64] The distinguishing feature of the new textiles lay in the type of wool used in their production, no longer short-staple and carded, but 'worsted', i.e. long-staple and combed, which was generally considered to be of inferior quality. This might lead one to suppose that the initial stimulus to the production of the 'new draperies' was not so much contact with the Mediterranean countries, but an effect of the continuing policy of enclosure in central and western England from the second half of the sixteenth century onwards; this brought about changes in the traditional production of English wool, which in turn led to the manufacture of new textiles, for which it then became necessary to find new markets.[65]

It is important to understand that the diversification of the English textile industry away from the traditional white broadcloths and kerseys was wide-ranging. There was a vast assortment of different textiles: Devon 'serges', made with a combination of combed and carded wools, or Suffolk 'says' made entirely of combed wool, or cloths made of fine Spanish wool, like the 'Spanish cloths' of Wiltshire, or, somewhat later, of local or Irish wool. There was also the manufacture of mixed fabrics, where wool was combined with silk, cotton or mohair, like the 'bombasines' from Norwich. The sheer variety of these products reveals how the English textile industry was aiming for a diversity of new markets and new categories of consumers which would supersede the traditional distinction of broadcloths intended for the affluent, and kerseys for the poorer social classes.[66]

In the second quarter of the seventeenth century, while new woollen cloths, finished in England, were sent together with the traditional kerseys for the Levant market in direct competition with Venetian textiles, the 'new draperies' flooded into Spain and Italy. In the 1660s

---

[63] Coleman, 'An innovation and its diffusion: the new draperies', 419.
[64] Fisher, 'London's export trade', 158.   [65] See Bowden, *The wool trade*.
[66] W. Minchinton, 'Patterns and structures of demand, 1500–1750' in Cipolla (ed.), *The Fontana economic history of Europe*, vol. II, pp. 130–6.

Table 5.6 *The Mediterranean markets for the 'new draperies', 1663–1669 (values in £)*

Country	No. of pieces	Percentage[a]	Total value	Percentage[b]	Percentage[c]
Italy	38,452	24.23	143,270	75.26	26
Spain	104,265	65.71	322,664	72.01	58
Portugal	15,949	10.05	90,887	58.21	16
Total	158,666		556,821		

Notes: [a] Percentage of total number of pieces.
[b] Percentage of domestic market.
[c] Percentage comprising the three countries.
Source: BL, Add. MSS 36785.

exports of the latter amounted to 158,666 pieces to a total value of £556,821 (see table 5.6). Spain was the largest market for all English goods absorbing 58 per cent of total exports, followed by Italy with 26 per cent; Italy, however, accounted for a higher percentage of textile exports in terms of the overall value of English exports, with 75 per cent as against 72 per cent for Spain.

If we examine what types of cloth were bought by Italian merchants in this period (table 5.1), we find a marked preference for the new products of the English textile industry: in 1663 and again in 1669, Devon 'serges' and 'perpetuanas' head the list, both in terms of their value and the quantity exported,[67] followed by 'Norwich stuffs', 'bayes' and 'minikins'.[68] 'Long cloths', with a high unit cost, are also prominent in terms of their export value; 'Spanish cloths' are comparatively limited in number. There may have been a market for both types in Italy itself, but

[67] The 'perpetuanas' proved to be the most successful of the 'Devon serges' despite predictions to the contrary. The name was of Spanish derivation and attracted potential buyers with its suggestion of a hard-wearing and good-quality cloth. In the eighteenth century the cloth was commonly known as 'long ells'. At the beginning of the seventeenth century, 'perpetuanas' measured 24 yards in length and 1 ell or yard in breadth. By the 1660s, however, they varied greatly in size, and the duty payable was assessed by weight. Customs officials estimated that a piece of serge or 'perpetuana' cloth weighed on average about 15 lbs. The manufacture of serges was restricted to the south-west, except for 'says', a lighter kind of serge, which was made at Sudbury in Suffolk. Between 1688 and 1715 the production of serge cloth was the most important branch of the English woollen textile industry and its foreign sales accounted for 28 per cent of all exported textiles. The sale of serges targeted, with considerable success, a large consumer market which wanted a cloth of average quality midway between the heavy and costly 'broadcloths' and the light cloth made in Norwich. Serges were economical, long-lasting, and well-made (Stephens, *Seventeenth-century Exeter*, pp. 4–5; Hoskins, *Industry, trade and people*, pp. 39–40).

[68] C. Wilson, 'Cloth production and international competition in the seventeenth century', *The Economic History Review*, ser. 2, 16 (1960–1), 211.

it is much more probable that they were merely in transit for the Levant, where there was a huge increase in demand for these two cloths in the second half of the century.[69]

Thus the English textile export trade had to deal with a variety of demands, dictated by distinct requirements, possibilities and tastes, within the two principal trading areas of the eastern and western Mediterranean. In 1661 Sir John Banks discovered how deep these distinctions were: in January of that year he arranged for a consignment consisting of 50 pieces of 'long cloths' in 10 bales, '20 Red, 27 Popinge and 3 French green', to be sent on his behalf to his correspondents in Aleppo, John Newman and Richard Sprignall, on the *Greyhound*.[70] Immediately after he had arranged this, the Levant Company issued an order that all textiles destined for the Levant could only be sent on ships belonging to the Company. The *Greyhound* was not a so-called 'general ship', nor did Banks wish to pay the 20 per cent fine which was incurred by all those who chose not to obey the Turkey Company's orders; he therefore asked his factors in Livorno, Lytcott & Gascoigne, to organise the sale of the 'long cloths' for cash or in exchange for organzine silk or some other kind of silk.[71]

By the end of August only one bale had been sold. Towards the end of November this state of affairs was unchanged, and Banks urged his correspondents in Livorno to sell the cloth as quickly as possible: 'I am sure itts not a trade that will answer and intrest your goods soe long lyeing and I had better know the worst you Did say you could barter them for silke I pray doe the best you Could . . .'[72] Shortly afterwards, he urged them to try to exchange the cloths for other goods, adding cash if necessary as an inducement to conclude the deal.[73]

It was a very different story for the 60 pieces of Suffolk cloth in 12 bales which Banks sent on his ship the *Virgin* in the autumn of the same year. Banks asked Lytcott & Gascoigne to sell them even before they had arrived in Livorno;[74] at the same time he instructed the ship's captain to seek out potential buyers in any of the ports of call on his route to Livorno. Banks advised Hendra: 'in case you touch Tituan sell them all any part the best you can there severall prices are in Invoice

[69] Clay, *Economic expansion and social change*, vol. II, p. 149.
[70] KCCRO, Aylesford MSS, U234/B3, Banks to Newman & Sprignall in Aleppo, London, 7 Jan. 1661.
[71] Ibid., Banks to Lytcott & Gascoigne of Livorno, London, 4 Feb. 1661; 18 Apr. 1661. 'General ships' were ships chartered by the Levant Company for the transportation to the Levant of goods belonging to members of the Company who requested the facility (see Wood, *A history of the Levant Company*, pp. 210–13).
[72] KCCRO, Aylesford MSS, U234/B3, 9 Dec. 1661.
[73] Ibid., 16 Dec. 1661.   [74] Ibid., 31 Aug. 1661; 28 Oct. 1661.

. . . and if you sell them let out the money for Legorne on Good security as you well understand'.[75] In March 1662, Banks received confirmation from Livorno that the cloth had been sold.[76]

In introducing their textiles into the markets of the western Mediterranean, the English employed methods which were not dissimilar to those they had already used to conquer the Levant markets. Their commercial strategy was based primarily on adaptation to the prevailing market patterns; what this entailed in the field of the manufacturing industries was first and foremost a careful analysis of the current situation followed by a distribution of articles similar to those already available but sold at a much lower price. The adoption of such a strategy frequently involved the production of counterfeit articles, a constant feature of the commercial rivalry prevalent in this period. The English introduced into the Levant several types of woollen cloth which closely resembled Venetian cloth, even on occasion stamped with the lion of St Mark on the edge, but sold cheaply; this influx of English textiles into the Levant probably contributed to the decline of the Venetian textile industry.[77]

In a similar way the 'new draperies' were not new to the markets of the western and central Mediterranean. Their production in England itself was not a sudden innovation brought about by the emigrant Flemish and Dutch textile workers, but developed from earlier techniques. Yet even though antecedents for the 'new draperies' can be found in English textile manufacture, their real origins are to be found in the foreign markets for which they were first produced.[78]

The English textile industry in the seventeenth century was in effect doing no more than turn the tables on the Italians, who in the fourteenth century had used the same strategy to oust the Flemish, who had until then enjoyed a monopoly over the textile trade within Italy. From 1320 onwards, the Florentines began to import English wool of good quality, while at the same time local textile production started to imitate the costly cloth imported from northern Europe, the so-called *panni franceschi*; the gradual process whereby locally produced cloth replaced its imported equivalent continued throughout the fourteenth century.[79] By the end of the century, when the 'grande draperie' of northern

---

[75] Ibid., Banks to Thomas Hendra, London, 29 Oct. 1661.
[76] Ibid., Banks to Lytcott & Gascoigne of Livorno, London, 14 Mar. 1662.
[77] Rapp, 'The unmaking of the Mediterranean trade hegemony', 512–13.
[78] See Coleman, 'An innovation and its diffusion'.
[79] Hidetoshi Hoshino, 'The rise of the Florentine woollen industry in the fourteenth century' in N. B. Harte and K. G. Ponting (eds.), *Cloth and clothing in medieval Europe: essays in memory of Professor E. H. Carus-Wilson* (London: 1983), pp. 185, 199, 203; Abulafia, 'Southern Italy and the Florentine economy', 384–5.

Europe had collapsed, the Florentine textile industry had built up an almost complete monopoly throughout the Mediterranean region, or more precisely, in the trade in luxury textiles to the Italian and Levant markets. However, Florentine textiles met with competition from Venetian woollens, which, as we have seen, went on to dominate the markets of the Near East by the end of the sixteenth century. Over the same period of time, certain specialised sectors of the textile industry had emerged into importance in Lombardy and in Cremona in particular, which was famed for its production of fustian, bombasine and linsey-woolsey, and, at the height of its prosperity, between the fourteenth and fifteenth centuries, exported 40,000 pieces of fustian to Venice as well as vast quantities of unspecified textiles to other cities in Italy and beyond, in France, Germany and the Low Countries.[80]

The English probably discovered these Italian textiles in the markets of Antwerp. Both necessity and chance contributed to the development of the 'new draperies'. The English textile industry needed new markets and new products in order to dispel the stagnation which afflicted it at the beginning of the seventeenth century, but favourable circumstantial factors also played a part, such as the emigration of Flemish merchants to regions like Suffolk, where independent moves to revitalise the textile industry had already begun to develop, or the peace treaty signed with Spain in 1604. England, moreover, possessed the raw material required for the manufacture of the new textiles, and was able to intervene in the Italian markets at a time when Italy's own industries could offer no real competition, for a variety of connected reasons, but partly because the country's industries were predominantly urban.

If the Suffolk 'says' imitated the earlier textiles from Hondschoote, which Florentine merchants had distributed throughout Italy in medieval times,[81] then the English bombasines from Norwich certainly owed something to Cremonese textiles.[82] Likewise the English term 'rashes' recalls the Florentine *rasce* itemized in the accounts of a textile workshop belonging to the Medici;[83] they were probably similar to what Thomas Mun at the beginning of the century termed 'Florence-rashes', which Tuscany exported to southern Italy in exchange for raw silk.[84]

[80] Sella, *L'economia lombarda*, pp. 43, 48.
[81] Coleman, 'An innovation and its diffusion', 422; Abulafia, 'Southern Italy and the Florentine economy', 385; R. de Roover, *Il Banco Medici: dalle origini al declino (1397–1494)* (Florence: 1970).
[82] Wilson, 'Cloth production and international competition', 211.
[83] Coleman, 'An innovation and its diffusion', 420.
[84] Mun, *A discourse of trade*, p. 16.

Confronted with an influx of English woollen cloth, Italian industries tried to keep it out. In Lombardy a decree was issued on 15 December 1646 which banned all foreign textiles which threatened to compete with local products from entering the region. However, warning voices had already been raised five years earlier in 1641: these dated the onset of the crisis in Lombardy's manufacturing industries to 1616, when duty had increased by a third, and they urged the imposition of 'a general ban on the import of all goods from abroad which are customarily manufactured within this state', in particular, 'woollens, silk cloth, woollen hats, and bombasines'.[85]

Similar reactions occurred in Venice and Florence; in the Tuscan capital the import of all English woollen products, and in particular woollen cloth, had been banned in 1663 or thereabouts.[86] The industrial cities of northern Italy therefore attempted to raise protective barriers against the newcomer, who offered textiles which were colourful, lighter and much cheaper than their own products. It was the cheapness of the English textiles which was their crucial advantage, one which was stressed by Finch when he wrote: 'Take Goodnesse for goodnesse we undersell them (as I know for certain) one third and this is the Reason that in the Mediterranean they are beaten out by us . . .'[87]

However, the policy of blocking English imports was not entirely effective in safeguarding the domestic industries, since it led to an increase in smuggling and at the same time did nothing to help those industries regain their foreign markets. Moreover, the political and commercial divisions of the country made it difficult to establish an effective nationwide system of protectionism. Imports of woollens continued to reach southern Italy, while in northern Italy Piedmont's establishment of the free port of Villafranca threatened to open up a new channel for the entry of foreign goods, since it was possible that the English would decide to move their trading base there in order to take advantage of the freedom to sell their cloth which it guaranteed. Finally, in Naples complete freedom for imports had been established by the commercial treaty which England had signed with Spain in 1664.[88]

It is therefore a plausible hypothesis that the greater part of English textile imports into Italy in the 1660s was absorbed by the south. Such a

[85] Sella, L'economia lombarda, pp. 126–7, 137–8: 'un bando general di tutte le merci forestiere solite a fabricarsi dentro questo Stato'; 'le pannine, i drappi di seta, cappelli di lana e robbe bombacee'.
[86] PRO, SP98/6, Finch to Arlington, ? Dec. 1665; SP98/9, Finch to Arlington, 8 May 1668; 12 Feb. 1668.
[87] PRO, SP98/6, Finch to Arlington, ? Dec. 1665.
[88] PRO, SP98/9, Finch to Arlington, Livorno, 5 Mar. 1668; 12 Mar. 1668.

deduction is borne out by events in Naples in 1668 when, in the words of the English Consul, Brown, there was an attempt to close the frontiers against the importation of English woollens on the part of 'moneyed Persons, Princes, Dukes and Barons, who had in their territories great incomes from the wools of the kingdom, now much abated and almost brought to nought by reason of the plenty of forreigne woollen goods'.[89] These members of the Neapolitan nobility had been encouraged to make their move by a prohibition issued by the Papal State against imports of silks from the kingdom of Naples. The promoters of the protectionist measures guaranteed that the losses sustained by the customs in Naples would be compensated for by the customs revenue in Foggia. After a series of tumultuous sessions, the Consiglio del Collaterale in the city decided to await a final verdict on the question from Madrid. The English consul was confident that the decision would be favourable to the English, since a similar proposal had once been made during the reign of Charles V and had been rejected. The ban on imports of woollens into southern Italy would, if implemented, have had serious consequences not only for the English merchants resident in Naples, but also for those based in Livorno, 'this kingdome being the cheife consumer of their woollen goods . . .'[90]

A certain Andrea del Rosso, a Florentine merchant resident in Naples, was also a firm believer in the commercial advantages of the southern Italian market. He had had personal experience of it in the 1650s, during the conflict between England and Spain, when he had acted as the correspondent and man-of-straw for the English merchants based in Naples,[91] who with this ploy avoided the danger of having their assets sequestered.[92] Del Rosso was thus aware of the immense profits which could be derived from the trade, with the result that he set up by himself and succeeded in outdoing the English. He had undertaken a similar activity in Sicily in the hope of excluding English commercial interests there as well. His profits from the sale of English cloth in southern Italy must have been immense, to judge from the commis-

---

[89] PRO, SP93/1, 206, Consul Brown to the Secretary of State, Naples, 20 Nov. 1668. See above, p. 20.
[90] Ibid.   [91] PRO, SP98/8, Finch to Arlington, Florence, ? Aug. 1667.
[92] PRO, SP104/173, 133–4, Charles II to the Viceroy of Naples, Conte di Penaranda, Whitehall, 4 May 1664; SP104/173, 163–4, Charles II to the Viceroy of Naples, Cardinal d'Aragona, Whitehall, 31 Oct. 1664. ASBN, Banco di S. Giacomo, 'giornale copiapolizze' 'matricola 235', partita di ducati 40 del 23.6.1657; matricola 238, partita di ducati 668 del 18.8.1657; Banco del Salvatore, 'giornale copiapolizze' 'matricola 63', partita di ducati 12 del 18.12.1657; Banco dei Poveri, 'giornale copiapolizze' 'matricola 341', partita di ducati 20 del 13.3.1658. See also G. Galasso, Napoli dopo Masaniello (Naples: 1971), p. 71.

sions which Vandeput, the London merchant who acted as his agent in the City, received – between 3,000 and 5,000 crowns annually.[93]

The reduced resistance which southern Italy offered to the import of English textiles, in comparison with the north of the country, can be traced back to the role traditionally occupied by the south in the economic and commercial division of the country. Lacking its own textile industry, except for the production of ordinary cloth, it had always relied on imports of high and average quality cloth from the cities of northern Italy, which in their turn depended on the south for supplies of agricultural produce and raw materials. Antonio Serra wrote in 1613:

> it is apparent that no woollen cloth for fine clothes is manufactured within the kingdom but comes from outside . . . on a rough estimate, if we calculate that there are a million households in the city, including those who are exempt from domestic tax and those who evade it, and estimate the number of people in each household who can afford to wear fine clothes, not forgetting that this figure includes not only the nobility and merchants and wealthy citizens but also ordinary working people who need to wear good clothes on feast-days, and work out how much a suit of clothes costs and how long it lasts . . . an overall estimate [of the potential market] might reach three million; even if we say that this category comprises less than two million, we still need to add the priests, friars, monks and suchlike, most of whom wear clothes manufactured elsewhere: when all these are taken into account, the above-mentioned figure is more likely to fall short of the real total than exceed it.[94]

Southern Italy had always had to buy the cloth it needed from outside its territory; with no local industries to defend, it is obvious that it turned to the supplier able to supply the goods at the best available price.

RE-EXPORTS

In the seventeenth century woollen cloth continued to be the staple of the English export trade. As we have seen, however, over the course

---

[93] PRO, SP98/8, Finch to Arlington, Florence, ? Aug. 1667.
[94] Serra, *Breve trattato*, p. 56: 'cosa chiara è che in regno non vi è artificio di lana per panni fini e il vestire vien da fuori . . . e giudicando all'ingrosso, essendo il regno di circa un milione di fuochi, compresi li franchi e fraudati, si faccia il conto delle persone per ogni fuoco e quanti possono vestire di panni fini, che oltre tutti i nobili e mercanti e cittadini ricchi ogni artigiano mediocre tiene vestiti di detti panni almeno per le feste, e vedasi a quanto ascende un vestito e quanto dura; e in tutto vollendo scandagliare bene arriverà a milioni tre, ma in contento si ponga questo esito di panni meno di milioni due, ed a questo si aggiungano preti e frati con monaci, e quali tutti la maggior parte vestono di panni da fuori, che importa alcuna cosa; sì che la somma che si è detto, più presto poca che soverchia si può dire'.

Table 5.7 *The composition of London's export trade by value (£000) and by percentage*

	1640[a]			Average 1663 and 1669		Average 1699–1701		
	Sterling	%	%	Sterling	%	Sterling	%	%
Woollens	1,150	94	88	1,512	74	2,013	73	45
Other manufactures	27	2	2	222	11	420	15	9
Raw materials	35	3	3	243	12	138	5	3
Foodstuffs	17	1	1	62	3	202	7	5
Total exports	1,229	100	94	2,039	100	2,773	100	62
Re-exports	76	—	6	—	—	1,667	—	38
Total	1,305		100			4,440		100

Note: [a] Exports handled only by English merchants; the value of exports handled by foreign merchants amounted to £89,160.
Source: Brian Dietz, 'Overseas trade and metropolitan growth', in Beier and Finlay (eds.), *London 1500–1700*, table 12, p. 131.

of the century, significant changes took place, such as the decline in the exports of raw materials and the appearance of the 'new draperies', which led to the creation of a new and advantageous trading link with southern Europe.

The figures in table 5.4 show how exports of woollen cloth continued to rise steadily until the end of the century; those in table 5.5, on the other hand, show that the proportion of national exports represented by woollens was in decline, which was compensated for by an increase in the exports of other manufactured goods as well as foodstuffs (fish, corn, etc.) and extracted metals and minerals such as lead, tin, coal, etc.

The figures in table 5.7, which includes figures for re-exports, show an even steeper decline in the proportion of exports of woollen cloth. Here the 74 per cent of the export trade for woollen cloth registered in the 1660s has declined to 45 per cent by the end of the century, as opposed to an increase in re-exports over the same period of time from negligible amounts to 38 per cent. According to Davis's calculations, imports rose by a third over this period while exports rose by over 50 per cent as the result of a steady increase in re-exports from the 1630s onwards.[95]

The growth in re-exported goods was a consequence of the expansion of English trading into areas outside Europe and it led to changes in

[95] R. Davis, 'English foreign trade 1660–1700', *The Economic History Review*, ser. 2, 7/2 (1954), 160–1.

the movement of imports and exports. For the first time English merchants could supply foreign buyers with vast quantities of goods which were not domestic products. This proved to be a real revolution in trade: certain of its effects, such as the sudden fall in the prices of products like sugar, tobacco and cotton which helped to create new mass markets for these commodities, resemble those of the Industrial Revolution a century later, when the mechanisation of manufacturing processes led to new patterns of domestic and foreign consumption.[96]

The origins of such a change can be traced back to the English effort to diversify its range of exports after the crisis of Antwerp had revealed the defective organisation of the English export trade, based as it was on one leading commodity. The problems which afflicted English foreign trade at the end of the sixteenth century had a double effect. English merchants started to explore the new markets of Spain, the Baltic and the French Atlantic coast, while long-distance trade was encouraged in an effort both to find new markets for English cloth as well as new sources of supply for those goods which had previously been imported through Antwerp.[97] As a direct result of these moves, various monopoly trading companies were established in the last quarter of the century.

England only fully succeeded in diversifying the range of goods which formed the substance of its foreign trade in the second half of the seventeenth century. The first indications of its subsequent success can be seen much earlier, however, in the triangular routes worked by the ships from the south-western ports, for example, which sailed to Newfoundland for fish which they then sold in the Mediterranean, or, even more notably, in the return of the pepper trade to the Atlantic route round the Cape of Good Hope under the control of the East India Company.

English pepper began to appear in Italy, in Livorno and Naples in particular, after 1610;[98] it was a welcome addition to the staple cargoes of fish, tin and lead. Pepper was an extremely useful commodity for foreign trade on account of its volume, its value, and the ease with which it could be marketed. Italian demand for the condiment was high, and consignments could easily be divided up into smaller quantities. Serra wrote that throughout the kingdom of Naples, 'there was not a single household which did not consume more-or-less half-a-ducat's worth [of pepper]'.[99] Pepper was also a speculative commodity with

---

[96] Ibid., pp. 153, 162.
[97] Chauduri, *The English East India Company*, pp. 5–6.   [98] See chapter 1.
[99] Serra, *Breve trattato*, p. 57: 'non vi è fuoco che sotto sopra non ne consumi circa mezzo ducato'.

which it was possible to guarantee maximum profits, since it could easily be kept in store and sold on the market when the time was judged to be right.[100]

With the pepper trade, the English transformed their role from buyers to sellers and began to reverse the unfavourable trade balance with Italy, managing to take away from Venice this profitable part of the re-export trade.[101] Pepper became a standard item in the cargoes of the English ships bound for Italy; between 1659 and 1661, Sir John Banks sent approximately 1,000 sacks of pepper to Livorno on various ships, all of it paid for in silver pieces of eight.[102]

The establishment of the East India Company in London meant that the city could start to build up, from the beginning of the century onwards, an almost complete monopoly over the re-export trade; by the end of the century, 84 per cent of it passed through London.[103] If the trade had been allowed to develop naturally, it would doubtless have avoided the London entrepôt and gone straight to the Mediterranean markets which it served. The first two ships to arrive in Livorno with cargoes of pepper in 1610 had both sailed directly from the East Indies and Goa.[104] Fifty years later, at a time of some disarray in the operations of the East India Company, Banks and his partners chartered two ships, the *Bantam* and the *Francis & John*, to sail to Asia for pepper and convey it from there straight to Livorno.[105] Such a route, however, would have reduced the customs revenue for the government, while the problem of how to make up the cargoes of the ships leaving English ports would have remained unsolved. As Finch observed in connection with a merchant ship which had arrived in Livorno carrying a cargo of sugar from Barbados:

> it was infinitely prejudiciall to England that these ships should be permitted to come directly to any foreign Ports; in regard that the mony they sell theyr sugars and Cargo for, they reinvest in forraign Commodityes; which otherwise would be spent in the Native Commodityes of England, and next England looses the Vent of so many Provisions as the Ships have need of which in so great a number of vessells as Come from

[100] K. Glamann, 'The changing patterns of trade' in Rich and Wilson (eds.), *The Cambridge economic history of Europe*, vol. IV, p. 283.
[101] Serra, *Breve trattato*, pp. 56–7.
[102] KCCRO, Aylesford MSS, U234/B2–B3, *passim*.
[103] Dietz, 'Overseas trade', p. 130.
[104] Braudel and Romano, *Navires et marchandises*, p. 130.
[105] KCCRO, Aylesford MSS, U234/B2, John Dethick, John Banks, Edward Mico, Edward Balle . . . to Thomas Dethick & Co of Livorno, London, 27 Nov. 1657.

the Western Plantations is a great consumption of the flesh and Corn of England.[106]

The problem arose in Livorno in 1667 with the arrival of the *Charles* which had sailed from the island of Nevis in the West Indies via Tangiers. The ship's owners were Francis Sampson and Joseph Rookby, the leading plantation owners on the island; Rookby was also the island's chief customs officer.[107] The *Charles* was carrying 100 barrels of sugar and other goods, the equivalent of 30 tons, which had remained on board after part of the cargo had been unloaded in Tangiers.[108]

Sugar, along with tobacco, cotton, indigo, ginger and other products which were 'grown, produced or manufactured in English colonies', could only be exported to England or one of its colonies. Whoever arranged for the transport of these goods had to pay a bond or sum of money as a guarantee that he would observe the law. Merchants in the American colonies had devised a way of avoiding the legal restriction of trading with the Mediterranean only via the entrepôt of London by sending their goods first to Tangiers, since the port was considered to be a colony, and subsequently from there to the various markets of the Mediterranean.[109]

Finch was faced with this problem when he received information in letters from Tangiers that two small vessels had arrived in the port from Jamaica with a cargo of cocoa, with more to follow in the coming months: he therefore turned to the authorities in London with a request that they explain how the law should be applied.[110] The Treasury replied that no ship was allowed to sail from Barbados to other English colonies before paying a deposit against its return with its cargo intact; the matter was one of great importance for His Majesty's customs and for the prosperity of the kingdom.[111] The *Charles* had to pay a fine of 400 pieces of eight, or £100, before leaving Livorno with a cargo of silk, oil, wine, earthenware, soap and paper to a value of £10,000.[112]

While ships working the sea routes from Asia converged on London under the auspices of the East India Company, an attentive legislative

[106] PRO, SP98/8, Finch to Arlington, 20 Sept. 1667; Florence, 24 Sept. 1667.
[107] Ibid.
[108] PRO, SP98/8, Chellingworth to Arlington, Livorno, 8 Aug. 1667.
[109] PRO, SP98/9, Finch to Arlington, Florence, 24 Sept. 1667.
[110] CSP Treasury Books, 1667–8, p. 106, 'Out of the letter from Sir John Finch, Sir George Downing (is) to extract what command the ship that went from Barbados to Leghorn', 14 Oct. 1667.
[111] CSP Treasury Books, 1667–8, p. 198, 'The treasury to Sir John Finch . . .', 29 Oct. 1667.
[112] PRO, SP98/8, Finch to Arlington, 20 Sept. 1667; Chellingworth to Arlington, Livorno, 3 Oct. 1667; Finch to Arlington, Florence, 15 Nov. 1667.

policy, reflecting the allied interests of government, merchants and shipowners, together with a newly created bureaucracy deployed in key
trading positions and responsible for seeing that the legislation was
observed, ensured that those ships sailing the Atlantic routes were
obliged to call at London. The state began to assume many of the
responsibilities which had previously been left to the trading companies;
the increasingly active role of government played a crucial part in the
country's commercial recovery between the mid-century recession and
the Dutch War of 1689.

CONCLUSION

In the course of the seventeenth century the established pattern of Mediterranean trade, under the control of the cities of northern Italy, went into irreversible decline, to be gradually replaced by a new and much wider structure, of intercontinental dimensions, centred on the trading nations of north-western Europe, Holland and England. The age-old pattern of Italian commerce suffered its first reversal in the age of the great geographical discoveries, with the sudden rise to importance of Antwerp as an entrepôt not only for European and Levantine commodities but also for those products which began to arrive from Asia, Africa and the colonies of the New World. However, Genoese and Florentine merchants were still dominant in Antwerp: this, and other characteristics of the period – such as the prominent role which Venice continued to play in the Levant trade, the late flowering of the Venetian textile industry, Genoese control of the Spanish financial world, the huge expansion of the Florentine silk industry and the creation of the free port of Livorno – demonstrate that Italy's commercial resources were still capable of transformation and adaptation to the new situation. On the other hand, the Italians were disadvantaged by the country's political divisions which led to a fragmented economy, by its geographical distance from the new transoceanic trading routes, and by the very fact of its long-established commercial success which meant that the country's merchants were less open than they might have been to the need for radical change.

Antwerp was also the headquarters of the Merchant Adventurers, who were responsible for the European distribution of the woollen cloth produced by the English textile industry and who were keen to encourage a national policy whereby English commercial dependence on foreign merchants acting as intermediaries was diminished or removed altogether. Until this period, England had been weakened by internal divisions and the country's commercial influence abroad had been marginal; now peace together with a new political unity and stability began to bear fruit, while the new trade routes to Asia and America encouraged the development of the national fleet.

Yet the parallel decline and rise of the Mediterranean and Atlantic worlds extended over the course of the century. Contemporary observers continued to regard the Mediterranean as the most prosperous and the most populous of trading areas: as trade evolved eastwards and westwards, the Mediterranean remained a key area in its development.

As one part of the whole pattern of changes taking place, the expansion of the English presence within the system of Mediterranean trade was the most significant and the most long-lasting in its effects, yet it took place gradually over the course of the century and in various stages. The first phase can be said to commence in the 1570s and continued until the beginning of the seventeenth century. English ships began to sail southwards to the Mediterranean; once English merchants had rediscovered the routes, they continued to use them and established themselves in the principal Mediterranean ports. They were thus able to dispense with their reliance on Italian ships and Italian merchants in trading with the countries of the Mediterranean. The goods which were bought and sold remained essentially the same, yet the new possibilities of access to the sources of direct supply of the Oriental and luxury commodities which were in demand on the English market tended to shift the focus of growth from exports to imports.

Italy's commercial power remained substantial: Venice retained its foremost position both as an industrial city and as an entrepôt for Oriental spices; Genoa, with its almost total control of Spanish finance, was at the peak of its power; while the banking activities of Florence meant that its presence was felt in every important market, above all in France. The first indications of a developing crisis, however, can also be seen in the Italian fleet's loss of its leading position and the increasing preference on the part of the country's merchants to invest their capital in financial speculation rather than in commercial activity.

From the outset, Italy played a key role in England's developing commercial strategy. At a time when England was in conflict with Spain, Italy provided the money which the English needed for the markets of the Levant, acquired largely through the chartering of armed ships which were capable of defending themselves against the increasingly numerous attacks of North African pirates.

The second phase of English expansion can be said to begin in the third and fourth decades of the seventeenth century, although certain key events, such as the reopening of trade with Spain, the return of pepper to the sea route under the control of the East India Company, and the ban on the export of raw wool, pre-date this period. Yet in the 1630s the wars in which both Holland and France were involved effectively ended their role as potential commercial rivals: England's way was clear to laying an enduring foundation for its trade in the Mediterranean. The sea routes of English ships focused on the free port of Livorno, which became the centre for the commercial activities of English merchants as well as a source of the valuable currency they needed for the markets of the Levant and the Far East and which they acquired by selling the cargoes their ships brought with them. The growing power of the English commercial network did not restrict Livorno, but on the contrary enabled it to prosper – English merchants were able to use the port to redistribute exports and imports, and to obtain credit, and it also functioned as the centre for the Mediterranean carrying trade. Livorno proved more welcoming to the English than either Genoa, whose very prosperity induced it to put its trust in its own commercial and maritime revival, or Venice, which was ferocious in the defence of its own ever-decreasing area of influence and sought to stem the advance of the English as much as possible. These two decades see the first signs of those economic changes which were to transform Italy by the second half of the century from a leading industrial power to a country reliant on the export of raw materials or semi-finished products.

The pattern of English trade in the Mediterranean was firmly established from the 1670s onwards, helped above all by the clear distinction which was created between the functions of the mercantile and military fleets. This separation enabled England to increase the efficiency and continuity of its transportation and improve the system of protection, and thus exploit to the full its control of the Mediterranean carrying trade. The Second Dutch War is generally judged by historians to have been less beneficial to English interests than the first, yet it served both to demonstrate and to stimulate the new capabilities of England's commercial organisation. In the earlier phases of English expansion in the Mediterranean, the English merely tended to replace or substitute the Italians; in this final phase, their innovations, when these occurred, were on an intercontinental scale. England followed the example of Venice in preceding centuries but translated the model from Mediterranean into global terms: its economic development followed two parallel yet mutually supportive paths: industrial production and trade in re-exports. Italy became a leading market not only for English textiles, but also for the spices and colonial products which arrived from the Far East and the New World via the burgeoning entrepôt of London. It was perhaps ultimately the lack of such a close connection between commercial and maritime expansion and industrial growth which was responsible for Holland's failure to resist the encroaching domination of English commercial power, despite the fact that the Dutch at times enjoyed a greater share of Mediterranean trade and freight than the English.

From the middle of the seventeenth century onwards commercial activity in the cities of northern Italy came increasingly under the control of London, working through the communities of English merchants in Livorno and other Italian ports. Italy had a part to play in a wider intercontinental commercial strategy directed by the City of London; Italy and the Mediterranean were indeed essential elements in the strategy, both as a market for goods and a source of raw materials. The dual economy of Italy, based on the complementary roles of north and south, was sundered; northern Italy's progressive abandonment of the south, which had begun in the early decades of the century, was complete. Southern Italy remained on the periphery of the English trading area, left to face the irreversible consequences of isolation and under-development.

SELECT BIBLIOGRAPHY

ARCHIVAL SOURCES

Archives Nationales de France: Affaires Etrangères
Archivio di Stato di Napoli: Fondo notarile: notaio Hieronimo de Roma
Archivio di Stato di Pisa: Consoli del Mare
Archivio Storico del Banco di Napoli
   Banco dell'Annunziata o Ave Gratia Plena
   Banco di San Giacomo
Biblioteca Nazionale di Napoli: Sezione Manoscritti
British Library: Department of manuscripts
   Additional MSS 36785
   Egerton 2524
Calendar of State Papers Domestic
Calendar of State Papers Venetian Treasury
Calendar of Treasury Books
Calendar of Treasury Papers
Kent County Council Record Office
   Aylesford Manuscripts
Public Record Office, London
   Colonial Office
   High Court of the Admiralty
   State Papers Foreign: Entry Books; Levant Company; News Letters; Sicily
     and Naples; Treaty Papers; Tuscany
   State Papers Supplementary

BOOKS AND ARTICLES

Abulafia, D., *The two Italies. Economic relations between the Norman kingdom of
   Sicily and the northern communes*, Oxford, 1977.
   'Southern Italy and the Florentine economy, 1265–1370', *The Economic
   History Review*, ser. 2, 34/3 (1981), 377–88.

Albion, R. G., *Forests and sea power. The timber problem of the Royal Navy, 1652–1862* . . ., Cambridge (Mass.), 1926.

Andrews, K. R., 'The economic aspects of Elisabethan privateering', Ph.D. thesis, University of London, 1951.

Aston, T. (ed.), *Crisis in Europe, 1560–1660*, London, 1965.

Aymard, M., 'Commerce et consommation des draps en Sicile et en Italie méridionale', in M. Spallanzani (ed.), *Produzione, commercio e consumo dei panni di lana (nei secoli XII–XVII)*, Florence, 1976.

'La transizione dal feudalesimo al capitalismo', in *Storia d'Italia, Annali*, vol. I, Turin, 1978.

Barbour, V., 'Dutch and English shipping in the seventeenth century', *The Economic History Review* 2 (1930), 261–90.

Battelli, G., 'Il porto di Livorno alla fine del secolo XVII', *Bollettino storico livornese* 1 (1937), 80–82.

Baugh, D. A., *British naval administration in the Age of Walpole*, Princeton, 1965.

Baumann, W. R., *The Merchant Adventurers and the continental cloth-trade (1560s–1620s)*, Berlin and New York, 1990.

Beck, C., 'Eléments sociaux et économiques de la vie des marchands génois à Anvers entre 1528 et 1555', *Revue du Nord* (1982), 759–84.

Beier, A. L. and Finlay, R. (eds.), *London 1500–1700. The making of the metropolis*, London and New York, 1986.

Benedetto, M. A., 'Appunti per una ricerca sul contratto di assicurazione marittima', in *Studi in onore di Giuseppe Grosso*, vol. IV, Turin, 1971.

Blanchard, I., 'English lead and the International Bullion Crisis of the 1550s', in D. C. Coleman and A. H. John (eds.), *Trade, government and economy in pre-industrial England – essays presented to F. J. Fisher*, London, 1976.

Bowden, P. J., *The wool trade in Tudor and Stuart England*, London, 1971.

Braudel, F., 'L'Italia fuori d'Italia', in R. Romano (ed.), *Storia d'Italia*, vol. II, part II, Turin, 1974.

La Méditerranée et le monde méditerranéen à l'époque de Philippe II (1949), Paris, 1979.

Braudel, F. and Romano, R., *Navires et marchandises à l'éntrée du Port de Livourne (1547–1611)*, Paris, 1951.

Brenner, R., *Merchants and revolution: commercial change, political conflict, and London's overseas traders, 1550–1653*, Cambridge, 1993.

Britannia Languens or a Discourse of Trade: shewing the grounds and reasons of the increase and decay of land-rents, national wealth and strength; with application to the late and present state and condition of England, France, and the United Provinces, London, 1680.

Brulez, W., 'Les routes commerciales d'Angleterre en Italie au XVIe siècle', in *Studi in onore di Amintore Fanfani*, vol. IV, Milan, 1962.

Carr, L. G., *Old ships' figure-heads and sterns*, London, 1925.

Carus-Wilson, E. M., 'The origins and the early development of the Merchant Adventurers' organization in London as shown in their own medieval records', *The Economic History Review* 4 (1932–4), 147–76.

Castillo, A., 'Les banquiers portugais et le circuit d'Amsterdam', *Annales ESC* 19 (1964), 311–16.

Chaudhuri, K. N., *The English East India Company: the study of an early joint stock company, 1600–1640*, London, 1965.

Chaunu, H., *Séville et l'Atlantique*, Paris, 1955–59.

Chorley, P., *Oil, silk and enlightenment: economic problems in XVIII century Naples*, Naples, 1965.

Ciano, C., *La sanità marittima nell'età medicea*, Pisa, 1976.

Cipolla, C. M., 'The decline of Italy: the case of a fully matured economy', *The Economic History Review*, ser. 2, 5/2 (1952), 178–87.

Istruzione e sviluppo, Milan, 1971.

Ciriacono, S., *Olio ed Ebrei nella Repubblica Veneta nel Settecento*, Venice, 1975.

Clay, C. G. A., *Economic expansion and social change: England 1500–1700*, Cambridge, 1984.

Coleman, D. C., 'An innovation and its diffusion: the New Draperies', *The Economic History Review*, ser. 2, 22/3 (1969), 417–29.

Sir John Banks, Baronet and Businessman (1963), Westport (Conn.), 1975.

Corbett, J. S., *England in the Mediterranean*, London, 1904.

Corfield, P. J., 'Economic growth and change in seventeenth-century English towns' in P. Clark (ed.), *The traditional community under stress*, Milton Keynes, 1977.

The impact of English towns, 1700–1800, Oxford, 1982.

Croft, P., *The Spanish Company*, London, 1973.

David, R. (ed.), *Hakluyt's voyages*, London, 1981.

Davis, J., *Società e imprenditori nel Regno Borbonico – 1815–1860*, Bari, 1979.

Davis, R., 'English foreign trade, 1660–1700', *The Economic History Review*, ser. 2, 7/2 (1954), 150–66.

'England and the Mediterranean', in E. J. Fisher (ed.), *Essays in the economic and social history of Tudor and Stuart England: in honour of R. H. Tawney*, Cambridge, 1961.

'English foreign trade, 1700–1774', *The Economic History Review*, ser. 2, 15 (1962), 285–303.

The rise of the English shipping industry in the seventeenth and eighteenth centuries, Newton Abbot, 1962.

Aleppo and Devonshire Square: English traders in the Levant in the eighteenth century, London, 1967.

English merchant shipping and Anglo-Dutch rivalry in the seventeenth century, London, 1975.

Day, J., 'Strade e vie di comunicazione' in R. Romano (ed.), *Storia d'Italia*, vol. v, Turin, 1973.

De Maddalena, A., 'Il mondo rurale italiano nel Cinque e nel Seicento', *Rivista storica italiana* 76 (1964), 349-426.

'Rural Europe 1500–1750', in C. M. Cipolla (ed.), *The Fontana economic history of Europe*, vol. ii, London, 1974.

de Roover, R., *Il banco Medici – dalle origini al declino (1397–1494)*, Florence, 1970.
'A Florentine firm of cloth manufacturers: management and organization of sixteenth-century business' in J. Kirshner (ed.), *Business, banking and economic thought in late medieval and early modern Europe: selected studies of Raymond de Roover*, Chicago and London, 1974.

Defoe, D., *Extracts from a plan of English commerce being a compleat prospect of the trade of this nation, as well as the home trade as the foreign – humbly offered to the consideration of the King and Parliament* (1728; 1730) in J. R. McCulloch (ed.), *Select collection of scarce and valuable tracts on commerce*, London, 1859.

Delumeau, J., *L'alun de Rome (XV–XVI ième siècle)*, Paris, 1962.

Earle, P., 'The commercial development of Ancona, 1470–1511', *The Economic History Review*, ser. 2, 22/22 (1969), 28–44.

Corsairs of Malta and Barbary, London, 1970.

The making of the English middle class: business, society and family life in London, 1660–1730, London 1989.

Edler de Roover, F., 'Andrea Banchi: Florentine silk manufacturer and merchant in the fifteenth century', *Studies in Medieval and Renaissance History* 3 (1966).

Fasano Guarini, E., 'La popolazione', in *Livorno: progetto e storia di una città tra il 1500 e il 1600*, Pisa, 1980.

Felloni, G., *Gli investimenti finanziari genovesi in Europa tra il Seicento e la Restaurazione*, Milan, 1971.

Filippini, J.-P., 'Il porto di Livorno e il Regno di Francia dall'editto di porto franco alla fine della dominazione medicea' in *Atti del Convegno 'Livorno e il Mediterraneo nell'età medicea'*, Livorno, 1978.

Fisher, F. J., 'London's export trade in the early seventeenth century', *The Economic History Review*, ser. 2, 32/2 (1950), 151–61.

Fisher, H. E. S., *The Portugal trade: a study of Anglo-Portuguese commerce, 1700–1770*, London, 1971.

Friis, A., *Alderman Cockayne's project and the cloth trade*, Copenhagen and London, 1927.

Galasso, G., *Napoli dopo Masaniello*, Naples, 1971.

'Momenti e problemi di storia napoletana nell'età di Carlo V' in G. Galasso, *Mezzogiorno medievale e moderno*, Turin, 1975.

'Social and political development in the eleventh and twelfth centuries' in *The Normans in Sicily and southern Italy*, Lincei Lectures, Oxford, 1977.

Gasti, C. (ed.), 'Scrittura in materia di nautica del Cavaliere Giovan Francesco Bonamici di Prato', *Archivio storico italiano*, 16 (1885).

Gibbs, L. (ed.), *The Tatler*, London and New York, 1953.

Glamann, K., 'The changing patterns of trade' in E. E. Rich and C. H. Wilson (eds.), *The Cambridge history of Europe*, vol. IV, Cambridge, 1967.

Goodman, J., 'The Florentine silk industry in the seventeenth century', Ph.D. thesis, London School of Economics, 1976.

'Financing pre-modern European industry: an example from Florence, 1580–1660', *Journal of European Economic History* 10 (1981), 415–35.

Goris, J. A., *Etude sur les colonies marchandes méridionales à Anvers du 1488 à 1567*, Louvain, 1925.

Gould, J. D., 'Cloth exports, 1600–1640', *The Economic History Review*, ser. 2, 24/2 (1971).

Grendi, E., 'Traffico portuale, naviglio mercantile e consolati genovesi nel Cinquecento', *Rivista storica italiana* 80 (1971), 593–638.

'I Nordici e il traffico del porto di Genova: 1590–1666', *Rivista storica italiana* 83 (1971), 25–73.

Grimaldi, D., *Memoria sulla economia olearia antica e moderna e sull'antico frantojo da olio trovato negli scavamenti di Stabia*, Naples, 1783.

Guarnieri, G., *Livorno Medicea*, Livorno, 1970.

Hamilton, E. J., *American treasure and the price revolution in Spain (1501–1650)*, Cambridge (Mass.), 1934.

Harper, L. A., *The English navigation laws*, New York, 1939.

Hebb, D. D., *Piracy and the English government, 1616–1642*, Aldershot (Hants.) and Brookfield (Vt.), 1994.

Heers, J., ' Les Génois en Angleterre: la crise de 1458–1466', in *Studi in onore di Armando Sapori*, vol. I, Milan, 1957.

Hobsbawn, E. J., 'General crisis of the European economy in the 17th century', *Past and Present* 5 (1954), 33–49.

Hornstein, S., 'The deployment of the English Navy in peacetime, 1674–1688', Ph.D. thesis, University of Utrecht, 1985.

The Restoration Navy and English foreign trade, 1674–1688, Aldershot (Hants.) and Brookfield (Vt.), 1991.

Hoshino, H., 'The rise of the Florentine woollen industry in the fourteenth century' in N. B. Harte and K. G. Ponting (eds.), *Cloth and clothing in medieval Europe: essays in memory of Professor E. H. Carus-Wilson*, London, 1983.

Hoskins, W. G., *Industry, trade and people in Exeter 1688–1800*, Manchester, 1935.

Houghton, J., *A collection for improvement of husbandry and trade.*

Innis, H. A., *The cod fisheries*, Toronto, 1954.

Israel, J. I., *The Dutch Republic and the Hispanic world, 1606–1661*, Oxford, 1982.

'The phases of the Dutch *straatvaart* (1590–1713)', *Tijdschrift voor Geschiedenis* 99 (1986), 1–30.

Dutch primacy in world trade, 1585–1740, Oxford, 1989.

Jones, D. W., 'The "hallage" receipts of the London cloth markets, 1562–c.1720', *The Economic History Review*, ser. 2, 25/4 (1972), 567–87.

Kamen, H., *Spain in the later seventeenth century, 1665–1700*, London, 1980.

Kellebenz, H., 'Le déclin de Venise et les relations de Venise avec les marchés au Nord des Alpes', in *Decadenza economica veneziana nel secolo XVII*, Venice, 1961.

Kellenbenz, H., 'Technology in the age of the Scientific Revolution' in C. M. Cipolla (ed.), *The Fontana economic history of Europe*, vol. II, London, 1974.

Kirby, P. F., 'Robert Dudley e le navi granducali' in *Atti del Convegno 'Gli Inglesi a Livorno e all'Isola d'Elba'*, Livorno, 1980.

Koenigsberger, H. G., 'English merchants in Naples and Sicily in the seventeenth century', *The English Historical Review* 62 (1947), 302–66.

Laloy, *La Révolte de Messine. L'expédition de Sicile et la politique française en Italie (1674–1678)*, Paris, 1930.

Lane, F. C., 'Venetian shipping during the Commercial Revolution', *The American Historical Review* 38 (1933), 219–37.

Venice. A maritime republic (1973) Baltimore and London, 1977.

Laras, G., 'I Marrani di Livorno e l'Inquisizione', in *Atti del Convegno 'Livorno e il Mediterraneo nell'età medicea'*, Livorno, 1978.

Latimer, J., *The Annals of Bristol in the seventeenth century*, Bristol, 1900.

Lewis, B., 'Some reflections on the decline of the Ottoman Empire', *Studia Islamica* 9 (1958).

Lithgow, W., *Travels and voyages (1609)*, Leith, 1814.

Lloyd, T. H., *Alien merchants in England in the high middle ages*, Brighton and New York 1982.

Luttwak, E., *The Pentagon and the art of war*, New York, 1984.

Luzzatto, G., 'Per la storia delle costruzioni navali a Venezia nei secoli XV e XVI', in *Miscellanea di studi storici in onore di C. Manfroni*, Venice, 1925.

Storia economica dell'età moderna e contemporanea, Padua, 1955.

McCusker, J. J., *European bills of entry and marine lists: early commercial publications and the origins of the business press*, Cambridge (Mass.), 1985.

McCusker, J. J. and Gravestein, C., *The beginnings of commercial and financial journalism*, Amsterdam, 1990.

McGrath, P. (ed.), *Records relating to the Society of Merchant Venturers of the City of Bristol in the seventeenth century*, Bristol Record Society, vol. XVII, Bristol, 1952.

Merchants and merchandise in seventeenth-century Bristol, Bristol Record Society, vol. XIX, Bristol, 1955.

Macry, P., *Mercato e società nel regno di Napoli. Commercio del grano e politica economica nel '700*, Naples, 1974.

Malanima, P., *La decadenza di un'economia cittadina – l'industria di Firenze nei secoli XVI–XVIII*, Bologna, 1982.

Mallett, M. E., *The Florentine galleys in the fifteenth century*, Oxford, 1967.

Malloch, A., *Finch and Baines: a seventeenth-century friendship*, Cambridge, 1917.

Marino, J., 'Economic idylls and pastoral realities: the "trickster economy" in the Kingdom of Naples', *Comparative Studies in Societies and History* 24 (1982), 211–34.

Masi, C., 'Relazioni fra Livorno ed Algeri nei secoli XVII–XIX', in *Bollettino storico livornese* 2 (1938), 183–84.

Masson, P., *La Compagnie du Corail – étude historique sur le commerce de Marseille au XVIe siècle et les origines de la colonisation française en Algérie – Tunisie*, Paris and Marseille, 1908.

Matthews, H. E. (ed.), *The Company of Soapmakers – 1562–1642*, Bristol Record Society, vol. X, Bristol, 1940.

Mazzauti, R., 'Il territorio livornese', in *Livorno: progetto e storia di una città tra il 1500 e il 1600*, Pisa, 1980.

Melis, F., *Origini e sviluppo delle assicurazioni in Italia (secoli XIV–XVI): Le fonti*, vol. I, Rome, 1975.

Michell, A. R., 'The European fisheries in early modern history', in E. E. Rich and C. H. Wilson (eds.), *The Cambridge economic history of Europe*, vol. V, Cambridge, 1977.

Millard, A., 'The import trade of London, 1600–1640', Ph.D. thesis, University of London, 1956.

Minchinton, W., 'Patterns and structure of demand – 1500–1750' in C. M. Cipolla (ed.), *The Fontana economic history of Europe*, vol. II, London, 1974.

Morineau, M., 'Il secolo', in P. Leon (ed.), *Storia economica e sociale del mondo. Difficoltà di sviluppo, 1580–1730*, vol. II, Bari, 1980.

Mun, T., *A discourse of trade from England unto the East Indies* (1621), in J. R. McCulloch (ed.), *Early tracts on commerce* (1856), Cambridge, 1970.

'England's treasure by forraign trade', in J. R. McCulloch (ed.), *Early tracts on commerce* (1856), Cambridge, 1970.

Nef, J. U., *The rise of the British coal industry*, London, 1932.

Nicolini, N., 'Il Consolato generale veneto nel Regno di Napoli', *Archivio storico per le province napoletane*, 13 (1927), 59–119.

North, D. C., and Thomas, R. P., *The rise of the western world. A new economic history*, Cambridge, 1973.

North, R., *Lives of the Norths*, London, 1890.

O'Brien, P., 'European economic development: the contribution of the periphery', *The Economic History Review*, ser. 2, 35/1 (1982), 1–18.

Oppenheim, M., *A history of the administration of the Royal Navy and of merchant shipping in relation to the Navy*, London and New York, 1896.

Oppenheim, M. (ed.), *The naval tracts of Sir William Monson*, Navy Records Society, vol. V, 1902.

Pagano de Divitiis, G., *Il Napoletano Palazzo di Venezia*, Naples, 1980.

'Il Mezzogiorno e l'espansione commerciale inglese', *Archivio storico per le province napoletane* 21 (1982), 125–51.

'Il Mediterraneo nel XVII secolo: l'espansione commerciale inglese e l'Italia', *Studi storici* 1 (1986), 109-48.

'L'arrivo dei nordici in Mediterraneo', in R. Romano (ed.), *Storia d'Italia*, vol. V, Milan, 1989.

'Il porto di Livorno fra Inghilterra e Oriente', *Nuovi studi livornesi* 1 (1993), 43–87.

Pagano de Divitiis, G. (ed.), *Il commercio inglese nel Mediterraneo dal '500 al '700*, Naples, 1984.

Palmieri, G., *Pensieri economici relativi al Regno di Napoli*, Naples, 1789.

Osservazioni su vari articoli riguardanti la pubblica economia, Naples, 1790.

Parker, G., *The army of Flanders and the Spanish road, 1567–1659*, Cambridge, 1972.

Parry, J. H., 'Transport and trade routes', in E. E. Rich and C. H. Wilson (eds.), *The Cambridge economic history of Europe*, vol. IV, Cambridge, 1967.

Piancastelli Politi, G., 'I Bottini dell'Olio', in *Livorno: progetto e storia di una città tra il 1500 e il 160*, Pisa, 1980.

Pinna, M., 'Sulle carte nautiche prodotte a Livorno nei secoli XI e XVII', in *Atti del Convegno 'Livorno e il Mediterraneo nell'età medicea'*, Livorno, 1978.

Ponting, K. G. (ed.), *Baines's account of the woollen manufacture of England*, New York, 1970.

Poyser, E. R., 'Anglo-Italian trade from the reign of Elisabeth to the French Revolution with a special reference to the Port of Leghorn', M. Litt. Thesis, University of Cambridge, 1951.

Ramsay, G. D., 'The undoing of the Italian mercantile colony in sixteenth century London', in N. B. Harte and K. G. Ponting (eds.), *Textile history and economic history: essays in honour of Miss Julia de Lacey Mann*, Manchester, 1923.

The Wiltshire woollen industry in the sixteenth and seventeenth centuries, Oxford, 1943.

The City of London in international politics at the accession of Elizabeth Tudor, Manchester, 1975.

The English woollen industry, 1500–1750, London, 1982.

Rapp, R. T., 'The unmaking of the Mediterranean trade hegemony: international trade rivalry and the commercial revolution', *The Journal of Economic History* 35/3 (1975), 499–525.

Industry and economic decline in seventeenth-century Venice, Cambridge (Mass.) and London, 1976.

Richardson, S. (ed.), *The negotiations of Sir T. Roe in his embassy to the Ottoman Porte, from the year 1621 to 1628 inclusive, containing . . . his correspondence, etc.*, London, 1740.

Roberts, L., *The treasure of trafficke or a discourse of forraigne trade* (1641), in J. R. McCulloch (ed.), *Early tracts on commerce*, (1856), Cambridge, 1970.

The merchants map of commerce, London, 1677.

Romanin, S., *Storia documentata di Venezia*, vol. VII, Venice, 1858.

Romano, R., 'Tra XVI e XVII secolo una crisi economica: 1619-1622', *Rivista storica italiana*, 74 (1962), 480–531.

'Encore la crise de 1619-1622', *Annales ESC*, 19 (1964), 31–7.

'L'Italia nella crisi del secolo XVII', in R. Romano, *Tra due crisi: l'Italia del Rinascimento*, Turin, 1971.

'La storia economica. Dal secolo XIV al Settecento' in R. Romano (ed.), *Storia d'Italia*, vol. II, part II, Turin, 1974.

Napoli dal Viceregno al Regno, Turin, 1976.

Roserveare, H. (ed.), *Markets and merchants of the late seventeenth century: the Marescoe-David letters, 1668–1680*, Oxford, 1987.

Ruddock, A. A., *Italian merchants and shipping in Southampton, 1270–1600*, Southampton, 1951.

Sachs, D. H., 'Bristol's "Little Businesses" 1625–1641', *Past and Present* 110 (1986).

Scrosoppi, P., 'Il porto di Livorno e gli inizi dell'attività inglese nel Mediterraneo', *Bollettino storico livornese* I (1937), 339–77.

'Attività commerciale nel porto di Livorno nella prima metà del secolo XVII', *Bollettino storico livornese* 3 (1939), 41–65.

Sella, D., *Commerci e industrie a Venezia nel secolo XVII*, Venice, 1961.

'European Industries, 1500–1700', in C. M. Cipolla (ed.), *The Fontana economic history of Europe*, vol. II, London, 1974.

L'economia lombarda durante la dominazione spagnola, Bologna, 1982.

Serra, A., *Breve trattato delle cause che possono fare abbondare li Regni d'oro e d'argento dove non sono miniere con applicazione al Regno di Napoli*, Naples, 1613.

Steensgaard, N., *The Asian trade revolution in the seventeenth century*, Chicago and London, 1974.

Stephens, W. B., *Seventeenth-century Exeter: a study of industrial and commercial development, 1625–1688*, Exeter, 1958.

Stone, L., *An Elizabethan: Sir Horatio Palavicino*, Oxford, 1956.

The crisis of the aristocracy 1558–1641, Oxford, 1967 (1st edn 1965).

Taylor, H., 'Trade, neutrality and the "English Road", 1630–1648', *The Economic History Review*, ser. 2, 25/2 (1972), 236–60.

Tenenti, A., *Venezia e i Corsari*, Bari, 1961.

Texeira de Mota, A., 'L'art de naviguer en Méditerranée du XIIIe au XVIIe siècle et la création de la navigation astronomique dans les océans', in M. Mollat (ed.), *Le navire et l'économie maritime du moyen-âge au XVIIIe siècle principalement en Méditerranée*, Paris, 1958.

The Diary of Henry Teonge, Chaplain on board his Majesty's Ships Assistance, Bristol, and Royal Oak anno 1675 to 1679 . . ., London, 1825.

The Harleian Miscellany: or, a collection of scarce, curious, and entertaining pamphlets and tracts, as well in manuscripts as in print found in the late Earl of Oxford's library, vol. IV, London, 1745.

Thirsk, J., and Cooper, J. P. (eds.), *Seventeenth-century economic documents*, Oxford, 1972.

Tucci, U., *Mercanti, navi, monete nel Cinquecento veneziano*, Bologna, 1981.

Visceglia, M. A., 'Il commercio nei porti pugliesi nel Settecento. Ipotesi di ricerca' in P. Villani (ed.), *Economia e classi sociali nella Puglia moderna*, Naples, 1974.

Vivanti, C., 'La storia politica e sociale, dall'avvento delle Signorie all'Italia spagnola' in R. Romano (ed.), *Storia d'Italia*, vol. II, part I, Turin, 1974.

Willan, T. S., *The Muscovy Merchants of 1555*, Manchester, 1953.

Wilson, C. H., 'Cloth production and international competition in the seventeenth century', *The Economic History Review*, ser. 2, 13/2 (1960), 209–21.

England's apprenticeship, 1603–1763, London, 1965.

The Dutch Republic, London, 1968.

'The historical study of economic growth and decline in early modern history' in E. E. Rich and C. H. Wilson (eds.), *The Cambridge economic history of Europe*, vol. v, Cambridge, 1977.

Witsen, N., *Aeloude en Hedendaegsche Sheepsbouw en Bestier*, Amsterdam, 1671.

Wood, A. C., *A history of the Levant Company* (1935), London, 1964.

Wrigley, E. A., 'A simple model of London's importance in changing English society and economy, 1650–1750' in P. Abrams and E. A. Wrigley (eds.), *Towns in Societies*, Cambridge, 1978.

Wrigley, E. A. and Schofield, R. S., *The population history of England 1541–1871*, London, 1981.

INDEX

CAMBRIDGE STUDIES IN ITALIAN HISTORY AND CULTURE